T0291236

PRAISE FOR *BUILT FOR PEOPLE*

"At last, new thinking on operationalising HR. We needed this. If you're thinking about how to take your people team to the next level, read this! Jessica Zwaan's fresh thinking is the energy we need in an often predictable domain."
Ben Branson-Gateley, CEO and Co-founder, CharlieHR

"A thoroughly enjoyable read. *Built for People* delivers a practical guide to unleash the true power of the people team. Jessica Zwaan lays a clear path for us to follow, and it leads to people teams delivering measurably more business impact."
Huw Slater, COO, Travelperk

"*Built for People* is an indispensable tool for you and your team that offers a fresh approach to solving new and old issues in the workplace. It offers a clear and concise framework for rethinking how we approach and design programmes with and for employees."
Lars Schmidt, author, Redefining HR and founder, Amplify Academy

"Jessica Zwaan not only offers a more humane and durably effective approach to acquiring, growing, and managing great talent, but also in the fundamentals of great product management, unpacked in highly-relatable terms. With this book people leaders will take away a fresh approach to building teams, and product managers will view their discipline through a novel lens. Rarely are these two disciplines discussed in the same place but Jessica Zwaan delivers a masterclass in both."
Andy Tyra, Chief Product and Technical Officer, Whereby

"Jessica Zwaan doesn't just tell us how important people operations should be: she urges us to make that a reality by leveraging principles used by the world's best product teams, often the same principles that our companies are already using, right down the hall."
Michael Wolfe, Co-founder, Gladly and Adviser, Point Nine Capital

"Productivity and performance gains are guaranteed by following Jessica Zwaan's powerful and deeply practical advice. Her experience in such a diverse range of organizations enables her to recommend an engaging approach to people operations that is applicable to all, whichever sector and whether you're an established or emerging entity. It's fantastic that her innovative ideas are now accessible to a wider audience thanks to this excellent book."
Abbie Pugh, Head of Leadership Development, Kindred Capital

"With brutal efficiency, accessible clarity and smart framing, this book has given people operations and HR professionals no excuse to opt out of "productising" the things it creates. Jessica Zwaan describes herself as a terrible (but very passionate) crafter which is almost poignant because this book creates craft from process, policy and protocols that are the HR hallmark. Smart and snazzy you will change forever how you view the products that are necessary to enable your people to do their best work. The future of work may be human, but the future of people operations is product management. It's the clarion call we needed."
Perry Timms, Founder, Chief Energy Officer, PTHR

"Jessica Zwaan's book offers strategies that will encourage current and emerging leaders to question the status quo. Change driven by COVID-19 and economic downturn makes this book essential reading for modern leaders who are required to manage transnational companies."
Dr Jeanne McConachie - Previous Manager, Griffith Honours College

Built for People

*Transform your employee experience using
product management principles*

Jessica Zwaan

KoganPage

Publisher's note

Every possible effort has been made to ensure that the information contained in this book is accurate at the time of going to press, and the publishers and authors cannot accept responsibility for any errors or omissions, however caused. No responsibility for loss or damage occasioned to any person acting, or refraining from action, as a result of the material in this publication can be accepted by the editor, the publisher or the author.

First published in Great Britain and the United States in 2023 by Kogan Page Limited

Apart from any fair dealing for the purposes of research or private study, or criticism or review, as permitted under the Copyright, Designs and Patents Act 1988, this publication may only be reproduced, stored or transmitted, in any form or by any means, with the prior permission in writing of the publishers, or in the case of reprographic reproduction in accordance with the terms and licences issued by the CLA. Enquiries concerning reproduction outside these terms should be sent to the publishers at the undermentioned addresses:

2nd Floor, 45 Gee Street	8 W 38th Street, Suite 902	4737/23 Ansari Road
London	New York, NY 10018	Daryaganj
EC1V 3RS	USA	New Delhi 110002
United Kingdom		India

www.koganpage.com

Kogan Page books are printed on paper from sustainable forests.

© Jessica Zwaan, 2023

The right of Jessica Zwaan to be identified as the author of this work has been asserted by her in accordance with the Copyright, Designs and Patents Act 1988.

ISBNs

Hardback	978 1 3986 0804 7
Paperback	978 1 3986 0802 3
Ebook	978 1 3986 0803 0

British Library Cataloguing-in-Publication Data

A CIP record for this book is available from the British Library.

Library of Congress Cataloging-in-Publication Data
Names: Zwaan, Jessica, author.
Title: Built for people : transform your employee experience using product
    management principles / Jessica Zwaan.
Description: 1 Edition. | New York, NY : Kogan Page Inc, 2023. | Includes
    bibliographical references and index. | Summary: "Taking the best elements of a product-led approach and applying them to HR activity can transform the people function. This book shows you how. Written for all HR professionals, Built for People explains how to improve workforce and business performance by developing agile ways of working, evidence-based decision making and a culture of continuous feedback and iteration. It explains everything from what this approach means for HR, what the benefits of it are and how to do it effectively. It covers how to proactively develop an employee experience which attracts, engages and retains the talent the business needs and supports them to operate at their full potential. There is also practical guidance on the importance of user research and how to encourage a continuous feedback loop as well as advice on how to build and improve employee experience at scale, the importance of testing and iteration and how to define metrics for success. Most importantly, this book provides expert guidance throughout on how to embed evidence-based decision making and develop agile HR working practices to improve both employee and business performance. Full of tools, tips, case studies, exercises and interviews with HR leaders who are already seeing the benefits, this is essential reading for all HR practitioners needing to develop an agile, innovative and evidence-based approach to their people operations"– Provided by publisher.
Identifiers: LCCN 2023004071 (print) | LCCN 2023004072 (ebook) | ISBN
    9781398608023 (paperback) | ISBN 9781398608047 (hardback) | ISBN
    9781398608030 (ebook)
Subjects: LCSH: Personnel management. | Employee motivation. | Employee
    retention.
Classification: LCC HF5549 .Z893 2023 (print) | LCC HF5549 (ebook) | DDC
    352.6–dc23/eng/20230306
LC record available at https://lccn.loc.gov/2023004071
LC ebook record available at https://lccn.loc.gov/2023004072

Typeset by Integra Software Services, Pondicherry
Print production managed by Jellyfish
Printed and bound by CPI Group (UK) Ltd, Croydon CR0 4YY

To my husband who managed to be nothing but generous
as I demanded he confirm figures, offer synonyms and conjure
up words that were just on the tip of my tongue.

CONTENTS

LIST OF FIGURES AND TABLES

ABOUT THE AUTHOR

Jessica Zwaan is a start-up and technology executive with a colourful background in operations, people, and talent spanning across three continents. She has served as Chief Operating Officer at Whereby, a fully remote video meetings company. Prior to this she served as Chief People and Operations advisor for start-ups across Europe, Group Head of Talent at McCann Worldgroup and VP People and Talent at Wonderbly.

She has a first class honours law degree from the University of Law in London, focusing her dissertation on the legal implications of remote working cross-border. She is a diploma-member of CIPD and has a bachelor of Communications Journalism from the University of Queensland, Australia.

Jessica can often be heard on podcasts talking about transformative approaches to operations, people and talent. She loves a good yarn about scaling leadership and her Twitter DMs are always open. Outside of work, she is a cyclist, vegan foodie, amateur comedian and terrible (but very passionate) crafter.

FOREWORD

What does it mean to practice HR? Does it differ from People Operations? Are they the same? Perhaps a better question is, does it matter?

The field of HR is deeply rooted in conventional practices. We do things, well, because that's the way they've always been done. Conventional practices are conventional because of how consistently they're applied.

The principles and practices of conventional HR were often adhered to with dogmatic devotion. It's what kept the field stagnant for so many years. Then 2020 came along and upended the field ... and the world. Our legacy practices and systems buckled under the crushing weight of Covid-19 and the assorted calamities that followed it.

We began questioning whether those legacy practices served us. We began embracing design thinking to re-engineer our practices from the employee's point of view. We got much better at social listening and user research. We embraced agile programmes and the 'move fast' thinking principles of ship it, learn, iterate.

In short, we began thinking like Product Managers.

Jessica Zwaan was at the forefront of this evolution long before Covid-19. Her practical and actionable blog posts provided a roadmap for HR and people practitioners to embrace product management thinking and approaches. *Built for People* takes the next steps with a clear and concise framework for rethinking how we approach designing people programmes for, and with, our employees.

This book is not a HR book. It's not even a product management book. It's a book about how to build better products and programmes. In the hands of HR, this book is a key to unlocking our potential and elevating our impact.

Gone are the days when HR earnestly references a 'seat at the table'. Our function is firmly a business function delivering business results through people. Why? Due to our ability to embrace concepts, practices and results that Jessica so clearly breaks down in this book.

Built for People is built for you. It's a masterclass on bringing a different approach to solving problems old and new and it is an indispensable tool as we build this new world of work.

Lars Schmidt, Author of Redefining HR and founder of Amplify Academy

PREFACE

While this book was in final edits, I was asked by a podcast host what led me to this way of thinking. 'Was it a Newton under the apple tree moment?' It wasn't.

Everything I wrote in this book is the product of years of working in businesses large and small. It's been a gradual set of realizations over some key moments in my career; working with a strat at Goldman Sachs, running our employee value proposition project at Box, building a truly exceptional cultural point of view at Wonderbly, and launching the squad model in its full form at McCann Worldgroup. Indeed, I am still learning more every day, and I seek to poke and augment this approach with time to better serve the needs of our beloved colleagues.

This means that this book comes with a warning (and a hope!) that all contained within it is iterative and adapting. I wrote a blogpost on which this book was based in 2020 and from there I have had hundreds of HR and business leaders reach out to me, ask for advice and let me know they are implementing People Operations as a product way of working themselves. What a joy to know that my opinion is one of many in this newly emerging way of approaching People Operations! I hope that in the coming years we will have plenty more to share as businesses see success in the approach.

I invite you to discover things with me through reading this book, but also to hold them against your own experiences along your journey and challenge what I say. Then, I would love you to share those with me so that we can all benefit.

Mostly, I hope you enjoy anything new I can possibly teach you – that you are able to read this book with the kind of ardent curiosity I try to adopt in my work, inspired by so many product leaders I've been privileged enough to work with.

ABOUT THIS BOOK

Embracing a product management approach within People Operations will transform your business. This book shows you how.

In this book written for HR professionals, but which should also be read by founders, operators, and business leaders, Jessica Zwaan explains how adopting a Product Management approach to People Operations will make your business perform better. The book explores what the core product management strategies and frameworks are and guides you on how to apply them to People Operations in order to establish an incredible employee experience.

It explains everything from what this approach means for People Operations and business leaders, what the benefits of this approach are and how to install it effectively. It covers how to proactively develop an employee experience which attracts, engages and retains the talent the business needs and supports them to operate at their full potential. There is also practical guidance on some of the key elements in product management, such as the importance of user research, sprint planning, vision development and how to encourage a continuous feedback loop in your team. The book does not shy away from problems of scaling sustainably, organizational change and culture clash, and provides advice on how to build and improve employee experience whatever your size or stage, including the importance of testing and iteration and how to define metrics for success.

Full of tools, tips, exercises and practical advice from those who are already seeing the benefits, this is essential reading for all business leaders seeking to develop an agile, innovative and evidence-based approach to their people operations to compete in the marketplace of culture.

ACKNOWLEDGEMENTS

I would like to send a thank you to everyone who read, contributed, brainstormed, deliberated, argued, or inspired the work in this book. There are too many people to list (a thing I have to say because I will inevitably miss someone), but I would like to thank Lars Schmidt for believing in my approach so much that he introduced me to the team at Kogan Page. Abbie Pugh for editing, discussing, and helping me build this way of working in reality (and for being an angel among mortals). Øyvind Reed for allowing me the space and time to write this book while working in his team. Ben Gately, Matt Bradburn, Andreas Bovens, Joel Overton, Andy Tyra, Ingrid Ødegaard, Abby Hayes, Mum and Dad (thinking of your proud reaction to me writing a book will always warm my heart), Kevin Hanna, Hélène Pichon, Jesse David, Ashley Williams, Roxanne Robinson, Max Warren, Serena Pettitt, Sophia Benedictsen, Charlotte Bailey-Wood, Kat Denham, Rune Kvist, Anders Krohn, Lily Smith, David Cadji-Newby, Tal Oron, Asi Sharabi, and *YES!* even Nick Marsh. The team at Kogan Page; Lucy, Zexna, and Anne-Marie. My final acknowledgement is for my aunty, Dr Jeanne McConachie, who has been a source of inspiration to me as I moved through every stage of my life – I hope I make you proud.

LIST OF ABBREVIATIONS

ATS	Applicant tracking system
ENPS	Employee net promoter score
EVP	Employee value proposition
FAANG	Facebook, Amazon, Apple, Netflix, Google. See MAGMA.
HR	Human resources
HRBP	Human resources business partner
HRIS	Human resources information system
IC	Individual contributor
KPIs	Key Performance Indicators
LTV	Lifetime value
L&D	Learning and development
MAGMA	Meta, Apple, Google, Microsoft, Apple
MLP	Minimum loveable product
MVP	Minimum viable product
OKRs	Objectives and Key Results
OD	Organizational design
PM	Product management
POPs	People operations
RACI	Responsible, accountable, consulted, informed
ROI	Return on investment
SaaS	Software as a service
SMART Goals	Specific, measurable, achievable, relevant and time-bound goals
VC	Venture capital
USP	Unique selling point
UX	User experience

LIST OF CONTRIBUTORS

Lars Schmidt; Foreword
Ryan Bonnici; Quotes
Laura Tacho; Quotes
Abbie Pugh; Advisory
Icons within figures from Flaticon.com

01

Why change how we execute? The need to think like a product manager

In 1911, IBM commanded us to 'THINK'.[1] Almost 100 years later, Steve Jobs at Apple asked us to 'Think Different.'[2]

It may be difficult to imagine today, but in late 1996 Apple was facing staggering losses and on the verge of financial ruin. In 1997, Steve Jobs engineered the award-winning advertising campaign that urged potential customers to buy Macintoshes and 'think different'. Jobs saw Apple was in a unique position to innovate. He understood the marketplace for consumer technology was multidimensional and personal, and therefore that an end-to-end experience could be created by taking control of both the hardware and software, and building integrated systems. He challenged the team at Apple to continuously ask not just *what* they were building, but *why* they were building it in the first place. This approach required the team to strip away anything unnecessary in the pursuit of simplicity, to develop a beautiful and loved product. Jobs demanded they go back to the drawing board. Pushed until magic happened.

In the 1990s, leaders like Jobs began encouraging businesses to apply customer product management principles to their software products. The concept wasn't new – it was invented at Proctor and Gamble a century earlier in the form of 'Brand Men' and used to sell more soap[3] – tech products began commandeering product management principles in an effort to become more consumer-focused. In 2001, Jobs began again, using more modern product management principles, to reinvent Apple products for the twenty-first century. That same year, Apple introduced iTunes, a now ubiquitous force in the cultural zeitgeist. The introduction of iTunes was a great example of end-user thinking from Steve Jobs. Apple solved a niche problem for the users: there was no easy way for users to license individual songs on their devices. It provided users with an effortless and elegant way to purchase songs of their choice and listen to them on their devices anytime, anywhere. It changed the way we listened to music.

Since the 2000s, a Product Manager's role has evolved as dramatically as the technology they are responsible for developing. Most companies tend to create their own rules; Amazon, Google, Apple and Facebook have shaped their modern-day Product Manager and ended up setting the trend for product development in technology. Despite the differences in the roles across these businesses and markets, they all deal with three main areas: design, engineering and the customer voice.

Now it is time for us in People Operations to 'think different'.

Time to 'think different'

While the objectives of Human Resources leaders and teams are often noble, if we were to ask our businesses today, '*What does the HR Department do?*' or ask our peer leaders, '*Does HR add value?*' the responses may not always please those of us who have committed our professional lives to this work. Intention *matters*, and many of us working in HR have good intentions, but somewhere along the way we may have felt, or been told, that the output of our work is policing, bureaucracy, or administration – directly contradicting our intentions of value, engagement, and commerciality.

I imagine you joined a People Operations team or became a business leader because you care about people and you want to make a difference – many of us do. You want to ensure your team and colleagues have a great experience at work, that you build a culture which is productive, engaged and safe. When I started working as a HR graduate, inspired by my studies and the interviews I'd been a part of, I entered the working world with this vision: to build a working world better than the one I entered. Along the way I found my peers' shared-vision somewhat eroded by the realities of budgets, siloes, administration and other such obstacles to our own success.

In 2017, I attended a conference in London with many motivated and ambitious HR practitioners who were gathered to learn about innovation within the industry. Over a break between sessions, I found the conversation moving quickly from compelling advances in software and tools to how we felt day-to-day. 'I find myself arguing with the CEO about the most basic ideas like working from home,' one admitted. 'I never get invited to strategy meetings, although I am meant to be on the management team,' was rebuffed with, 'At least you're in the management team. I report into the Finance Director and spend most of my time organizing our office.' It was clear that even the most ambitious and aspirational of us felt that, though the industry had made great strides in the tools we use and how we learn from each other, something was failing us in the way we worked within our businesses.

Key moments in the history of HR

Although sometimes it can feel like business is operating at some kind of peak, with machine learning, automation, and instant communication at our fingertips, history and progress have been shamefully slow. At almost every point, change met with both despair and longing for the improvements still to come, and exaltation of the 'end of all of our problems'.[4] It is crucial to note, at the beginning of any overview of history, that much of the world's history is written from a European perspective. While efforts have been made to describe the forthcoming book's content with a decolonized approach, a Eurocentric view remains the primary lens through which this book was written.[5]

The history of modern Human Resources as we now know it starts, rather grimly, within the miserable history of labour abuses in the British Industrial Revolution. During this time, factories across Britain recruited thousands of workers, including children, who worked up to 16 hours a day in unsafe and unsanitary conditions.[6,7] In a direct response to the harshness of industrial conditions, the influence of trade unions and the labour movement, the kindling of HR began to gain momentum. Through campaigning for what was called 'industrial betterment', welfare officers, or welfare secretaries, came into being.[8] These roles can be seen to be the birthplace of some elements of HR, including employee counselling.[9]

Unsurprising to us today, workplace owners began to see that oppressive workplace environments were *not only* directly obstructive towards societal good, but they were not benefiting business. The connection between happiness, satisfaction and work performance was beginning to be understood.

The first developments Robert Owen and Charles Babbage shared a simple idea that people were crucial to the success of an organization.[10] Together, they sparked the revolutionary hypothesis that the improved wellbeing of employees led to an improvement in work quality and output (another reason I would perhaps rather forward over backward should we ever invent time travel). The idea that without healthy workers, the organization would not survive was a catalyst for monumental change. Some factories began to introduce programmes for employees to increase their comfort and satisfaction, and to make standards less inhumane.[11] Moreover, British, American, and European governments began to intervene to introduce some fundamental human rights, child labour laws, and work safety legislation, such as the Representation of the People Act 1867.[12]

The move from welfare to personnel administration   The second rapid development of Human Resources started in the 1920s to 1930s. Jobs with the titles of Labour Manager or Employment Manager were introduced to the engineering industry and other industries where there were large factories. These roles involved handling recruitment, workplace absences, dismissal and compensation queries. Employers' federations, particularly in engineering and shipbuilding, negotiated national pay rates with the unions. The growing size of businesses and the pressure placed on them to improve efficiency and production lead to a greater need for recruitment, control, training, etc. These tasks fell on welfare officers, as they had relevant experience. However, the roles were changing rapidly in terms of scope – no longer busy with matters purely of employee safety and wellbeing, the role had a new dimension of administration.[13] At the same time, academics around the world in the fields of sociology, philosophy and psychology, such as Kurt Lewin and Abraham Maslow were publishing the work in human sciences that would one day become the fabric for the HR Management we now see taught at university, which began in the 1940s.

By 1945, employment management and welfare work had become integrated under the broad term 'personnel management' or 'industrial and labour relations'.

A Royal Commission under Lord Donovan was set up in the 1960s in the UK after years of poor industrial relations. The Royal Commission on Trade Unions and Employers' Associations, known as the 'Donovan Report', was issued in 1968.[14] It was critical of both employers and unions. Personnel managers were criticized for lacking negotiation skills and failing to plan or deliver robust industrial relations strategies. A silver lining for our early HR pioneers, Donovan suggested these deficiencies were a consequence of management's failure to give personnel management sufficiently high priority. The recommendations of the Commission made way for some ground-breaking improvements in the mechanics of industrial relations in the United Kingdom, and indeed many of the procedures embodied in the original 1974 legislation remain in effect today in the form of The Trade Union and Labour Relations (Consolidation) Act 1992.

The Women's Liberation and Civil Rights movements dramatically changed social and business climates, and alongside them, workforce demographics. These much-needed changes and introduction of Anti-Discrimination and Equal Pay Legislation such as the United States Equal Pay Act of 1963, and Race Relations Act 1965 forced employers to radically reconsider how they prioritized workforce planning, recruitment, wellbeing and compensation. At the same time as these crucial changes in legislative and social fabric, personnel techniques further developed using theories from psychology and the social sciences. HR Practitioners began to explore concepts such as organizational behaviour and individual career motivations.[15] During the 1970s and into the 1980s, specialisms started to develop with reward, learning and development, and resourcing.

People Operations as we know it today   In the late twentieth century, development in transportation and communications greatly benefitted workforce mobility and collaboration. Businesses began, at least in name, viewing employees as their property, and the term 'Human Resource Management' became the dominant nomenclature. However, it wasn't long before a new era of change began. In the early 2000s, mirroring the great strides taken within technology, the term 'Human Resources' began to phase further into the past.

I've always had some resistance to the term Human Resources, and the relationship with the concept of Human Capital. Both of these imply that people are 'resources' that are to be used just like machines or commodities. This opinion seems shared, and many professionals agreed that 'HR' didn't align with a world where we were working to emphasize holistic employee engagement, talent, development and motivation. People Operations, Employee Experience and People and Culture departments were born in the Silicon Valley and have since spread across the globe.[16,17]

A brilliant future   There is no doubt that Human Resources, now People Operations (or POPs, as it is often known), has been changing and evolving in a direction which is both inspiring and reassuring. In many technology companies and scale-up businesses, the People Operations teams I've worked with speak passionately about their role as one with deep, tangible impact on human beings, businesses and customers. Indeed, over the last 20 years, modern HR has been rapidly ushered into strategic focus – moving from administration and bureaucracy to strategy in only a few decades. Practices which now seem table stakes were forged: developmental plans, work shadowing, 360-degree feedback, assessment centres and succession plans.

Throughout the 2010s, some of the old complaints about the HR function have touched a new nerve in POPs. The kinder critics say that POPs teams focus too much on bureaucracy and administration, that we act only in self-interest and lack vision and strategic insight.[18] The most unsympathetic online audiences call HR the 'fun police' at best, and at worst purposely corrupt and manipulative corporate mouthpieces, lacking in value or integrity.[19]

In 2022, the radical shift to hybrid and remote working, ushered in by the devastation of coronavirus in 2020, ignited what many were calling 'the great resignation' or 'the big quit'.[20] Millions of people each month are changing jobs to improve their pay and lifestyles. Millions of others appear to have quit work entirely. From 1971 until 2021, Labour Force Participation Rate in the United Kingdom averaged 76.77 per cent, reaching an all-time high of 79.80 per cent in January of 2020. In 2021, the rate was only 2 points above the record low in 1983.[21]

What now?   It seems clear a new age of People Operations must rise to the challenge. I believe the secret lies in Product Management. Product Management is a discipline of its own, living within the technology and product function of your organization. Many of you reading may be well versed in what Product Management is and does, how the teams work, and the way they think about delivering value. However, there is much to explore before we can begin weaving this into our People Operations practice.

The discipline of Product Management

To begin to understand product management, one must understand what it is to work through 'Product Thinking'. Product Thinking is a methodical approach which starts with a user problem, and arrives at a solution that bridges the gap between a need and business value. Product thinking, therefore, aims to solve real problems by building meaningful solutions. True to this, product managers are information gatherers, defining the strategic direction of their products through the lens of knowledge about their business's strategic goals, the market's demands and opportunities, and the technological and financial resources available to them to make the product a reality.

Crucially to what we must understand about Product Managers (PMs, for short), is that they aren't operators themselves. Once they have analysed all of the available data and determined a strategic direction for the product they are responsible for, the product manager's job is to communicate this strategy to many stakeholders and to earn buy-in. They then ensure the appropriate teams understand their roles and have the tools they need to execute the product strategy moving forward. Sometimes this involves building internal tools and processes, but the machinery of these is almost never operated by product managers themselves.

Product management has, in recent times, become a momentous force in technology companies. Before the introduction of agile ways of working, product management was still a part of the Marketing or Engineering functions, reporting up through those hierarchies.

Today, product management is increasingly a standalone function with a seat at the management table and reporting directly to the CEO, sitting on boards, or as founders in successful businesses. This shift has been critical because it aligns the product team directly with the business vision and goals, serving to improve the capacity to succeed in their aims. It also makes the product team an internal as well as external evangelist of that vision, offering the necessary independence to make tough prioritization calls.

Product management practice is widely written about and evangelized. Product management professionals flock to events like Mind the Product, and platforms like Productboard in order to learn best practice, influence the future of the discipline and share their wins. The communities around product management are vibrant and innovative. If you feel you still don't know all you need to, Chapter 4 of this book gives a more thorough overview of the approach and maxims of product management which should be adopted by People Operations teams.

Craft your culture like a Product Manager

In 2015, I was responsible for a project distilling the employee value proposition (EVP) of Box's European enterprises. Box is a Silicon Valley founded tech start-up developing and selling cloud document storage to enterprise businesses and I worked in the European HQ in London during the company's 2015 IPO. During the EVP project I conducted a number of surveys, fact-finding interviews and workshops in order to better understand what it was which made Box a compelling and vibrant place to work.

Before I had even commenced the project, I had my own preconceived understanding of what I may find on my investigation. I was unsurprised to hear my peers speak of Box's impressive customer-portfolio, interesting technological marketplace and internal thought-leaders as being key triggers for joining the team. I understood there was clearly something compelling and disruptive about our *product* and the space in which we were operating which was unique and held value to our team.

However, when I began to try to understand what about the *culture* of Box inspired and retained our best employees, I found myself looped in a spiral of buzzwords and sentimentality. I knew we had generous perks and benefits, but so did our competitors at Salesforce, Google and Facebook. I myself appreciated the commitment to work-life balance, but found even our most earnest description of that approach sank into the white-noise of other companies paying lip service – ping pong tables, snack walls, gym memberships. Myself and the team became awakened to the fact that a recruitment strategy balanced on showcasing a company's perks and fun-loving lifestyle would not be enough to stand out in the marketplace of employers.

What felt novel and exciting in the late 2000s and early 2010s – sleep pods, snacks and bean bags – has now become passé or even cautioned against as a band-aid solution to a potentially toxic workplace.[22] Thinking almost a decade later, in 2022, the COVID pandemic proved that, if Friday beers and gym membership wasn't culture before the pandemic, then virtual paint nights and video-call beers won't do the trick now. People Operations teams have to do the work that defines what brings your employees, their work and the customers together.

WORKPLACE CULTURE IS A MARKETPLACE

Culture has always been a hard thing to define. Sure, we know a great culture when we see it. Often, however, we're unable to describe exactly the inputs or specifics, using words like 'transparent' and 'rewarding' which lack substance and shared definitions.

Culture is, primarily, a marketplace and I am a firm believer that (outside of toxic outliers) there is no such thing as 'good' or 'bad' culture. For some, a highly hierarchical structure gives security and confidence. For others, it breeds paranoia and unhealthy power dynamics. Autonomy and ownership can bring some individuals great senses of responsibility, empowerment and satisfaction in their work, but for many I've worked with it may also drive insecurity, anxiety in ambiguity and ultimately cause great unhappiness.

Individuals need to seek out a workplace with a culture that offers them the opportunity to do their best work and workplaces need to be honest and focused about building something specific to their needs and strategy, and then projecting that effectively into the world.

Being recruited by a business, working inside their walls and growing your career according to their values, policies and programmes form some of the biggest 'purchasing decisions' you will make in your life. The product we buy when we join a new company is not a laptop, or a coat (and developing those products is complex enough!). *It is a subscription to an experience, an opportunity and a path in life.* The work an effective People Operations team does is building, maintaining and iterating on that subscription product.

Because of this, it is my firm belief the best People Operations teams in the world run like product management functions. That may not be how they describe themselves, but it is often one of the reasons that they are successful, admired and do innovative work. It's also how I choose to operate when I build a company.

The employee experience as a product

The way we think about employee experience, and our role in crafting it, needs to change. We can no longer see the employee experience as a series of independent mechanisms to run a business; recruitment, training, onboarding and the like. Instead, each of these steps is a part of a whole, the product. This product is what we are convincing talented candidates out there in the market to buy into and remain engaged in.

Imagine a world where a business considered Sales, Engineering, and Marketing as entirely independent and relatively unrelated mechanisms. Sales are aggressively approaching B2B enterprise clients, Engineering is building a platform so technical it seems impossible to use without deep expertise and Marketing has elected to take a low-brow, tongue-in-cheek tone steeped in memes only understood by TikTok users and Twitch streamers. Standing alone, each of these strategies may not be discouraged, in fact many successful businesses do take approaches listed above with great effect. However, the sum of these strategies together is confusing and disjointed. We understand that what may appeal to one customer may repel the other and business units are becoming well trained on how to synchronize their efforts to target their key demographics.

I have seen many People Operations teams fall at this hurdle – finding themselves selling a confusing and unpredictable employee experience which results in poor hiring, disengaged teams and regrettable churn. An example: the employer branding messages preached 'self-driven learning and development' and 'progression, and quick promotion'. However, upon entering the company the new recruits discover a different story: performance reviews and performance assessments are bureaucratic and happen yearly, forcing the most aspiring in the team to a rigid annual schedule of growth. Self-driven development is a wonderful concept, and structured yearly reviews can be incredibly effective, but it should come as no surprise that they go together chalk and cheese. Another example is managers talking of a deeply empathic leadership style, involved and human-first, encouraging hour-long weekly 1:1s, growth and career planning and line-manager coaching. Meanwhile the organizational design and planning enforces a strict 15:1 manager ratio, squeezing the margins within leadership's capacity to deliver on these cultural and management aspirations. The crucial thing here is that all of these strategies, taken on their own, have credence. Together, they spell *fiasco*.

We must, as People Operations teams, begin at first principles (the idea of thinking without assumptions, which I discuss in detail in Chapter 4) when we build a business and understand what kind of product *we want to be in the market*. That initial work is how we can be informed and capable enough to deliver a cohesive, effective, and admirable brand and employee experience. The internet is flooded with millions of resources on how to position your product. Culture, like product positioning, is a market force; there is no right or wrong answer. It is the role of someone doing a good job to work out the most efficient approach to aid in reaching whatever goals you have as a company.

In Chapter 3, this book goes into further detail on how and when to draw the Product analogy to your employee experience.

This book

A company's Product Management function is now considered a real and competitive advantage and the practice of Product Management is continuing to evolve through meaningful thought leadership. What is key for people operations practitioners to learn is not just the way in which product management has come to take their seat at the table, but how the day-to-day of their work can influence a better approach to improving the employee experience as a whole.

This book aims to help those responsible for working in People Operations, building businesses and leading teams, and includes founders, C-suite leaders and business advisors. In adopting a product management approach to the work we do in People Operations, I believe we have a better chance of successfully doing what I aimed to do as a young HR graduate: build a better working world than that which we entered.

In part, this book is about drawing connections between two disciplines within a business, understanding the similarities in the work done within them and using these similarities to encourage new ways of approaching modern challenges. For some, just understanding more about these similarities with Product Management is enough, but what I also aim to do is give practical guidance on how to use product management disciplines to structure your teams, plan your work, and operate day-to-day.

Throughout the book I will refer to two fictional businesses which I have invented with the purpose of guiding the reader through the practicalities of implementing this approach. Not all of the suggestions I make and paths I lead you down may suit your business or your team. However, I hope that what everyone can take from this book is some inspiration and food for thought. My greatest joy would be having you close the final pages with a curiosity about the other functions of the businesses you work in and a plan to aim for a more commercial and strategic place for the People Operations team.

You can read this book cover-to-cover, and indeed the order I have aimed to write this book in does lend itself to revealing crucial information in a way which is easy to understand. However, once complete, I encourage you to return to it from time to time (and wherever within strikes you most pertinent) in order to prompt reflection on how you can improve your product management practice in your own career in People Operations or Leadership.

Case Studies

As mentioned, throughout this book it is important you are able to understand the practicalities of this way of working. For this purpose, I have created two fictional companies which will be referred to throughout the book. Both of these companies and the situations they face are entirely fabricated, but attempt to give you a 'sand pit' for which to apply your new found product thinking, with what I am calling a 'people operations as a product' methodology.

CASE STUDY

Sprintbox

Sprintbox, and its two founders Abby May and Kevin Hanna, do not comfortably fit into the stereotypes of a successful digital start-up.

The business was founded from a personal need to easily, and without cost implications, return purchases to brick-and-mortar stores while balancing complex work-life balance. The app and service offering is such that you can purchase products online or instore from any participating business, pay nothing up front and, should the purchase not be ideal, easily return them using the Sprintbox packaging and drop for collection at almost any location, without any cost to the consumer. If you do not return the product within 14 days, payment is taken from your credit card or via direct debit.

The business obtained an astonishing $100 million in their Series A after an incredibly successful launch in London, UK. The platform was seemingly instantly successful, filled a market need, and was initiated by using common locations (receptions, mail-boxes and post offices) as post-points for returns, where Sprintbox couriers could easily collect items through an app. Dubbed the 'Uber of mail and e-commerce' by *The Times*, the company reached their valuation of almost $500 million within two years of operations and with 240 employees based entirely on site. The People Operations team of Sprintbox consists of one HR Manager who has also been managing the London HQ Office facilities.

The business is now, however, seeing e-commerce retailers begin to build their own in-house version of Sprintbox, which is seeing a down-turn in revenue. Sprintbox has made four strategic decisions to combat revenue contraction: international expansion to France, Netherlands and Belgium; to increase their product offering to bus stops and public transport (named SprintBoxStop); to employ 30 new marketing team members to drive customer engagement and brand awareness; and finally, to increase the technology team by 100 per cent to support the new product lines. To support this growth, the founding team have decided to expand the People Team and will be looking for a new Chief People Officer to sit in the executive team and build the People Strategy.

CASE STUDY

BloomLabs

BloomLabs is a 60-person digital advertising and app-development agency. The agency was founded in Edinburgh almost 30 years ago and has seen many iterations of their offering, team structure and ways of working. Today the agency is fully remote, with one 'HQ' office in Edinburgh for client meetings and events. BloomLabs has a number of large clients and is a profitable business, producing some award winning digital creative work at Cannes in the previous two years. However, BloomLabs has no venture capital funding and is entirely self-funded, so although the business is profitable the margins are tight and the CEO cannot afford to see the company burning cash unnecessarily.

The split of their headcount is mostly Creative and Technology, and for several years the kinds of team working at BloomLabs have been those coming from more traditional advertising or in-house digital marketing teams. The BloomLabs HR team (one Recruiter, one HR Director (HRD), two People Partners and one Learning and Development Partner) have been able to attract and retain talent from within the agency ecosystem relatively confidently due to their interesting client portfolio and flexible culture. In recent years, however, big-tech companies have begun to approach BloomLabs's team members. This has resulted in an alarming increase in churn of 200 per cent year-on-year for the last two years, with over 50 per cent leaving to larger tech companies which have previously not been considered competition.

The Executive Team has been concerned for 12 months, but recently the problem became more acute when it became clear that the technology companies are actively employing out of traditional digital advertising businesses, posing a threat to both current employees' retention, and hiring competition within BloomLab's suitable candidates. BloomLabs has seen an increase in rejected offers to candidates, but is also proving unable to attract candidates from technology companies or start-ups.

The HR Team is beginning to appreciate that perhaps some bigger changes need to be made in order for BloomLabs to compete within the current market. The HRD, Lottie, is not afraid to turn their ways of working on their head as she sees this as an existential threat to the business should it continue for another 18 months.

With the introductions and base knowledge under our belts, we should be ready to begin diving into the belly of the work we're doing in People Operations as a Product. I am so excited to hear your feedback and implementation stories once you've finished reading. *Now, let's get started!*

The key points from this chapter

- Human resources and management have changed significantly over the last 200 years.

- New challenges, such as remote working, Covid-19 and 'the big quit' are forcing HR practitioners to move quicker and be more creative.
- Candidates and employees understand that culture is more than ping pong tables and beer-fridges, and are seeking compelling differentiators from the People Teams.
- There is mounting frustration from business leaders and employees about how HR has evolved and the discipline is due a reframing of the problems we solve in order to be more effective as business leaders and functional experts.
- Product management is the practice of looking for challenges and problems within a market and creating solutions to serve those needs.
- Product managers are not *operators* themselves of the tools they build and must think of themselves as conduits for the business, the customer and the available resources.
- Product management and design thinking can be used to find needs within candidates and employees, work to create solutions and then fill needs in the marketplace of culture.
- This book aims to help you take this product thinking and apply it to People Operations problems, solving problems for the market needs of candidates.
- Throughout the book we will refer to two fictional case studies from Sprintbox and BloomLabs.

Endnotes

1 Aswad, Ed; Meredith, Suzanne M (2005) *IBM in Endicott*. Arcadia. p. 18

2 Clifton, Rita; Ahmad, Sameena (2009) Brands and Branding. *The Economist*. Bloomberg Press. p. 116

3 Mcelroy, Neil (1931) Brand Men Memo. Available at: https://upload. wikimedia.org/wikipedia/commons/7/70/Neil_Mcelroy%27s_1931_Brand_ Man_Memo.pdf (archived at https://perma.cc/GX3S-ZTWM)

4 Despite the fact the fabric of our problems seems to remain the same throughout time: employee engagement, talent attraction, well-being and training. Friedman, Eric (2021) *Top 10 Issues Facing HR Leaders Heading Into 2022*, Forbes https:// www.forbes.com/sites/forbeshumanresourcescouncil/2021/12/07/top-10-issues- facing-hr-leaders-heading-into-2022/?sh=62f228f9474e (archived at https:// perma.cc/8WKZ-89HL)

5 Itika, J (2011) *Fundamentals of human resource management: emerging experiences from Africa.* Leiden: African Studies Centre / University of Groningen / Mzumbe University https://scholarlypublications.universiteitleiden.nl/access/item%3A2888137/view (archived at https://perma.cc/Z6TR-W6GE)

6 Cruickshank, Marjorie. (1981) *Children and Industry.* Manchester University Press, Manchester

7 Kydd, Samuel (Writing as Alfred) (1857) *The History of The Factory Movement from The Year 1802, To the Enactment of The Ten Hours' Bill In 1847.* Simpkin Marshall & Co, London

8 Newcomb, Elizabeth D (May 1922) *Industrial Welfare Work in Great Britain,* the International Labor Review. Vol. 14, No. 5, pp. 18–24

9 Eilbirt, Henry (1957) *Twentieth-Century Beginnings in Employee Counseling;* Business History Review, Volume 31, Issue 3, Autumn 1957, pp. 310–322 https://doi.org/10.2307/3111835 (archived at https://perma.cc/M357-LCKH)

10 Wagner-Marsh, Freya (2022) *Pioneers of Management: Reference for Business* https://www.referenceforbusiness.com/management/Or-Pr/Pioneers-of-Management.html (archived at https://perma.cc/RJ74-7U7S)

11 Ward, Marguerite (3 May 2017) *"A brief history of the 8-hour workday, which changed how Americans work".* CNBC. https://www.cnbc.com/2017/05/03/how-the-8-hour-workday-changed-how-americans-work.html (archived at https://perma.cc/LBP2-2Y5N)

12 Tolman, William Howe. (1900) *Industrial Betterment.* The League for Social Service, New York

13 Cuming, Maurice W. (1985) *The Theory and Practice of Personnel Management.* Heinemann, London

14 Donovan, (1968) *Report of the Royal Commission on Trade Unions and Employers Association,* Industrial Relations, Volume 23, Number 4, pp 686–698

15 Mills, D Q (1979) Human resources in the 1980s, *Harvard Business Review,* Jul-Aug; Volume 57 (4) pp 154–162

16 Manjoo, Farhad (2013) *The Happiness Machine;* Slate technology https://slate.com/technology/2013/01/google-people-operations-the-secrets-of-the-worlds-most-scientific-human-resources-department.html (archived at https://perma.cc/E79S-ZK2F)

17 Janzer, Cinnamon (2021) *Why Did Google Invent the Term "People Operations" — and Did It Work?,* Workest https://www.zenefits.com/workest/why-did-google-invent-the-term-people-operations-and-did-it-work/ (archived at https://perma.cc/9ACZ-QT4B)

18 Cappelli, Peter (2015) Why We Love to Hate HR…and What HR Can Do About It, *Harvard Business Review* https://hbr.org/2015/07/why-we-love-to-hate-hr-and-what-hr-can-do-about-it (archived at https://perma.cc/FC8K-N5NH)

19 Ryan, Liz (2016) Ten Reasons Everybody Hates HR, *Forbes* https://www.
    forbes.com/sites/lizryan/2016/07/27/ten-reasons-everybody-hates-
    hr/?sh=196a15585af4 (archived at https://perma.cc/G7RN-LVK4)

20 Klotz, Anthony, (2021) Transcript: The Great Resignation with Molly M.
    Anderson, Anthony C. Klotz, PhD & Elaine Welteroth *Washington Post* https://
    www.washingtonpost.com/washington-post-live/2021/09/24/transcript-great-
    resignation-with-molly-m-anderson-anthony-c-klotz-phd-elaine-welteroth/
    (archived at https://perma.cc/BT35-3QZA)

21 CEIC Data (2022) United Kingdom Labour Force Participation Rate https://
    www.ceicdata.com/en/indicator/united-kingdom/labour-force-participation-rate
    (archived at https://perma.cc/TF7L-JVPJ)

22 Lindzon, Jared (2017) How to Identify a Toxic Culture Before Accepting a Job
    Offer, Fast Company https://www.fastcompany.com/40476040/how-to-
    identify-a-toxic-culture-before-accepting-a-job-offer (archived at https://perma.
    cc/Z3KH-B3DX)

02

What is the product?
The employee experience

One of the best gifts I've ever received was a subscription to an alcohol-free wine box. When I decided to stop drinking alcohol, it was clear that my weekly trip to the local wine merchant was no longer going to be a part of my routine. I lamented the loss of that little joy, and so a kind friend had thoughtfully arranged for the subscription for a few months. Every month, six bottles of carefully selected alcohol-free wine were delivered to my house in London in environmentally considerate packaging. The team running the service had put considerable thought into the selection and frequently asked me my thoughts on the previous offerings to improve forthcoming deliveries.

I loved that subscription and kept it up for several years before my husband and I made the decision to move internationally. It was at this point that we discovered not only did I no longer need the subscription (the stores near my new house had a wonderful variety), but it was not practical for my lifestyle or values to have the wine shipped across borders. I cancelled my subscription but remain an avid supporter of the service and every year during Dry January I send many of my family and friends to their website.

But what does this have to do with culture and the employee experience? Well, understanding the idea of how a subscription product works is the first step in understanding the mechanics of how to reconsider the employee experience in a product-mindset. Through this chapter we'll be discussing the culture of your business as a subscription product and analogizing your work in People Operations to managing a product of that nature.

What is a product?

Like many common words in our daily vernacular, the word 'product' is one you've likely applied little thought to. It may be something which feels easy to understand, but almost impossible to define. This may be because a product can take many different forms. Products can be physical objects, media, music, events, services, experiences, information and ideas. So, if you seek a simple answer to the question '*What is a product?*' you may find yourself more confused than when you started out.

It may also be difficult to define a product because it is not as simple as what the item or service tangibly represents. If you go into the candle section of a department store you can understand that, even when buying something which may seem straightforward, we are really buying a collection of benefits, which always includes some tangible aspects and some intangible aspects. A candle is a candle, but they may also have scent, may make you feel calm, celebrate a birthday, make a space feel beautiful, expensive or match a certain aesthetic. The infinite options for candle purchasing feels beyond comprehension and all of these products have been designed to fit a niche need in the market.

A simple way I try to define a product is as follows:

A product is (1) the result of a process, which (2) offers something useful.

A wooden stick is not a product until it becomes a *walking* stick, processed and marketed as giving you something you need. A tree isn't a product until it's cut, stripped and sold as wood for your project. The kind of products that spring to mind when I say 'what is a product?' can be as simple as a plank of wood, or as complicated as the platform used to book a package holiday. Your business almost certainly has a product they are offering the world (or else, what are you selling?!). You will know from working in your business that a product is more than what you see, touch or feel. A product is actually a multi-layer concept and even if they're not always obvious, three distinct 'levels' of products are nearly always present: the Core Value, the Actual Product and the Augmented Product. These are shown in Figure 2.1.

CORE PRODUCT

The core product is not necessarily a physical object. It is the product's *benefit* to the consumer. For example, thinking about our case study for BloomLabs – an app created by BloomLabs will make a brand resonate further with a younger clientele. BloomLabs is selling *relevance and awareness*.

FIGURE 2.1 Core, actual and augmented product layers

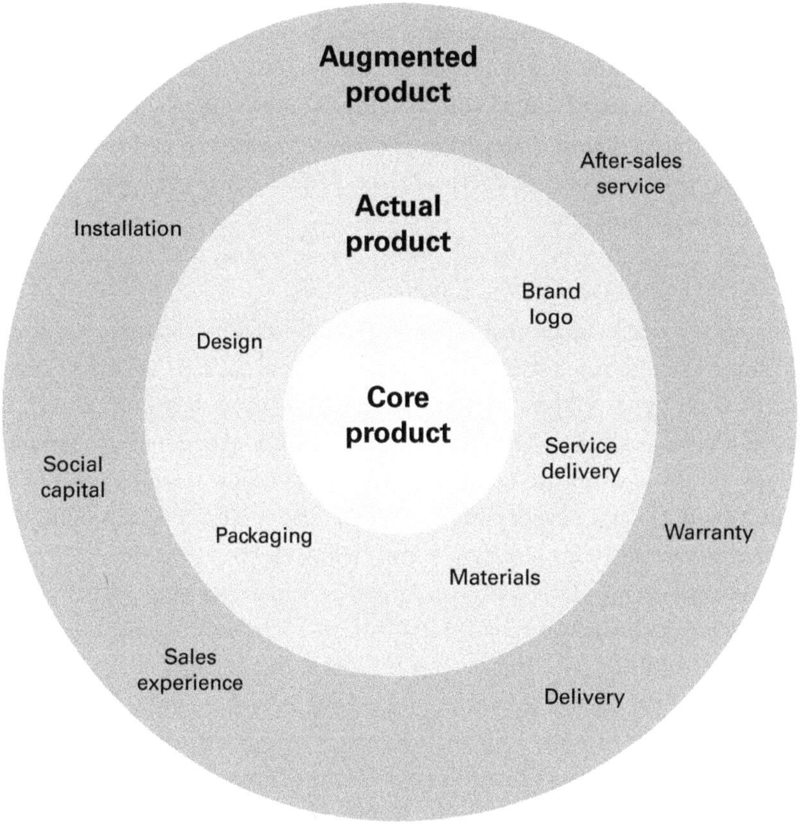

ACTUAL PRODUCT

The actual product is what is *actually* for sale. This can include the unique branding, experience, design and packaging that is associated with it. The actual product and its features should deliver on the core-product expectations that consumers want from the product. In the case of BloomLabs, this would be the quality and usability of the application and digital work developed.

AUGMENTED PRODUCT

The augmented product adds features and services that distinguish it from similar products offered by the competition, however these add-ons don't change the actual *product* itself. What is important to know is that an augmented product may have a perceived value that gives the consumer a reason to buy it beyond the actual product. The added value associated through an Augmented product may also allow the seller to command a premium price. A great example here is the kind of social capital someone may get from purchasing a limited edition set of sneakers or a designer handbag. Examples of augmented product aren't confined to fashion and BloomLabs, for example, may offer the opportunity to win a Cannes Lion or offer an enhanced client experience like lunches and theatre tickets during pitching and production.

PEOPLE OPERATIONS THROUGH A PRODUCT LENS

When we are thinking about People Operations as a product, we are thinking about what your team is buying into every month. This 'product' can be described as the employee experience and is what you are building as a People Operations team. Thinking of the employee experience as a product means you must adopt (to some degree) the process of creating and maintaining products as a part of how the People team define, build and improve that experience for your customers (our fellow employees).

Breaking it down a little more, the employee experience also offers the same Core, Actual, and Augmented product elements found in any other product:

The core product we offer in People Operations is *paid employment*.

The actual product is something inherently useful: a career and a job to be done! And not just any job, but a role in an organization where one feels motivated, included and effective, part of a profession you enjoy and in an industry you believe in; this is the augmented product. Just like the creatives and developers at BloomLabs working on building a compelling advertising product, the People Operations team is obliged to build an employee experience which is equally competitive in order to hire, engage and retain the best talent in the team in order to achieve better business outcomes.

Finally, the Augmented product is the sense of culture, prestige or pride an employee has from working in your team. When you see someone proudly stating 'ex-Netflix' in their Twitter bio, you know that the augmented product has power. It was more than just paid employment to them; it is a part of their career identity.

Subscription products and the employee experience

I also find it helps *even more* to refine your understanding of the employee experience as a product by likening it to a subscription product. Like a subscription product, when you join a company and 'buy into' the employee experience, you continue to make that purchasing decision on a regular basis. Any month in which you choose to remain employed by a company is another month in which you are subscribing to that specific employee experience. The month you decide to hand in your notice is you severing that subscription. Thinking of your employee experience this way is highly effective as there is a vast array of research and advice around how to product manage a subscription product which can be valuable to your People Operations practice.

Each stage of the subscription lifecycle can, in some way, correlate with the People Operations lifecycle. The analogy stretches at points, and, like all good analogies, sometimes when taken too far it can break. That said, we should deeply explore the similarities where they are there, so that we are able to optimize our ways of working by learning from those teams who own parts of the product funnel, as seen below in Figure 2.2.

FIGURE 2.2 Comparing the Product and People funnel

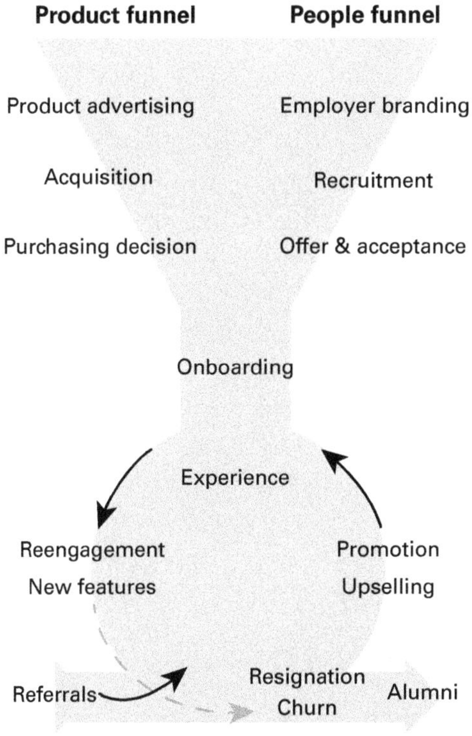

> Many of the stages of the lifecycle have ambiguous beginnings and ends, cross-overs and similarities. For this reason, for a shared understanding I have defined each of the stages in my own words at the beginning of each comparison section. It may not be exactly how you define this section, but I encourage you to try to think in those terms for the benefit of the analogy.

PRODUCT ADVERTISING AND EMPLOYER BRANDING

> **Employer Branding:** The strategy that aims to influence the ways in which potential candidates and current employees perceive a company's brand, culture and value proposition.
>
> Employer branding for recruitment purposes, as I see it for the purposes of this book, is everything before an employee enters a recruitment funnel, i.e., before they apply or respond to a sourcing outreach.

Your subscription product can be the best in the world, but if no one has heard of it there is almost no chance it will be flying off the shelves. Thinking of my wine subscription, the friend who purchased this as a gift for me saw the box advertised on Instagram through influencer marketing. The ad was good enough to get their attention and then describe the ways in which the subscription was a good fit for me.

It is no great revelation that recruitment advertising and employer brand efforts share a broad cross-over with more traditional marketing efforts. Employer branding is an interesting and modern field in businesses and employer branding teams are popping up in innovative organizations across the world. Employer branding specific agencies are also established businesses, servicing the company's needs for more compelling collateral without the need to build the in-house capabilities.

Just like the wine-box fighting to have their name stand out in a stream of products, your company must attract the attention of potential employees, share your compelling culture and ways of working and appeal to candidates who may be a great fit for the needs of the business. Recruitment is notoriously competitive and phenomena such as the big quit, as discussed in Chapter 1, is making things even more difficult. Employer branding is one way a company can swim upstream in this competitive market.

CASE STUDY

Wonderbly is a personalized technology-enabled children's book publisher based in East London. The team is built as a typical platform e-commerce business with a consumer brand directed entirely to parents and young children. When I joined Wonderbly as the Head of People we encountered an odd recruitment pickle: talented adults struggled to take our business seriously as a place for grown-ups to work. We were attracting creatives who had a history working in children's publishing, but often struggled to employ into engineering, finance or data.

The roles at Wonderbly were adult jobs, of course, and presented real career benefits and interesting technical problems. Despite this, we struggled constantly with the juxtaposition between our employer voice and our consumer brand. It felt odd to go against that consumer brand and develop a deeply serious employer brand. We knew that our mission to inspire magical bedtimes was a competitive advantage if presented correctly. It was also clear to us that the product we were offering our candidates: an ambitious workplace with interesting problems and a kind, family-friendly culture, was something that was possible to share in a single voice. We didn't have to pick between one or the other.

In 2017, my team and I embarked on an employee value proposition project and began to build employer brand positioning for the company. We decided upon a direction which totally embraced and even poked fun at the idea that the business was grown up. The team went about creating a recruitment branding video starring exclusively children doing grown-up work, as dev-ops, finance and even executives. The video was tongue-in-cheek, demanding the viewer to confront the presumption that a children's book publisher wouldn't have grown-up jobs. It worked fantastically. Not only was the video a brilliant attraction tool, increasing our candidate engagement at the early stages of recruitment, but it was a good way to break the ice about the kinds of roles we had in our business. We were able to show our kind, curious and courageous values while talking more about the way we work and the problems we were working on solving.

The video went on to win Gold at the Inhouse Recruitment Awards in 2018 – a great achievement for the team and a demonstration that careful employer branding is an effective way to sell the unique cultural product your company is building.

Some companies have employer brands so strong that they have thousands of people engage with, follow and 'peek into' the employee experience from afar. It is an interesting phenomenon and something fairly new since the term 'Employer Branding' was first coined by Simon Barrow in 1990 and published alongside Tim Ambler in 1996.[1] In 1990, an employer brand was something bidirectional and quite transactional. An employee seeking a job would actively engage with an employer brand primarily during recruitment. Today, potential employees engage with an organization's employer branding efforts despite perhaps never working for the business. An example is Google's employer brand, which continues to dominate on a mass scale. In 2021, Universum surveyed over 110,000 business students from 10 of the world's largest economies to learn about what makes an employer attractive to them and what companies they wish to work for.[2] Google was not only named the most attractive employer among business students surveyed, but the tech giant also landed the top spot in the engineering student and IT student rankings. Google's 'Life at Google' Instagram has over 675,000 followers peeking into the daily life working at Google and because of these efforts to develop a following of potential employees, Google receives thousands of applications every day.[3, 4]

CONSIDERING THE IMPORTANCE OF EMPLOYER BRANDING

In 2016, 65 per cent of Talent Acquisition leaders said that employer branding was one of their key focuses.[5] Most organizations focus employment branding efforts on becoming better known as 'a great place to work' or something similar. However, as more and more competitive companies fight for relevance in the crowded employer marketplace, 'branding for appeal' is not enough. Increasingly sophisticated employer branding strategies are becoming more crucial towards creating a robust and attractive employer brand. Furthermore, just like a product or marketing, your employee experience must live up to the advertising or it will fail you in time. No Product Manager worth their chops will advise you to lie, obstruct or inflate your product beyond reality. To have strong retention statistics, you must have a product which fits with your price and advertising. In our work in People Operations, thinking like a Product Manager, we also have to use that same pragmatism.

Before the Coronavirus pandemic, many companies advertised themselves as being 'flexible' in their approach to working. What it is to be a flexible employer has changed significantly from 2020 to 2022. What was previously flexible, such as working from home a day a week, is now table stakes in many industries, and may even be quite *un*competitive. If a company who did not allow remote or home working referred to the ability to work compressed hours for less pay as being 'flexible', it may appear to be the modern equivalent of fast-food advertising of a $2 hamburger; glorious in photos, but disappointing in the hand. You may attract some subscribers, but your onboarding, retention and engagement stats are bound to suffer as the truth is revealed.

To complicate matters further, Glassdoor and other recruitment and review platforms are giving voices to unsuccessful candidates, ex-employees and current 'subscribers' in order to challenge and give nuance to your employer branding efforts. Seventy-five per cent of job seekers research employer brand and reputation before they apply,[6] and 50 per cent said that they wouldn't work for a company that has a bad reputation, even if they'll receive a higher salary.[7] Many marketing teams have robust programmes in place to manage their presence on Trustpilot or Yelp, but I have seen recruitment teams stumped by how to approach Glassdoor. In fact, product and marketing functions may give us in HR a new perspective on how to approach these new ways of engaging with our market.

CASE STUDY
When employer branding goes wrong

An example of an employer branding exercise turned PR disaster is that of Bon Appétit. Bon Appétit is a part of the Condé Nast company and is an online and print foodie magazine. In 2012, Bon Appétit launched their YouTube channel for recipe tutorials. It started out as what the industry calls 'hands and pans' videos, which are the shot-from-above videos we've come to know from brands like Buzzfeed's Tasty. In 2016, the first episode of *It's Alive* debuted as Bon Appétit's first hosted show, presented by editorial employee Brad Leone. In 2017, *Gourmet Makes*, hosted by editorial employee Claire Saffitz, followed. The company continued to expand, using their employees in their videos where the team represented a wholesome and relatively diverse mix of employees. The ways of working in the company seemed to be relaxed and joyful, with many of the videos showing positive and refreshing interactions between the kitchen and office teams. The channel made an effort to showcase the diverse backgrounds of their employees, celebrating motherhood, culture and ethnic diversity. At its peak, the YouTube channel had almost six million subscribers and over 1.3 billion views (not to mention a dedicated meme account with over 400,000 Instagram followers). The employer brand benefited from the aura of the channel's success, with searches for 'Bon Appétit jobs' peaking in 2018 and 2019.[8]

In June 2020, in a *Business Insider* article, Bon Appétit was publicly criticized over its mistreatment of BIPOC employees and the magazine released multiple statements committed to equitable change in the workplace.[9] This led to a deluge of public criticism after many former and current staffers described a culture of racism and inequality at the brand and its parent company, Condé Nast. Three of a handful of non-white stars which had regular appearances on camera spoke publicly about being paid less to host videos than their white colleagues, feeling pigeonholed within their respective cultural cuisines and being tokenized to increase the publication's appearance of diversity. Nearly two months after Bon Appétit's public reckoning, multiple members of the team announced they would no longer make content for Bon Appétit's YouTube channel.[10]

Today Condé Nast is still recovering from the scandal, and Bon Appétit is working hard on improving their internal 'product' for minorities and women. Dawn Davis, a black woman, was named the new editor-in-chief on 27 August, effective 2 November 2020.[11] Searches for jobs at Bon Appétit have declined and the company continues to focus its efforts on improving their internal culture. Some have applauded the publication for making strides toward a more diverse workplace, while other viewers continue to openly criticize the company for tokenizing BIPOC workers. An introduction video for the kitchen's new stars, titled *Why We Joined Bon Appétit*, has 5,900 likes and 48,000 dislikes. The comment section isn't particularly positive, either: almost universally, comments are critical of the channel's new approach in the wake of the scandal. With users referring to the video as tip-toeing around the issues and covering up the scandal with new employees. Reading through Reddit threads covering the situation, commenters describe themselves as heartbroken to discover the environment differed so significantly from what was advertised.[12]

This story is not unique. In the wake of the global reaction to George Floyd's murder, the Black Lives Matter movement demanded more of employers, and employees began to publicly criticize the gaps between employer branding efforts and actual work done by People Operations teams in order to keep their black and brown colleagues safe at work.

These stories are only one part of many layers of the employee experience and many companies were seeing the same backlash to their employer branding not fitting the reality of the experience, and continue to do so. As consumers of workplace culture and even as viewers of media, we're becoming fed-up: corporate lip service isn't enough and we are becoming more adamant about legitimate promises our employers are expected to deliver. It is our role in People Operations to rise to those expectations.

PURCHASING DECISIONS AND RECRUITMENT

> **Recruitment**: The shared process between an employee and business, towards successfully identifying suitability for the role, analysing and assessing competencies and exploring a cultural connection between the company and the employee's values and ways of working.
>
> The recruitment process, in this analogy, begins when an employee applies for a role or begins interviewing and ends when an employee is offered a role.

Let's start at the very beginning. One of the most important points in a product user's journey is where it begins. After all, you never get a second chance to make a first impression. In People Operations, recruitment and onboarding is as much the company identifying a candidate's fit as it is the individual understanding if the employer is right for them. Gone are the days where a recruitment process was a formal one-hour drilling of a candidate's experience and skills. Companies are now expected to spend time answering questions about the ways of working, benefits, projects and company plans. I've even had candidates request to sign non-disclosure agreements in order to obtain copies of shareholder updates and company engagement surveys; candidates are demanding higher levels of education before making a choice about a new role and People Operations teams should be ready to answer or lose out.

For a long time, employment didn't have much of an element of choice or availability. Ask most folks born in the years after the Second World War and you will hear that jobs were something for (at least close to) life and were often in an industry close to your home or which was familiar. As discussed in Chapter 1, in many capital cities around the world the idea of 'choice' began to emerge in the early 2000s alongside employer branding, when forward-thinking companies began to aggressively develop a more holistic 'employee value proposition' (EVP) in order to attract the most talented candidates as a competitive advantage.[13] In the wake of the Coronavirus pandemic, and in the face of changing working expectations, many organizations in the global north suffered in mass labour shortages. The absence of workers in critical industries such as meat production, agriculture and transportation lead to reports of wage increases to attract workers to key industries like hospitality.[14] Alongside an increase in demand for knowledge workers, and more choice and competition within employer's employee value propositions, there are structural and socioeconomic challenges facing Europe, the United States and the United Kingdom, namely inflation and a slow in working-age population growth over the next decade.

Recruitment trends reports in 2022 were topped with the confirmation that we are in a 'candidate driven market' where applications are falling and candidates are swiftly moving through recruitment processes in order to 'win' the ubiquitous war on talent.[15] This leads to recruiters and talent acquisition professionals having to work harder to stand out and appeal to top talent, and the same tried and tested tactics may no longer be enough to win the race for in-demand talent. The recruiters and HR professionals must employ more creative problem-solving in recruitment from sourcing tactics, data-driven recruitment sourcing or asynchronous interviewing.

Using product management as a competitive advantage   Product management thinking can be an effective tool in elevating a HR team's capacity to rise to these challenges. When comparing recruitment to a product purchasing flow, a People Operations team should (just like a product manager) pay close attention to the process of *qualifying leads* in order to swiftly move a candidate through a process. Using data-informed decision making, a POPs team may be more capable of acting swiftly in a volatile and liquid employment market.

Where traditional product management and marketing relies heavily on data and experimentation, recruitment marketing has often failed. Speaking at a conference in 2021, I asked the recruitment leaders present where they believed their recruitment efforts were compared to marketing teams doing similar work in their organizations; several suggested that the function is about 10 years behind consumer marketing in the way we measure success and learn from data analysis. It seemed the team agreed there was an ambiguous fear of iteration and experimentation in People Ops teams. Not necessarily because of lack of intention, but due to budget cuts, structural disempowerment or lack of knowledge. There is so much to learn and improve in recruitment marketing, process and reporting and I am confident that we can unlock a wealth of benefits through the People Operations as a Product approach.

ONBOARDING AND, WELL, ONBOARDING!

Onboarding: The process where a new hire is integrated and embedded into the organization.

This process begins on acceptance of the offer letter or contract of employment and ends when the employee completes their 'ah ha' moment, which can come at probation passing, or the completion of their first effective and independent output in the role.

Onboarding, too, is a place where an employee's commitment to their purchasing decision can be further embedded. In product management and in people operations, successful onboarding drives new users to experience 'aha' moments, or the personal realization of a product's value proposition or fulfilment of marketing's promise (we'll talk a bit more about these in Chapter 10 too). Welcome kits and swag are attractive and offer a good start to impress new recruits, but are they enough to promote your company's values and really ensure commitment? For years, Product Managers have been thinking about onboarding and the effects it has on retention.[16] It is time for People Operations teams to adopt the rigorous and data-driven approaches of product teams to the process of employee onboarding. The unfortunate reality is that most companies – by their own admission – pay little to no attention to their onboarding or reboarding (when returning from long-term leave, such as parental).

Much like product management acquisition funnels and onboarding, recruitment and onboarding processes in POPs can give insight into your candidates and team's long-term commitment and ROI. You can use these insights to develop repeatable, intelligent strategies that give you a competitive edge and improve your people strategy. If we can somewhat master using product management principles, as this book aims to do, recruitment and onboarding will become a more exciting and forward-thinking element of People Operations.

THE EXPERIENCE

The Employee Experience: Your team's perceptions about the company, career and journey through all the touchpoints in your organization.

I consider, in this analogy, the experience starting with role efficacy through to the exit from the company.

Great. So, you've understood how employment branding, recruitment and onboarding relate to a subscription product, you can hopefully identify that you have some subscribers in the form of your employees. However, in attracting and onboarding them, you've only scratched the surface, and now the real work begins. In product management, the key to subscription models is that the benefits continue evolving to remain relevant and support the subscriber's ongoing needs and goals. At the same time as optimizing for your existing subscribers, you have to continue to stay relevant for your future customers and changes in the market. The same is true for People Operations and the employee experience.

Many product management teams have squads specifically focused towards customer engagement, optimizing benefits to retain customers as well as attract new customers to unlock growth for the business. As we discussed, having great acquisition stats is important, but focusing solely on acquisition would be the equivalent of attracting and employing excellent candidates and then watching them leave in month three when they realize they have no career opportunities. Within a subscription product and model, it's just as important – if not more important – that your users continue using and engaging with the product to improve their LTV (LifeTime Value). This means that the product-market fit and EVP development needs to be ongoing, or you're going to lose your subscribers as quickly as you sign them up. In people operations, this is where we should be using product management methodologies to track, manage, and optimize for engagement and retention.

Ideal customer profile   In people operations it is likely that your best and most valuable subscribers (employees) conform to a range of patterns of behaviours which you can begin to understand and optimize for. This means you can leverage these employees to share these experiences with others in the team, or work with your People Operations team, to develop your employer brand to more effectively attract the ideal employee profile (with a keen eye on DEI statistics as you go! A diverse team is a healthy team). In Chapter 8, I will talk a lot more about how to stand out to your ideal customer.

Shipping new products   We must never consider our employee experience as a complete but holistic product. As our company changes and grows and our teams and colleagues mature in their lives and careers, the People Operations teams must continue to refine and improve their product line in order to retain our ideal customers. In product management, this work is done in an iterative and gradual pattern, including user research and phased over incremental releases.

This is a way of working often avoided in People Operations, causing ineffective traps such as launching new projects in silo and over long-time horizons such as a year or several months. Doing this work effectively, in a data-driven and user-centric way, is crucial to the engagement and retention of your key employees. We talk more about embedding agility in Chapter 4.

Engaging the customer Product management teams, like People Ops teams, should spend a great deal of time thinking about engagement. They have clear metrics and patterns for what an engaged customer looks like.

> Do you know what that engagement in your team looks like (or should look like) over time?
>
> I mean *really* looks like? Do you have a specific metric? Do you expect that to stay static or move in certain periods? Why?

Beyond probation passing in the first few months, early behaviours can be indicators of engagement.

- How many times did they participate in team coffee-meets?
- How many Slack channels did they join and participate in?
- Did the team get value out of engaging with your benefits offering?

Each of these behaviours has potential to increase the value of the employment relationship and may serve as great markers of an engaged employee. A product-management thinking HR leader is capable of developing hypotheses about these early indicators and tracking them. We will spend more time thinking in detail about metrics for success in Chapter 10.

As a product manager of the employee experience, you have many levers to help your employees remain in their roles in your team and increase their LTV. But you are not the only one who can influence that key performance indicator (KPI) of retention – managers are key in your ability to control and manage churn. A 2018 Udemy study found that nearly half of employees surveyed had quit because of a bad manager, and almost two-thirds believed their manager lacked proper managerial training.[17] Now, adopting a product management mindset, you may find it is a good time to bring together managers and colleagues from across the organization to look at all of the drivers of churn, and determine what tactics each of you might be able to apply to improve retention.

REFERRALS

Considering again my wine subscription box, when I became a subscriber to the product, I began to receive it each month and joyfully awaited its arrival. I was invited to join a referral programme, something many People Operations teams today utilize in recruitment efforts. Like in employee recruitment, customers who participate in referral programmes are much more likely to stay with your company.

Referral programmes also don't have to be financial; many businesses have great success in encouraging referrals by custom company merch or pizza parties. Employee referrals eliminate or greatly reduce the time spent sourcing new applicants. They allow recruiters to start their candidate search much further down the funnel, eliminating time-consuming outreach activities, and typically take 29 days to become new hires, compared to 39 days for job boards and 55 days for career sites. Eighty-two per cent of employers report that referrals offer the highest ROI as a result and save about $3,000 in recruiting costs per hire.[18]

Employee referral programmes help to strengthen your employer brand. As employees become ambassadors for your company, they will spread authentic, social-proofed messaging about your culture and workplace. One of my favourite niche People Operations metrics is referrals via rejected job applicants. If you can build a recruitment process compelling enough that even unsuccessful candidates are advocating for your employer brand, then you're doing something very, very right!

EXITS

When I moved countries the need and interest in my wine subscription diminished. I began to reconsider if the product was fit for my needs, and ultimately decided to cancel my subscription. In product management this could be resolved through efforts on improving my retention via new features or product offerings, as discussed in the section prior, but subscriber churn is also a well-documented area of product management operations. In product management, teams think about subscriber churn and cancellation as areas to optimize and improve upon in order to learn more about how to successfully build a great product with high lifetime value (LTV).

You may have seen subscription products ask for surveys on churn, something HR teams have done through exit interviews (and often incredibly poorly, through bad question formulation and process design). Understanding regrettable and non-regrettable attrition, the markers for churn and building a robust process for identifying 'at risk' employees is key to building a people operations function which operates like a product management squad.

Alumni   After I churned from my wine box, I still subscribed to the newsletter to keep an eye on upcoming changes to the product and I continue to refer folks to the product even years later. This is an area where more HR teams can still develop: alumni programmes. These aren't new, and universities have built successful alumni programmes for centuries. Experience and learning products have been effective in building communities of alumni and subscribers in order to optimize engagement, encourage referrals and bolster employer brand. The world of people operations is slower to the mark, but they do exist. Xoogler is one of the most famous employee alumni programmes, describing itself as, 'a group of Google alumni and current Googlers who have come together to help each other advance our ambitions in the start-up ecosystem'.[19] Xoogler boasts over 10,000 members of their community, all ex-Google. As a matter of fact, you may often see ex-FAANG (or MANGA, now with Facebook's name change to Meta) employees proudly stating their previous workplaces on their LinkedIn and Twitter.

This may have felt like a somewhat rushed or even patronizing chapter, and I appreciate your patience while we worked through this analogy. Some of these concepts aren't easy to connect on the surface and we are only at the very beginning of our journey into interlinking our People Operations and culture-building into product management principles.

Right, so now you have a good understanding of how you should be thinking about your product as an analogy for a subscription product. Already you may have some inspiration swimming around on how you think about metrics, user research or even just campaign ideas from the product side of your team. There is still plenty to wrap your head around, from how to build your team to how to scale. In the next chapter, we will begin to unpick the role of People Operations teams in light of this new approach to the employee lifecycle as a subscription product.

The key points from this chapter

- The employee experience can be considered a subscription product, something which is subscribed to each month and must both expand (new customers) and retain old customers in order to be successful.

- The product we are building in People Operations should be analogised as such:

  o Advertising the product is like employer branding.

  o The acquisition funnel is analogous to the recruitment process.

  o Onboarding exists in both product and people operations.

  o The experience of using a product, and how product managers approach that stage, can be used to approach the employee experience.

  o Churning from a product, and how product management teams think about the stage, can be used to inform your decisions around employee exits.

  o Some other analogies exist, such as referral programmes and alumni programmes, both of which exist in some capacity in subscription products.

- The above-mentioned stages of the employee lifecycle are important to the success of the people operations team, and may not be as effectively managed when thought about in silo. This new way of thinking asks you to think of each stage as a contributing part of the whole subscription product.

- Employees demand an accurate and compelling employee value proposition and any deviation from truth may end in disaster.

- Platforms like Glassdoor make it more complex for people operations teams to manage their employer brand without being deeply honest and articulate about their employer brand and how it matches to the employee experience.

- I believe, through experience and working with experts in the field, that recruitment advertising is around 10 years behind consumer marketing, and there is much to learn about data analysis, campaign management and value propositions.

- The labour market is incredibly competitive and People Operations teams must begin to think about recruitment and onboarding like a product onboarding, with the room to learn more about cohorts, ideal candidates and to further engage the employee as they move through the product cycle.

- Employee engagement is not just asking who is engaged through surveys, but also understanding what engagement looks like through regular and robust talent calibrations and performance expectation-setting.

- Employee referral programmes are very similar to those in product management and marketing and should be key elements of a modern HR practitioner's approach to attracting talent and understanding who in the business is engaged.

- Alumni programmes are underutilized by HR teams and are effective tools to build employer brand and increase engagement.

- All of these stages should be thought about as the product, but the way you operationally approach this to effectively embed product management principles is to be discussed throughout the remainder of this book.

Endnotes

1 Barrow, Simon; Ambler, Tim (1996) The Employer Brand, *The Journal of Brand Management* Volume 4 (3), pp 185–206 https://julitadabrowska.pl/wp-content/uploads/2018/08/1996AMBLERandBarrow.eb_.pdf (archived at https://perma.cc/ZY8L-URTG)

2 Hoff, Madison (2021) The 25 companies business students around the world most want to work for, *Insider* https://www.businessinsider.com/ideal-companies-business-students-around-the-world-universum-2021-10 (archived at https://perma.cc/T6QF-K8LG)

3 Randstad (2006) Case Study: Employer Branding at Google https://www.randstad.com/workforce-insights/employer-branding/case-study-employer-branding-google/ (archived at https://perma.cc/792H-38A9)

4 Google, Life at Google https://www.instagram.com/lifeatgoogle/ (archived at https://perma.cc/G5TQ-A8QV)

5 LinkedIn (2016) Global Recruiting Trends https://business.linkedin.com/content/dam/business/talent-solutions/global/en_us/c/pdfs/GRT16_GlobalRecruiting_100815.pdf (archived at https://perma.cc/SR8N-Y3GG)

6 LinkedIn (2016) Global Recruiting Trends https://business.linkedin.com/content/dam/business/talent-solutions/global/en_us/c/pdfs/GRT16_GlobalRecruiting_100815.pdf (archived at https://perma.cc/SR8N-Y3GG)

7 Betterteam (2017) Employer Branding https://www.betterteam.com/employer-branding (archived at https://perma.cc/8Y93-4MK2)

8 Datasource: Google Trends (2022) https://www.google.com/trends (archived at https://perma.cc/W73Q-L8N8)

9 Rapoport, Adam (2020) Bon Appétit's editor in chief just resigned – but staffers of color say there's a 'toxic' culture of microaggressions and exclusion that runs far deeper than one man; *Insider* https://www.businessinsider.com/bon-appetit-adam-rapoport-toxic-racism-culture-2020-6 (archived at https://perma.cc/7HJ8-NU5L)

10 Harris, Margot; Haasch, Palmer; Greenspan, Rachel E (2021) A new podcast is exploring the reckoning that happened at Bon Appétit. Here's how the publication ended up in hot water. *Insider* https://www.insider.com/bon-apptit-timeline-allegations-drama-culture-race-andy-alex-sohla-2020-6 (archived at https://perma.cc/2MDP-5RH4)

11 Tracy, Marc (2021) Bon Appétit's Next Editor in Chief Is a Book-World Star, *New York Times,* https://www.nytimes.com/2020/08/27/business/media/bon-appetit-dawn-davis-editor.html (archived at https://perma.cc/J9A2-4YRR)

12 Reddit (2020) www.reddit.com/r/bon_appetit (archived at https://perma.cc/KWE4-QFAC)

13 The Society for Human Resource Management (SHRM) (2022) Employee Value Proposition (EVP) https://www.shrm.org/resourcesandtools/tools-and-samples/hr-glossary/pages/employee-value-proposition-evp.aspx (archived at https://perma.cc/U2SV-EH34)

14 Causa, Orsetta; Abendschein, Michael; & Others (2022) *The post-COVID-19 rise in labour shortages*, Organization for Economic Co-Operation and Development (OECD) https://www.oecd.org/publications/the-post-covid-19-rise-in-labour-shortages-e60c2d1c-en.htm (archived at https://perma.cc/55LC-CXPX)

15 Friedman, Eric (2022) Hiring and Recruitment Trends to Expect In 2022, *Forbes* https://www.forbes.com/sites/forbeshumanresourcescouncil/2022/02/15/hiring-and-recruitment-trends-to-expect-in-2022/?sh=17cfe46b279e (archived at https://perma.cc/VJC9-65FX)

16 Appcues (2022) Why User Onboarding is the most Important part of Retention, Appcues Blog https://www.appcues.com/blog/user-onboarding-customer-journey (archived at https://perma.cc/9S44-85DA)

17 Udemy (2018) Udemy in Depth: 2018 Employee Experience Report https://research.udemy.com/research_report/udemy-in-depth-2018-employee-experience-report/ (archived at https://perma.cc/N6VB-PRV3)

18 Duke, Sarah (2022) 10 Employee Referral Program Fast Facts, Recruiter.com https://www.recruiter.com/recruiting/10-employee-referral-program-fast-facts/ (archived at https://perma.cc/7YQF-YQEU)

19 Xoogler Community https://xoogler.co/ (archived at https://perma.cc/96K8-XCSN)

03

The reconsidered responsibilities
of people operations

I am not going to surprise you when I say things have changed since I started my career in HR. In my first role I spent hours every day printing, scanning and mailing contracts of employment out to our new hires. Then, on receipt of the signed contract, I took them in to my Head of HR, had them counter-signed before scanning, uploading and mailing them again. It was 2011 and DocuSign had been invented but hadn't reached my corner of the business world yet. In fact, it would take until 2014 before I began to really see a future beyond the administrative, which was likely a joint outcome of the modernisation of HR tooling (such as DocuSign) and my moving out of more junior positions and deeper into tech.

Around the same time in 2014, Ram Charan wrote a rather disruptive article in *Harvard Business Review* suggesting to split HR into two factions: HR Administration (HR-A) and HR Leadership and Organization (HR-LO).[1] He proposed that HR-A:

> would primarily manage compensation and benefits. It would report to the
> CFO, who would have to see compensation as a talent magnet, not just a major
> cost. The other, HR-LO (for leadership and organization), would focus on
> improving the people capabilities of the business and would report to the CEO.

His proposal saw the HR-LO work as the central competitive-edge, the up-and-coming management candidates could move from Operations or Finance into roles where they built, 'their experience in judging and develop-ing people, assessing the company's inner workings, and linking its social system to its financial performance'. In other words, the HR-LO work would be entirely management and used as a fast-track to more senior leadership opportunities. The article seems to me to lack faith in the capacity and potential of the People Operations function, reducing it to either a path to management for folks outside of HR, or admin to be managed by HR folks. He further describes the HR-LO role as, '*a developmental step rather than a ticket-punching exercise*'.

I really love People Operations and this approach suggested by Charan seems somewhat disparaging to the capacity for People Operations teams to be deeply strategic, impactful and commercial. I am pleased to say that, for many of us working in POPs teams, the times of scanning contracts and manually adding data to HR and payroll systems are generally behind us. This means Charan's suggestion that HR should be split into HR-A and HR-LO is, for many of us, already feeling somewhat anachronistic.

One thing I will not argue with Charan is the need for two distinct areas of HR practice. However, the way I think about this split is within the single role of a People Partner, rather than splitting the responsibilities out and into two factions. Today, and in order to adopt product thinking, you must begin to understand that there *are* two sides to HR: People Operations and Human Operations. These two sides are performed by the same person in the one role as a People Partner. There is no separation into different role types, no alternative reporting lines, just a distinct definition of responsibilities as they relate to thinking about People Operations as a product.

Human operations

Human Operations is what I call the parts of our roles where you really need a *human*. Empathy, listening, coaching, supporting, making strong positions for a business's ethics and values. The reason *Human* Operations is my preferred nomenclature is because no bespoke algorithm or tool in the world can do what we do in Human Operations (not yet, anyway).

I don't think it is really possible to treat Human Operations as a *product*, because it's more ad hoc, bespoke, and because it's more like a service. Over the last few years, Human Ops has been getting quite a bit of screen-time in the POPs world.[2] There are blogs, products, conferences and books on how to be a better coach, run compelling one-to-ones, handle difficult feedback and support mental health (just to name a few). It is the area which is often held up and defended as the key area of responsibility of our teams.

Like so many of my peers and colleagues, you are potentially in your HR role *because* you love the Human Ops aspect of the work. Indeed, the relationships you can build with colleagues are what keeps many of us going when challenges feel insurmountable. There is no doubt that Human Operations is critically important to your business. Most of us in HR know that some of the most valuable time you can spend is time spent with your colleagues. Human Operations gives us the space to better understand our team's and business's needs, talk through difficult situations to deescalate future concerns, and to disseminate knowledge of how a business and its culture works. However, Human Operations can also be hard to prioritize because of the volume of work to be done everywhere else; performance calibrations, recruitment and reporting responsibilities consume a huge volume of our time in HR.

A CATCH-22

Complaints about HR teams include criticism of weak process design, reactive support, slow solution development and incomprehensible jargon-filled comms. One of the underlying reasons I believe these criticisms are able to gain traction is because HR teams are too focused on Human Operations and are not fully optimizing the other half of their duties (*hint*: not admin).

In my history, the least scalable HR teams have been those which overinvested in Human Operations at the expense of the other work they were responsible for. Due to the fact Human Ops work requires, well… humans; the only way to increase velocity is through hiring more people into the team. This presents a pinch-point scaling problem: to do more, you must hire more, but hiring, onboarding and engaging a team is time-expensive and dominates a HR team's calendar. From there, the roadmap of high-quality work is at jeopardy and you are left with slow process development, weak solutions and reactive projects.

CASE STUDY

BloomLabs

The BloomLabs HR team is struggling to keep up. In the last few years, the team has leaned-in deep on coaching and people partnering, but suddenly it feels like the current ways of working are no longer sustainable. Lottie, the HRD, has been given some clear instructions by the rest of the executive team: improve retention of *key talent*.

Sounds simple enough, but the challenge is huge. BloomLabs is lucky that they have a clear understanding of the job descriptions of everyone in their team, but that is where the HR-oversight erodes. Lottie and her two people partners have spent the last twelve months very much embedded in the teams, spending around 20 hours of their week in one-to-one discussions with team members in coaching sessions, training or exit interviews.

The current annual review cycle is entirely qualitative 360 feedback – it's very hard for Lottie to get a clear grasp on who exactly the 'key talent' is that they should be working to retain... particularly with things moving so quickly. There is no consistent levelling structure and the team are left with a lot of qualitative, wordy information and processes to unpick. It feels like the majority of the information about people management is stored inside Lottie and her two People Partners' heads.

The People Partners themselves feel overwhelmed and are constantly asking for Lottie to request a new People Partner headcount to relieve some pressure. With the current levels of churn, they are spending a huge amount of their time outside of one-to-ones deep in replicating onboarding documentation and reminding stakeholders of their to-dos. Lottie herself isn't convinced hiring a new People Partner is the solution. First, it would take between 5 and 10 hours of her week to stay on top of the recruitment, and then she has to think about onboarding and training them – how will she ever get all the information from one head to the other?

She knows the most important thing the team can do right now is identify who the key talent is, but that will take a huge amount of work: a levelling structure, performance framework and calibration process. Lottie is at a loss on how to find the time while she prioritizes the Human Operations work the team has come to expect from her HR team.

When a HR team begins with the foundations of their work as being Human Operations, it is not possible to unpick this problem outlined in the case study above. By thinking like a Product Manager, and embracing another side of responsibility, I believe we are able to better balance and make time for Human Operations. Further, we can use that Human Operations knowledge like user researchers: informing proactive, user-friendly processes which are effective and meaningful (but more on that in Chapter 5).

Thinking like a Product Manager requires us to tip our roles in HR on their heads; the basis of the work we deliver should be that of building our product. In building, we can make time for listening, applying and testing. We have to in order to build effectively. This means we have to move away from a Human Operations-centric approach, as hard as that can be, in order to prioritize it responsibly.

People operations

People Operations is Product Management of the employee experience; it is *building*. Our role in People Operations needs to be the number one priority in order to create more space and time for Human Operations work. Doing this also enables us to improve our velocity; it is the part of our role where we create the machinery by which managers can develop a safe, competitive and engaged culture and to expand the reach of Human Operations. In this work it is crucial we think like Product Managers. As discussed in Chapter 2, the product your team buys into is the employee experience. It is there during recruitment and then continues to be something your team subscribes to until they hand in their resignation and indeed even beyond in alumni programmes such as the Xoogler network.

This requires a total reframing of the job description of a People Partner. No longer are we Human Operations underpinned by administration; we are now Product Managers of the People Experience, who use our insights gathered in Human Ops work to inform and iterate on what we are building.

CASE STUDY

BloomLabs

Lottie decides to adopt Product Management thinking to solve the problem she and the BloomLabs team face. She decides to readjust the ways of working as a team starting from the basics. She begins to write her People Partners new job descriptions from the perspective of a Product Management lens. No longer will the central responsibilities of her People Partners be around Human Operations. She refocuses the roles on building what is needed in order for BloomLabs to solve their retention issues.

She writes the job descriptions for a 12-month trial period, with two key deliverables to aim towards. First, to use this new way of working to turn the tide on the retention trend (aiming for stable retention improvements month-on-month for six months). Secondly, to have an evidenced, replicable understanding of who the 'key talent' (ideal customer profile) in the business is.

Lottie starts from the very beginning of the People Partner's roles, removing everything. First thing to be introduced is that they should be spending at least 20 hours of their week building,

The People Partner is responsible for planning and execution of the People Operations roadmap, including: defining the vision, gathering feedback, prioritizing requirements, and working closely with managers to ensure team satisfaction and that goals are met. The People Partner is expected to:

- Define the strategy and roadmap (with a focus to improve retention).
- Deliver solutions and test them in order to see impact on our goals.
- Work with the team to understand their needs and feedback.
- Train managers and users on how to engage with proposed solutions.
- Prioritized features and defend the prioritization with evidenced justifications.
- Be an expert with respect to the competition.
- Act as a leader within the company.

This presented a huge change in the People Partners roles at BloomLabs, and one which Lottie knew she would need to work hard to implement effectively.

THE EMERGING ROLE OF A PRODUCT-MINDED PEOPLE PARTNER

This new way of framing our role brings some key responsibilities to the surface:

- Planning and prioritization
- Testing and measuring
- Research
- Building
- Communicating shipping
- Human Operations.

This clearly shows that, even when using a People Operations-centric approach, the role of your People Partners will still be human-heavy. Your team should be spending time thinking, talking with 'customers', managing change and gathering feedback. Your teams should, however, also be using their time to be analysing metrics, exploring market trends, doing competitive research, reviewing the backlog and roadmap and shipping iterative work. A benefit of not packing your calendar with Human Operations in favour of spending more time building products your teams love is that you should now have time to proactively communicate with stakeholders on an as-needed basis, including Human Operations emergencies.

The Product Management lens enables us to see our roles in a new way; one which liberates our time, connects us to the commercial needs of the business and delivers better solutions to the challenges presented to our teams. This can only be achieved by recentring our roles around People Operations, with Human Operations as an element of user research and as an auxiliary part of the role which enables better cultural cohesion for People Partners. Like any change, this may be painful for your team and your business. Many HR teams are feeling the sting of criticism around a lack of commerciality or strategy, but receive consistent feedback for their effective partnering, coaching and cultural engagement. It can feel incongruous, even impossible, to change what is working in order to fix the whole.

Each element of the People Operations role listed above may already sound familiar. Many of you reading may already be able to fit a large proportion of your day to day into a job description like that one written by Lottie at BloomLabs. Considering a role with the mindset of product management doesn't require a wholesale reconstruction of the People Partner role, just a reframing of it. This is a good thing for many reasons. You shouldn't need to dramatically change the skills and profiles of those in your team and you may be easily enabled to win buy-in from your executive leaders. However, the mindset change and reframing of this can be difficult to get on top of because the way we do these things – the *why* – has to change. We are no longer doing people operations with the same approach. Considering our organization like a subscription product requires a dramatic repositioning of the old habits and neural pathways we've built during our careers.

PLANNING AND PRIORITIZATION

We begin with the product roadmap for your employee experience. Your role as a people partner now includes a crucial element of contributing to strategic planning. Strategic planning is the process of defining how you will achieve your vision and mission for your employee experience.[3] Are you imagining topping *Fortune* Top 100 places to Work?[4] Are you aiming for 99 per cent retention of your top performers? Think about what your big picture vision is for your HR team and for your company. As discussed in Chapter 2, the goal of your product in People Operations is to generate value for your customers (employees) so that they continue to subscribe. This has the natural effect of driving meaningful results for the business as your team is able to fully engage and grow in the organization, increasing their LTV. So, it is essential to have a unified plan that ties company objectives to the product-level work. There is no point creating a vision which is contradictory or challenges your company's vision. If your Japanese head quartered company is aiming to grow their go-to market strategy in Asia, it may not make sense to aim to be a top 100 employer in the United States. If your company doesn't intend to recruit a significant portion of graduates, a mission of being a top company presence at campus recruitment fairs is likely not a strategic priority. I will talk more about what a vision is and how to set it in Chapter 4.

This process of planning is somewhat similar to the annual planning process for financial forecasting, but instead of working purely forward from where you are today and looking at budget and headcount as the key driver for the upcoming year, product planning should enable you and your team to move into a more strategic planning role. This means taking a higher degree of control over the *why* behind the work you're shipping as it connects to your overall plans as a company and team. By working backward from your desired end state, you and your team can set goals and initiatives to guide your strategy and a timeline to achieve them. That timeline is often referred to as a product roadmap and will be a crucial document which guides your team towards your vision for your employee experience.

As teams have adopted agile methodologies, the typical product planning cycle has become compressed and is now averaging nine months. It would be your responsibility as a Head of People Operations to have planning and prioritization lookahead of 9–12 months, with a rough view of what the future may look like in a year so further on. Further down the chain, your People Partner team should have 6–9 months of visibility, and your more junior members of the business should be looking 12 weeks ahead to what you have planned each quarter. This way of thinking about future roadmaps doesn't mean you have a perfect vision of 100 per cent of each project and deliverable, but rather that you can clearly project the milestones and achievements that would put you on track towards the vision.

Ruthless prioritization is needed in order to allocate budget and resources to shipping the highest impact work first. Building good products effectively means doing the things that create the most customer value first, even if it may be at the detriment of your team's comfort. Your team should be able to work together to assess relevant projects and pieces of work, while sequencing them in the most impactful way for your business. Brandon Chu (2017) took to the Black Box of PM to write a brilliant post called *Ruthless Prioritization: All high functioning teams must prioritize. Not once a month, not once a week – but rigorously, and ruthlessly.* In this article, he outlines the two scopes of prioritization for product managers: 'Prioritization between projects – this is about determining what project your team should do next. And prioritizing work within a project – this is about how efficiently you can execute a project'. [5]

People Partners must adopt this exact mindset in their role when using product management thinking, which is a unique set of skills that must be constantly at the forefront of the People Partner's mind. Planning and priority setting should be constant work your People team are engaging in on a weekly basis in order to swiftly identify and address high value work to improve your employee experience.

Required skills

People Partners in this framework should have a solid understanding of the employee life cycle, customer (ideal candidate) segmentation, the project management process, as well as budget and resource forecasting. Additional strategic thinking skills include problem-solving skills, mind-map software such as Miro, product planning tools such as Roadmunk or Trello, risk management and goal drafting.

Testing and measuring

Hypothesis testing is a concept which has found its way into technology development 101. Despite a simple premise, 'using data from a sample to draw conclusions about a population' there exists a wealth of experience and skills which are required in order to frame and run an effective test.

The real challenge is not as much in understanding how hypothesis testing works as it is in understanding how to frame the work: develop a hypothesis, outline the success criteria, design a test and interpret the results that emerge. Hypothesis testing is hard enough in technology development, but when applied to POPs it becomes even higher stakes. When building a test for software, you have to be aware of the impacts that test has on human subjects. Often that means they may 'churn' from the funnel or product, or be at a risk of a more negative experience. A test with a negative outcome on a select cohort is something which is not *ideal* per se, but a risk worth the reward of learning and being able to build better products.

In People Operations, when we test, we need to be cautious to build a test which is ethical and which does not have an impact on human beings' psychological safety, career, or relationships at work. For example, if you are testing a new policy on performance improvement processes and your hypothesis is that performance improvement processes are more likely to be successful if they are supported by the optional use of a mental health support service and coaching. Over the next three months you run six performance improvement plans, but what you don't tell the individuals is they are in a test – half are with mental health support and coaching and half without. This immediately identifies just why a simple A/B sample test may not be ethical under certain circumstances in HR. If those in the group without the coaching support are terminated, you are faced with the dilemma of wondering if you should have intervened earlier and supported them in a more suitable way. This highlights how scoping and designing of a test is a critical skill in People Operations.

In this instance, it would require the skill of understanding that this test is better run on previous data rather than a new A/B sample: assess a change of process against a new cohort, after running some 'safe' tests by asking individuals if they are willing to participate. Not all tests are that black and white. Some may be testing a recruitment campaign on various platforms and some may be testing a method of running social and special interest groups. However, what is crucial is getting your People Operations team into the headspace of understanding how to test a hypothesis and then comparing data to reach conclusions for further iterations of a solution or project.

Outside of ethical considerations, it is also very important for your People Partners to understand the methodology behind testing. This includes changing one variable at a time and being able to discern where that may not be possible. It means knowing how to design the practicalities of a test so that it is indeed measurable. Your team should be able to use logical thinking to develop a decision tree of outcomes to help you understand what to do if a test is successful and then feed those successful tests back into the roadmap they are developing (Figure 3.1). We talk more about testing in Chapter 6, but will briefly cover the high-level details for the sake of your People Partner's role overview.

CASE STUDY
Testing in Practice

Sprintbox has a £2,000 per annum learning budget which is shared to each individual in the team. In the last year, the budgets have been spent inconsistently and there seems to be no connection between performance and spend. Furthermore, engagement surveys show that employees have a lower level of satisfaction when they are not spending their L&D budget.

- **The hypothesis to be tested:** Employees are more likely to spend L&D budgets effectively when a curated learning list is shared by influential managers.

- **The test:** A control group of team members are sent a weekly L&D newsletter with books and learning opportunities as shared by influential managers.

- **Success metrics for the test:** Percentage increase in approved L&D budget spend.

- **Decision-making criteria for the test:** The test validates the hypothesis that team members show a higher L&D spend than those in the control group.

- **Metrics that need to be instrumented to learn from the test:** L&D spend approval values, L&D spends in prior year for the same segment, employee performance scores.

This test will help the People Team know if they should continue curating these weekly newsletters, or if they should try an alternative method to improve L&D budget spend.

FIGURE 3.1 Testing decision tree

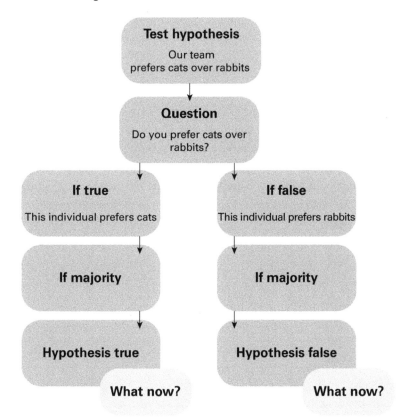

Measuring test performance   Measuring the performance of a test is nuanced and may not be as simple as a yes or no answer. It may be increasing the traffic on a landing page for an ecommerce. In some instances, a test may be one very similar to those of a traditional product manager: increasing traffic to your careers page, increasing qualified leads to job postings or increasing signed offers after sending a new benefits package document. However, sometimes it can be incredibly difficult; improving holiday booking forecasting with a new policy or increasing diversity in your promotion pipeline through a new coaching programme. These things are very complex to set up testing environments in (and in some businesses, it may not be possible to use testing alone to determine success or failure). In short, a People Partner's role to analyse and measure the success of a test may be even more complicated than some product managers out there.

It is really important you have a People Partner who is able to clearly understand which metric you are trying to improve and then use the data you have to monitor that change, while also assessing if any other key metrics are affected. One of the main reasons this can be very difficult with People Data is due to the huge volume of external variables which can creep into your tests. For example, even if you are testing something simple, such as qualified leads coming in for your open engineering roles, you will need to consider variables such as the experience of your hiring managers and recruiters, the time of year, the market shifts and changes. These things are true of many situations, and if you are dealing with already small data sets (3 engineering managers, 30 open roles, or 300 qualified candidates) it is crucial to understand how to interpret and prioritize the outcomes of these tests to better inform your actions. Building a small dashboard to look at data and trends can help and some snappy Google sheets skills or an understanding of Airtable, is a very valuable resource in these instances.

It is also worth saying that People Partners should be comfortable extending into the business to ask for support. Data analysts and data engineers are usually adept at identifying the right test designs and can guide your team, so make sure to utilize their expertise early in the process wherever possible.

Required skills

You should be hiring or training People Partners to have an understanding of how to identify a hypothesis, design an ethical solution, run a test in a logical and controlled way and then analyse the outcomes. Testing and measuring require a high degree of ethical awareness, statistical analysis, often Excel and Google sheets skills (perhaps even some basic SQL), dashboard development, experience and an awareness of hypothesis framing. Experience with tools like Airtable, Zapier and Google Analytics is also very useful for specific tests and outcomes.

RESEARCH

The end game of product development is to build something that resonates with your target customers, solves their problem, is delightful to use and is something they'll want to keep coming back to. The endgame of People Ops, like a product, is to build a culture that resonates with your target candidates and employees, offers them a delightful employment experience and ensures they will continue to subscribe to your company as they grow. Thinking like a product manager, this means one of your primary goals is to give your ideal customers what they want. Knowing what people want is a science in and of itself. The answer is, of course, user research methods.

I have already alluded to the fact that not everything in POPs can be tested. In fact, there are many places where testing is not possible and research is the only way to get an understanding of how successful a project can be. Even higher up the planning cycle, being able to scope out what a reliable test may be requires some understanding of the possible solutions. User testing is the best way to get under the skin of what may be a solution or testable hypothesis for your People Ops team.

Great Research 101

1 **Scope the problem:** Knowing the answers you want will help you to formulate questions. Figure out the answers you need before asking your questions. The simplest example: don't ask yes or no questions in your user interviews – prompt specific and actionable questions that have a chance to lead to answers which cover what you're looking to know.

2 **Don't contaminate the research**: Be cautious not to lead your interviewees, be neutral and objective when asking or referring to what you are asking for. If you feel you cannot be neutral, look to see if third party research or anonymous feedback may be more suitable.

3   **Vary your research:** Don't just use one method and try to conduct a mix of quantitative and qualitative user research. This will help enrich your outcomes and provide more beneficial data for your testing and planning.

4   **Confidentiality and data protection:** Data protection compliance isn't the most exciting aspect of building a product, but you're going to need it if you want to be successful. It's all about building trust and accountability for your People Team to continue running fantastic research.

User interviews, surveys, market research and usability testing are all formats of research which can be utilized by a Product Manager in order to better build a product to the needs of their target market. In Chapter 5, we will focus exclusively on testing, user research and evidence-based decision making.

Required skills

Look for People Partners who are able to run effective interviews, understand how bias influences conversations and are able to analyse qualitative and quantitative data. It would be very beneficial if your People Partners had experience building surveys or doing research, which can be something attained through practical experience or academic studies. Experience with statistical analysis is again beneficial for the outcomes of research, as is presenting that research in a clear and articulate outcome presentation or document.

BUILDING, SHIPPING AND COMMUNICATING

Planning, researching and testing are all crucial skills, but nothing is as critical as building. Actually being able to put pen to paper and make things happen is known as 'shipping'. This is one area where the role of Product Manager slightly deviates from our analogy. In Product Management, you may recall me saying in Chapter 1, it is rare (and discouraged) that a PM actually builds the product hands-on. In the framework of People Operations as a product, the presumption here is that the HR Team *does* build. However, they do not *operate* the machinery they build. This means that the People Operations team no longer turn the machinery of performance reviews, probation, recruitment, etc. This means that the POPs team needs to build tools that others want to use. Instead of authority or administrative bottle-necking, you must work to build tools with empathy, collaboration, influence and incentives to empower (not direct or instruct) your teams.

The good thing about this subtle adjustment to the perspective is that the POPs Team is empowered by the joy of the craft. People Ops teams should be motivated primarily by the desire to solve hard people problems by constructing something fit for purpose, something of their very own design, in order to solve it. This gives People Ops teams a huge amount of room for creativity, joy and expression. There is nothing more satisfying to see than to see a process or system you've built humming along making your team happy, delivering results.

Note here that it is your role as the leader of a People Ops team to guide and influence your team through the process of planning and shipping, so that they are able to build and ship great work quickly and in order to solve problems in the most pertinent order. Shipping fast is especially important for start-ups. If you are not shipping fast enough, your team faces the challenge of not meeting the dynamic needs of your business. You've likely seen examples of where People Teams have failed at this before. My mind takes me back to a Performance Review process which took a People Team I worked with over a year to build and ship. During this time, the high performers were told to wait until the process was complete before they would be entitled to pay changes or constructive feedback. Over the course of the year the high performers in the team churned due to the state of stasis, waiting for the 'perfect performance review process' (which turned out to no longer be scalable after another 18 months of growth, and had to be redesigned). What a waste of time and energy! If only the team had taken a different approach.

Of course, building and shipping something in 12 weeks which otherwise may have taken 12 months to get perfect means you are faced with a dilemma: the quality of the outcome won't be as good! It won't be complete! This is part of an iterative workflow, in which teams create a basic version of a product, test it and make changes to enhance it. Multiple iterations will be required to achieve practical insights and refine features. This approach favours ongoing improvement rather than working straight through and releasing a complete package without actionable feedback. People Operations teams who are able to identify the MVP (minimum viable product) and ship that earlier are much more successful, because they can learn and iterate as the product is in use.

It is no secret that this approach requires somewhat thicker skin. The 'shipped' product may be bare-bones. Releasing projects and processes that lack implicit features may mean initial feedback is overwhelmingly negative, with little constructive insight. When done right, though, using good user-research and testing structure, projects shipped early will lead to valuable iterations and an increasingly desirable work that aligns with your broader team's goals and outcomes.

Note: In Chapter 6 and 7 we will talk more about how to execute like a Product Squad, including how to adapt your way of working to iterate on your people practices and processes.

Required skills

Resilience is required, as is the ability to scope a minimum viable product, and be prepared to gather feedback and 'kill their darlings'. A bias to action is necessary for People Partners while building this kind of team and you should look for those who are motivated by feedback (positive and critical) in order to learn and grow.

How to make the transition

In your role in POPs, you will understand that changes within your business are necessary to adapt to changes in the business environment. When done well, change can help grow your business, engage your team and tackle new obstacles. However, when badly managed, it's also possible for you to introduce change in such a way that your employees can see change as an opportunity rather than a threat. Moving from a Human Operations centric or more traditional approach may feel like a threat to many on your team. As mentioned before, many of your teammates and colleagues may find their joy in Human Operations work – that may be where they receive most of their compliments and praise and it is likely to be an area which has served them well in their career thus far. It is important to say here not all change management should be the same. The circumstances at BloomLabs will not map perfectly against your business. Perhaps you have a team of 20 People Partners rather than 2, or have very different business challenges than those faced in any of the previously mentioned case studies. This doesn't mean this approach to People Operations won't work for you, but it does mean you will need to carefully adapt the transition to suit your needs.

An aspect of a Product Manager's job is a relationship with owning and managing risk through change. There are several stages in the product life cycle where PMs are expected to assess and call out risks and the same is to be said for HR professionals in this new Product Management mindset. Change management should be nothing new to you in HR, but during this transition you should take the opportunity to embrace your new product management mindset.

If you currently have a People Operations team, as there is at BloomLabs, you will see that you will be required to make some rather dramatic changes to the ways of working of your existing team. In the transition, you should be able to outline exactly what the issues are which you are trying to solve with this new approach and the changes you are proposing to rectify these. Communication during change is absolutely crucial. No matter how committed you feel to this new way of working, it will fail if your team is not fully engaged in understanding the benefits.

On your path to becoming a great product manager for the employee experience, you will encounter the need to develop your hard skills such as data analytics, process design and digital marketing. But developing your soft skills is just as important, especially as you continue to develop the Human Operations work your team engages in. Stakeholder communication is at the heart of any product manager's day-to-day life. Mastering this soft skill is one of the most important keys to success.

In times of change, it is important to remind your team of the skills they do have which are critical to the transition. For some in your team, learning road mapping, analysis and design thinking will be a difficult transition. For this reason, it's more important than ever to continue to recognize the interpersonal skills and attributes which will make your team successful and which many People Operations partners will already be adept in.

Soft attributes to cultivate and recognize in your HR Team:

- **Coordination**: Planning, scoping, and organizing is a critical part of People Operations as a product. Ensure your People Team has strong coordination and prioritization skills.

- **Empathy**: Keeping your Human Operations roots to understanding needs, strengths and personalities of the team.

- **Motivation**: It's all about keeping everyone in sync, pushing in the same direction. Moving through rapid product cycles with change and the momentum to ship constantly.
- **Perspective**: You need to both cultivate your stars and support the entire team. The role of People Partner requires shifting between the macro and micro with minimum context switching fatigue.

Note: If you are looking at hiring new People Partners Chapter 11 deals in detail with who to hire and how to interview for your new People Partner profiles.

THE PHASES OF TRANSITION

In Figure 3.2 you will see a visual of the stages of launching this kind of organizational change. You will notice this approach is not new and you may see several diagrams which are very similar to others you've encountered when approaching any kind of organizational change. I am going to avoid talking at length about the stages of organizational change and rather focus on which elements of the People Ops as a product mindset should be explored or focussed on during these stages.

If you would like to learn more about organizational change, I suggest a few titles:

- *Neuroscience for Organizational Change* by Hillary Scarlett (Kogan Page)
- *Leading Change* by John Kotter (Harvard Business Press)
- *Who Moved My Cheese?* by Spencer Johnson (Putnam Adult)

Prepare   So, you're ready to make the change to working like a Product Management team. Great news! You're about to embark on a process of change management with your People team (and the business) which may be difficult, but should also be inspiring and motivating when handled well. Successful change requires both careful planning and preparation. Before you get started communicating or implementing any changes, it is crucial you have:

- Buy-in from relevant leaders: Your manager and relevant leaders should be 100 per cent bought into your plan to move to this way of working.

FIGURE 3.2 Phases of organizational change

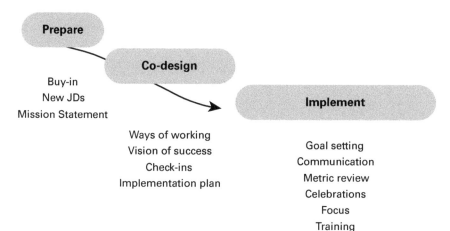

- A clear runway for this to land: There is no point trying to launch this during a competing change management project. Do your best to give this the space and time to breathe. Unlike the proverb about planting trees, now is not *always* the best time when it comes to change.

During this preparation phase, begin working on all of the documents and frameworks you will need to present to your team for their buy-in and understanding. I suggest you take a day or so away and begin writing new frameworks which you will share with your team before you work on co-designing how this change will be implemented:

- Overview of People Ops as a product: If you can share a copy of this book, it may be a good tool. Otherwise, I have some downloadable content in the form of presentations about People Operations as a Product and a quick-bite blog which is a useful initial read.

- Job descriptions: Your People Team will require new job descriptions to outline how their role will be transforming to meet the new approach. Job descriptions can be documents which are notoriously jargony and difficult to penetrate. I encourage you to avoid this pitfall and write these in plain language, giving tangible examples of how the day to day will look. This current chapter and Chapter 11 share an overview of job descriptions and some content to this effect.

- Mission statement: You will require a new mission statement and vision for your team. Perhaps you already have something which you can use or adjust to fit the new ways of working. Your mission should aim to describe the future state of your employee experience (or People Operations team, in some instances). As mentioned earlier in this chapter, it should match the core essence and direction of the business you are working in. Ideally, this piece of work will serve as a guide for the People Operations team, as it will remind them of the general direction they should be taking and be able to inform goals and decisions when they arise. Mission statements might seem like a simple sentence, but creating something that resonates isn't an overnight process. If you take a few hours over a week to write it, refine it and share it with stakeholders, it will end up being a powerful statement. Remember that we now work iteratively, so even if you launch something now, it is always something you can rework in the future.

- Examples of great product visions and missions:
  - **Google**: Organize the world's information and make it universally accessible and useful.
  - **Netflix**: To entertain the world. Whatever your taste and no matter where you live, we give you access to best-in-class TV shows, movies and documentaries.
  - **TED**: Spread ideas.

Note: In Chapter 4 we will talk about how to maximize impact to the mission, and then again in Chapter 8 we will talk in detail about how to stand out in the marketplace of culture. Both of these chapters include information on how to formulate and articulate a clear mission statement which works for your business.

Co-design   I am a huge advocate of co-designing as much as possible. This means you should spend time with your People Ops team having them contribute towards processes and ways of working as a method of increasing their motivation and buy-in. The auxiliary purpose of rolling out change through co-design is to discover unique perspectives through collaboration and to include diverse stakeholder opinions in key decisions.

During this co-design stage you should have already shared information about the new approach, perhaps any new JDs, and your new mission statement with your People Partners. At this point it is crucial you begin to plan how this implementation will work with your team and approach it like you would a project rollout: what are the metrics for success, how often will you have check-ins, how will you seek the team's feedback on how you are progressing? As we read further through this book you will develop a stronger sense for these kinds of questions, so don't be discouraged if you're feeling like you haven't got all the answers right now. This would be a great place to mark the book with a post-it and come back once you're ready to start implementing.

In Chapter 6, 'Execute like a Product Squad', we will explore the regular cadence of a product squad, from planning, quarterly retros and sprints. I encourage you to do this in collaboration with your team. This will give you some real teeth on how to design a working pattern which works for your team and business. During this period of co-design, work with your team to have them contribute ideas towards how you will work like a new product squad. Will you have daily stand-ups? How will your agenda change for your weekly or fortnightly team meetings? Ask them what their ideas are as you move into this new stage of implementing this way of working.

You're going to be busy working with your team on developing lots of new frameworks and during this period it is crucial you work with your team to design your initial set of quarterly goals. Many businesses use objectives and key results (OKRs) or SMART goals. Adopting either of these approaches is suitable in this instance. Writing a great goal is (like most things I advocate for!) an iterative process and – if you're doing it well – will probably take more thought and energy than you expect. In a well-written goal, every word carries specific meaning and it can be difficult to get them to drive the right kinds of behaviours. We will talk in more detail about how to write great goals in Chapter 6 and more about metrics in Chapter 10.

Implement   Preparation can only do half the heavy lifting in change management. Organizational change requires a steady hand during implementation of change. In my career, almost every terminal issue in change management comes down to two things: communication and focus. Good preparation will give you the tools to nail these two aspects of change, but it requires more than just good preparation – the heavy lifting doesn't end once you've launched.

Communication   This is more than just an operational update or implementation. This change will touch on the culture and behaviours expected in your team, their ways of working and even their career paths. This makes the communication complex. You aren't just sending out a new instruction manual; you're entirely rewiring how your People Operations team thinks about the work they do. That said, I don't want to cause concern where none is due. Communicating this kind of transformational approach should, above all of the hard work, be fun! If you are prepared and confident, the process of communicating your change is something which can be enjoyable and rewarding. Optimism and confidence go a long way in communications, so if you have received feedback before that you could improve your tone of voice or communication style, then don't be afraid of asking for some help from your internal communications or marketing teams.

Telling a story when communicating change may sound intimidating if you aren't used to using this style. If you have already spent time crafting your mission statement, you should be able to connect that easily to the larger story that involves both you (as a leader) and your business. Telling a story from the point of view of your mission enables everyone to easily imagine where the company needs to be, but also compare that against where you are currently and how they may see that transition. But storytelling isn't everything. When communicating these changes be sure to:

- **Be consistent:** Make an effort to use consistent names and conventions. If you are going to refer to this as 'People Operations as a Product' don't deviate from that and begin calling it 'New People Operations' or 'Agile HR'. Simple semantic changes like this can cause confusion with your team who are still trying to understand all of the new nomenclature.

- **Be detailed:** In order to get into the nitty gritty without swamping people with information, you should be laser focused on the details that matter. This is a delicate balance and requires skill in how you craft and architect documents. Try to avoid lots of word-heavy documents and try to share details in dot-points, images and tables. People need to hear details multiple times. This is where I suggest multiple 'ways' to communicate change: open hours, shared documents, Slack updates, etc.

- **Think of the human:** Every individual has a different capacity for change. Keep this in mind in all one-to-one communications and try to think of ways you may be able to influence or guide whomever you're speaking to in a way which works best for them. No business implements change in order to make things worse, however, there will naturally be some folk in your team who may have reservations or be sceptical of what is to come. Try to get under the skin of their concerns, show you understand that emotional investment is required from them and don't downplay that this might be difficult.

- **Give line managers and your team the tools to help:** You do not have to carry the burden of this communication alone. By equipping those around you with plenty of context and information, you are able to ensure you get the support you need to reach further into the organization.

- **Seek feedback:** Communication is never one way. Empower your team and employees to get involved and motivated with the changes that are happening by inviting their feedback and experiences. I'll share more on this below in 'Focus', but those in your team are often best placed to make recommendations on how to improve processes even more. It is a part of your role as a leader to encourage and reward your team to own these developments. Feedback makes people feel valued and appreciated, but only if you show you're listening and taking it on board, so be wary of asking for feedback you do nothing with. Even if you are just sharing the results back to your team, there are plenty of ways to show you value their voices.

Focus   No change process is ever truly 'over' at a predetermined point. Change is ongoing, and often the drive and momentum behind change wains towards the completion of the project, with even those most engaged team members becoming susceptible towards old behaviours and routines. Because of this, you should set some clear checkpoints and reviews where you are able to assess the success of the project, make adjustments where required and reinforce crucial messages so your team successfully transitions. To many folks in your team, the first year of any big change such as this will feel like a wonderful and needed breath of fresh air. Suddenly, bold ideas are at the forefront of how they work – they are learning new skills and adapting to exciting ways of approaching problems. Losing focus is particularly easy if you're confident that all is going well. One of the biggest risks at this point is to lose track of short-term results or to begin to lose focus on the details of the craft of this way of working. For this reason, I encourage you to set up mechanisms where you are forced to look at results, retrospect on failures, and celebrate wins.

It is highly important to evaluate outcomes against objectives: design and conduct some ongoing evaluation mechanisms such as goal reviews, KPI dashboard check-ins and team retrospectives. Chapter 6 will go into more details about how to 'bake' these into your ways of working.

Outside of your mechanism for reviewing goals, there should always be space for you to advocate for the consistent celebration of wins. Metric wins can be called out in goal reviews or KPI meetings, but you should make room for celebrations pointed in their aim to motivate behaviours as well as outcomes. Having a #Celebrations or #Appreciation channel on Slack is a good way to institutionalize this across your business, giving you space to recognize your team not just for work they have completed, but also things they do day-to-day to move you closer to your team mission.

The key points from this chapter

- There are two halves to the role of those in People Operations: Human Operations and People Operations.
    - ○ Human Operations is the work you do coaching, mentoring and guiding your team through interpersonal issues, values behaviours and difficult challenges at work.
    - ○ People Operations is what we call the product side of the work we do: building systems, processes, and tools for your team.
- If a team 'leads' with Human Operations then there is a chance that the team will bloat in size, due to poor process design and a lack of time to execute requisite changes.
- The People Operations (product) side of the work must be prioritized in order for more time to make room for better quality human operations.
- In order to be effective at this 'People Operations as a product' work, HR teams need to think like product management functions.
- The job description of the People Partner role changes and elements from product management are added or emphasized, such as:
    - ○ Planning and prioritization
    - ○ Testing and measuring
    - ○ User research.
- Making this transition is hard and requires careful change management.
- Change management is a field of its own, and much has been written about how to effectively implement organizational change.
- Document the case for change and the channels for reaching stakeholders with information they need to know.
- Prepare yourself and other key people for their role in this change. Preparation includes a new mission and vision statement, communication plan, tools and training on what is changing and why, guidance on handling employee questions and expectations they share feedback and are accountable for forwarding questions and responding to enquiries in a timely manner as appropriate.

- Execute a communications plan in a consistent and purposeful way, ensuring leaders are able to support you during this period of change, responding to employee questions and providing information in a timely fashion.

- Purposefully gather feedback from employees and respond to their input with adjustments and communication as needed. In the spirit of continuous improvement and design thinking, regularly examine lessons learnt and reinforce how you are responding to support the needs of employees.

- Develop metrics and goals and check your progress often and in an organized and consistent manner. More information on this in Chapter 10.

- Celebrate successes, recognize progress and reinforce consistently to help employees see their efforts matter.

Endnotes

1 Charan, Ram (2014) It's Time to Split HR, *Harvard Business Review,* July-August 2014 https://hbr.org/2014/07/its-time-to-split-hr (archived at https://perma.cc/JU3R-CY97)

2 Zwaan, Jessica (2020) People Operations as a Product, Medium https://jessicamayzwaan.medium.com/people-ops-as-a-product- 8976f70f025c (archived at https://perma.cc/HQQ2-64ZK)

3 Kerzner, Harold (2001) Strategic Planning for Project Management Using a Project Management Maturity Model. John Wiley & Sons, Hoboken, New Jersey. pp. 4

4 *Fortune Magazine* (2022) 100 Best Companies to Work For https://fortune.com/best-companies/2021/ (archived at https://perma.cc/T5KM-U4X9)

5 Chu, Brandon (2017) Ruthless Prioritization: All high functioning teams must prioritize. Not once a month, not once a week — but rigorously, and ruthlessly. https://blackboxofpm.com/ruthless-prioritization-e4256e3520a9 (archived at https://perma.cc/V5UG-QQYE)

04

Embedding agility with two maxims of product management

One of the things which has been most surprising to me as I've become more experienced in start-ups, is just how many 'truths' I have held and released at any point in time. I am sure that years from now when I read a quote from this book, I will be shaking my head in frustration at things I will vehemently disagree with. Such is life and such is gaining experience. It's always a humbling moment when I come face-to-face with a changed belief, reminding me that personal growth is often not just in one direction, but can step back, rewrite, cross-out, contradict and then take off in a new direction. It's the chaos and joy I find almost daily while working in fast moving businesses.

For a long time, if you would have spoken to me about communication, I would have preached the value of *nuance*. I've always been a big fan of writing and reading and I often find myself drawn to long, detailed, carefully structured explanations and communications. At work, reductive taglines irritated me and I found the idea of decisions being delivered via maxims and first principles as being *bad* communications. You would have seen this kind of communication before in statements like 'the customer is always right', 'it's a marathon, not a sprint' or – at the other end of the spectrum – 'move fast and break things'. I found using these kinds of statements to guide decision making and teamwork as being reductive, irresponsible, even unkind.

I now see that I was wrong, 'to paraphrase Oedipus, Hamlet, King Lear, and all those guys, "I wish I had known this some time ago"'.[1] Today I know that the more junior you are, the more you expect nuance and detail in all communications. Actually, you may believe it to be crucial. I've seen myself awakening to just how immature that thinking is if you are leading a business. I used to be frustrated and wanted management to show they understood the context and detail of every perspective in the team, not just leadership, but that was a selfish and stupid desire in retrospect. Of course, my leadership teams understood the nuance and complexity of decisions. (How could I trust our company to run otherwise?) It made no sense to demand them to then 'show their working out' as a vanity exercise for my comfort.

Simply put, nuance makes communication ineffective at scale and it is incongruous to both trust and pace. The more detail you put in the padding around your instructions, the less clear they become: 'prioritize efficiencies' becomes 'focus on efficiencies, unless you think that is going to have cost implications, in which case, think about cost but in a reasonable way'. Your team then reads this and sees different things, what is 'reasonable' in this context? What defines 'cost implications' – is it money or resources ... perhaps both? How much quantifies an 'implication'? A scale of risk which isn't clear leads to poor decision making and unsatisfactory team dynamics. Ironically, sometimes nuance makes things fuzzy and although it may be more comforting to read, it doesn't work at scale. More importantly, it definitely doesn't work in the types of cultures we're trying to build in high-velocity businesses like start-ups and scale-ups. Today, I see direct and simple instructions and decisions as *more respectful*. To me, it means those leading me trust that I can see into the detail of decisions, ask appropriate questions and prioritize according to the instruction. I no longer want detailed descriptions of decisions. I want simple instructions; give it to me in *maxims*, keep it consistent, keep it straight and let me ask questions.

First principles and the two maxims of product management

> 'We can't solve problems by using the same kind of thinking we used when we created them.' Albert Einstein

Technological innovation puts a premium on agility, and this is the reason most of the best engineers and PMs I know make their decisions based on first principles. A first principle is a basic, foundational proposition or assumption that cannot be deduced from any other proposition or assumption.[2] When product managers use critical questioning to challenge existing assumptions, they dig right down to the building blocks that those assumptions are based on. First principle thinking is starting from that initial position and working forward to a desired outcome or decision.

In People Operations as a product, when approaching new problems and coming up with your own ideas, you should think in terms of first principles to improve the clarity of your thinking. First principle thinking helps product managers and will help your People Team, because as companies scale, communicating simplified decisions is the most effective way to move quickly in the same direction, decouple, and make smart trade-offs without leadership presence. Then, once your team has simple instructions and maxims to guide thinking, they are able to use first principles thinking to simply break through the problem and test solutions.

This may all seem pretty abstract so far, so let's get stuck into something a bit less cerebral...

START WITH MAXIMS

Maxim, motto, axiom, epigram, catchphrase, truism – all of these terms mean essentially the same thing: a basic principle or truth, boiled down into a short and easy to remember phrase. Think of a maxim as a nugget of wisdom to continuously communicate in the quest for alignment. Maxims should be universal to your space and speak to the direction of the work you're delivering. In life, duelling maxims exist all around us. It's strange how both 'actions speak louder than words' while 'the pen is mightier than the sword'. Luckily, in Product Management and People Operations, you have the luxury of selecting which maxims will guide you as you move towards your goals. In People Operations as a Product, there are two which I use to centre all work we do (and which I have gratefully yanked directly out of the Product Management zeitgeist):

- Maximize impact to the mission.
- Achieve everything through others.[3]

Maximize impact to the mission   If your company's mission is to 'inspire every cat to be more majestic' then it's your People Operations team's role to do everything in their power to achieve that mission through their roles in the team. There is no point making a programme of work which offers your team the ability to craft the best pottery in Europe, unless of course somehow that pottery will be used to 'majestify' cats. Yes, this example is silly, but it gives a very clear alignment on what 'maximizing impact to the mission' *doesn't* look like.[4]

> **Vision:** A vivid and inspiring description of what you want your business to become in the future, such as the world you imagine existing because of your company's work.

> **Mission**: A concise, and often measurable, description pointing to the company's evidence of achieving their vision. Often these are lofty and may take several years or even decades to achieve.

Many companies interchangeably use the words 'vision' and 'mission' or you may not use definitions quite like mine above. In theory I don't actually really mind that, as I think most of your team will find the semantic details immaterial over the importance of having *a single, clear, lofty goal*. If you find yourself spending time arguing over the semantics of calling your goal a *vision* versus *mission* versus *purpose*, you're spending crucial time away from writing down what your goal actually is – then you can call it whatever you want.

As a minor aside, at Wonderbly we used the name 'reason to party' because once we reached the goal, we should throw a party. (I still happen to think that is the best description of a goal I've ever encountered.) Generally speaking, a mission statement is more pointed towards all the things your company is moving towards in the present, while a vision statement describes what your company is building toward in the future. If you haven't started using these terms before, go with the descriptions above if they feel appropriate. In my experience I've found that a team doesn't care what you call it, but they will care *what it is*.

Your company's mission statement may be something quite lofty or overtly aspirational, and in Chapter 2 I briefly explored creating a mission which was specific to the People Operations team, but which connected to the overall mission of your company. When I say 'maximize impact to the mission' in this book, for simplicity's sake I am referring to your company mission, but it could instead refer to your company mission through the proxy of your People Operations team's mission. Decide for yourself which structure is easiest to explain and understand.

In Chapter 2 I gave examples of missions for Google, Netflix and TED. Your company's mission may not be the right mission to guide your People Ops team. The reason for this may be that it is too separate from the day-to-day work the People Operations team does, such as Netflix's mission to 'To enter-tain the world.' If the Netflix HR team were to adopt 'To entertain the world' for their mission, it may be too easily confused that the HR team themselves should be the one entertaining, rather than enabling the organization to do so. For this reason, many People teams come up with their own mission statement, which guides them in the direction of the company mission through their teams' responsibilities.

For a long time, HR mission statements were little more than brochure-ware. Examples like 'enable performance' and 'create the best place to work'. Now, they address more critical issues, and I've consulted People Operations teams with missions as specific and inspiring as the company missions themselves.

> When thinking like a Product Manager you should ensure your mission is specific, inspiring and sometimes vulnerable (for example, when focusing on the crucial work to be done in diversity, equity, awareness and inclusion).

CASE STUDY

Sprintbox is on a mission to make buying, trying, and returning effortless for everyone, everywhere.

The new VP People, Yihana, has just started in the team. Yihana was hired due to her strategy pitch in her interview, which used the ideas of People Operations as a product to create the future of the Human Resources function at Sprintbox.

In her first month, Yihana and the HR manager, Jan, have been working together on fleshing out that strategy with people operations as a product in mind. During this work, they spent a day together at an offsite where they brainstormed and developed their mission for the People Operations team.

The activity they did was to write down a series of action words like create, seize, build; a range of audiences such as investors, candidates and team; and, finally, a range of input and output metrics like '100 new engineers', 'qualified applicants through careers page', 'Top 100 places to work', 'perfect ENPS' and 'balanced gender representation'. The output metrics have the effect of really ensuring the mission statements could be connected to something tangible. A mission statement like 'be cool' would be hard to pin down in a quantifiable way, however 'be a global catalyst for creativity' could be quantified by volume of new creatives hired, or a team's winning of creative accolades.

Yihana and Jan then went through each of these post-it notes and began to put them together into mini-missions, before grouping them into broad categories such as 'diversity', 'engagement', 'stakeholder satisfaction', 'performance'.

From there they found they had three mission statements which really appealed to them:

1   Build teamwork and joy into everything we do at work.

2   Develop an inclusive atmosphere that fosters challenge and personal growth.

3   Deliver excellent tech-enabled execution with a caring attitude.

Yihana really felt the third option spoke to the kind of culture Sprintbox was trying to deliver more broadly. The product was tech-enabled returns, with a caring human-first approach to the customer and the team. It seemed to fluidly flow from the company mission and she and Jan felt it would effectively guide the HR team in that direction organically.

It was settled, the HR Team at Sprintbox were on a mission *to deliver excellence: a tech-enabled execution with a caring attitude.*

Maximizing impact to the mission means justifying the work you do in terms of its impact. It is a method to enable prioritization. Human beings have a bad habit of prioritizing based on whatever is quickest to ship. This often means we end up prioritizing work that keeps us busy and moves us forward, but which may move us further from our mission or at a slower pace than if we prioritized using our first maxim.

Prioritization is almost never easy. Product leaders and POPs teams alike are subject to competing demands: what the customer needs, what your key stakeholders want to see, the organizational debt you have behind you. Sometimes these demands can be entirely incompatible. Even before you look at the list of suggestions and ideas from your team and through engagement surveys, it is easy to find yourself swamped under a mountain of expectations and 'to-dos'. From this position it is so easy to fall victim to the temptation of shipping whatever low hanging fruit appears to you. The desire for the thrill of finishing something is hard to resist, particularly when those around you are giving you advice like 'ship fast' and 'ship often'. However, Lewis Carroll comes to mind, 'If you don't know where you're going, any road will take you there'.[5] This is why we must prioritize impact on the mission, it gives us guidance and an anchor for prioritization decisions. There are many ways to score your initiatives and product managers have an impressive library of prioritization frameworks to borrow, of which my personal favourites are:

RICE[6]   The RICE framework scores features based on four factors:

1 Reach: How many customers the feature will benefit (in the case of People Operations think of customers as employees/candidates/managers).

2 Impact: A measurable impact to customers or the business, such as an increase in applications, or team engagement.

3 Confidence: What is your confidence in the success of this proposed value to the customer?

4 Effort: Resources needed to complete the project.

The MoSCoW method [7]   This method qualifies initiatives and features into four categories by grouping them into the area which is most relevant:

1 Must-haves: Here are initiatives which your product or team must deliver in order to succeed. If your team has no way to advertise open roles, a careers page may be a must-have.

2 Should-haves: Things the industry expects from your product or team. Not necessarily required to function, but which are industry practice. If your team has benefits but no 401K, this may be a project which is floated up here.

3 Could-haves: These projects are those which the team may be asking for, things like a four-day work week, or a new 'lunch and learn' calendar may be on this list.

4 Will not have at this time (nice to haves): Either direct 'no' projects, like a sauna in the office, or projects which are optimizing work you already have that you're happy with for now, like 'rewriting the expenses policy'.

Eisenhower's Urgent/Important Principle:[8]   Former U.S. President Dwight D Eisenhower, who was quoting Dr J Roscoe Miller, president of Northwestern University, said: 'I have two kinds of problems: the urgent and the important. The urgent are not important, and the important are never urgent'.[9] From here the Eisenhower Principle was born. It is said to be how he organized his workload and priorities. In this model, you mark if your project idea is 'urgent' or 'non-urgent' and 'important' or 'non-important'.

1   Important: These activities have an outcome that leads to us achieving the mission directly.

2   Urgent: Is where an activity demands immediate attention for compliance, administration, clarity, or some other non-mission critical purpose.

From there, each project is in one of four groups (Figure 4.1):

- If a project is *urgent and important*, it should be prioritized.

- Projects which are *important but non-urgent* should be planned or scoped.

- If a project is *urgent but not important*, you should consider how to outsource or address it in as little time as possible.

- And, hopefully obviously, projects which are *non-urgent and non-important* should be shelved.

Basic Initiative Scoring   If you don't love any of the above frameworks, you can also build your own. All this requires is for you to make a note of 3–4 themes or outcomes you're wanting to address or achieve. For example, 'tech-enabled', 'easy to implement', 'highly requested', and 'unblocks future projects'. Then, score each initiative on a 1–5 scale for what it contributes to that theme. Summed, plugged into a spreadsheet and sorted high to low, this is an easy way to provide a quick indication of which themes support the mission most effectively (Figure 4.2).

FIGURE 4.1 Eisenhower Matrix

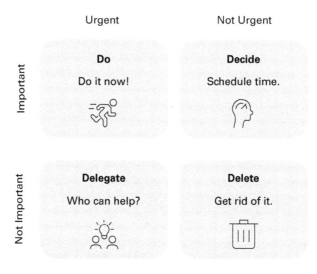

FIGURE 4.2 Basic Initiative Graph

	Theme 1	Theme 2	Theme 3	Theme 4	Theme 5
Option 1	✗	✓	✗	✗	✓
Option 2	✓	✓	✓	✓	✓
Option 3	✓	✓	✗	✓	✓
Option 4	✓	✓	✓	✗	✓
Option 5	✓	✗	✗	✓	✓
Option 6	✗	✗	✗	✗	✗
Totals	4	4	2	3	5

Almost everything can be connected back to the mission with enough creative mental-gymnastics. This is a dangerous place to be. When we justify insignificant tasks, we can lose sight of the overarching goal or mission, and we stop making the best decisions for the company we're building. If you find yourself in a place where you find it difficult to ignore 'urgent but unimportant' work, or where you find auxiliary work like employee socials being used as mechanisms to reach your mission through justifications of 'building team engagement' or 'benefiting retention', then our second maxim should provide a necessary tension point.

Achieve everything through others   Aligning things to the mission is not enough to ensure we are building the right things for the company long-term. Our second Maxim, 'achieve everything through others' offsets and compliments Maxim 1 by ensuring POPs teams are no longer the administrators of the projects they launch. There is a risky habit of some POPs teams I've worked with, where time is spent building pieces of work which genuinely *are* mission critical but which are built in a way which become ongoing responsibilities for the POPs team to run. Examples include team book clubs, planning and facilitating social events, owning the content and attendance of performance evaluation meetings. When a People team builds these new initiatives, but then is required to run them in order to maintain their success, we should consider that a failure at worst, or an incomplete project at best. That is why our second maxim empowers us to build systems and projects through mechanistic management.

Mechanistic management   Mechanistic management, in this context, is the idea of building 'machines' which other folks must run in order to meet their own performance expectations and outcomes. If a People Operations team builds a performance review process, but managers are not responsible for ensuring performance reviews are successfully completed, then the HR team will find a new ongoing task which appears in their job description.

When not building in a way which achieves through others it is easy for People Operations teams to become a source of their own constant administrative backlog and bottlenecks to progress. This leads People Teams down the path of hiring for the sake of hiring and often into roles which are weighed down by administrative burdens such as scheduling, chasing, documenting, updating and uploading. It's an easy trap to wander into and people teams using a product mindset are well placed to avoid it almost entirely. This means they are able to focus on maintaining lean teams who spend more time *building* and less time operating the machinery they've made because they have distributed the responsibilities across the organization in a way that benefits the whole.

Mechanistic management in practice

The RACI model is a system where responsibility is organized on the outset of a project or piece of work according to four categories: responsible, accountable, consulted and informed.[10]

Using the RACI model 'Employment policy clarity and understanding' is an area the POPs team is **a**ccountable for.

There is a world where the POPs team is also entirely **r**esponsible: sending out company-wide emails about policy changes, answering all questions and running Q&A sessions on new policies.

However, there are ways to offset that burden. By setting up a system where managers and executives are also **r**esponsible for the implementation of that clarity, enables the People Team to build with mechanistic management principles.

A very simple example of mechanistic management in this area is doing two things:

• Ensuring all managers have a written expectation in their role competencies that they are responsible for their team's understanding of company policies, and

• Setting up a regular calendar of senior leadership 'Ask Me Anything' or AMAs. Bonus points for having a rotating calendar selected through an automated system or Slack bot if you're really thinking like a PM!

These two actions create a negative incentive but also a positive incentive. Managers will want to meet their role expectations in order to receive strong performance outcomes, so should make efforts to ensure their teams are informed about policy outcomes in a way that works for them. In the AMA sessions, a question about a policy change may be brought up and whoever is hosting is incentivised to understand these policies and updates in order to be able to capably respond to the team. It is not enough to say, 'We will get the people team to get back to you,' unless, of course, the question is so complex or novel that it requires further consideration.

In this way, achieving everything through others means that you will spend your time acting as a coach in a sports team. Here's why, as described by The Product Index:

Coaches don't play: They enable and align the team to maximize their collective performance.

The players are celebrated, not the coach: When the team does amazing work, they deserve the spotlight.

Coaches let captains lead: When a captain emerges do whatever you can to capitalize on it.

Coaches make sure the team is in peak performance: They are responsible for the process that enables them to do their best work.[11]

Here you can see that achieving through others doesn't mean shifting account-ability – quite the opposite. People Operations teams now become accountable for capably informing others of their managerial responsibilities, coaching them, and developing processes which are easily adoptable, cohesive, efficient and value-adding. Achieving everything through others also allows the POPs team to ship iterative projects, using the management and teams who are interacting with them as sources of feedback for improvement.

THINKING FROM FIRST PRINCIPLES

I explained earlier that it's easy for teams to 'massage' ideas into reasoning they meet the criteria to maximize impact to the mission. Now, our second maxim of achieving everything through others offsets the damage somewhat by ensuring that, even if the People Team builds something superfluous, that it does not become their problem to be constantly running. Within this is the mechanistic assurance that a project that is not of high-impact to the mission, and not being run by the People Team, will eventually die as no one will be held accountable to its success. However, that doesn't always happen and even with things working as they should, this can become quite a serious waste of everyone's time. For this reason, I encourage all People Operations who want to operate from product principles, to begin cultivating their skills in first principles thinking, or *reasoning from first principles*.

First principles thinking is a problem-solving technique which requires the thinker to break down a complex problem into its most basic, foundational elements. Aristotle called these foundational elements, 'the first basis from which a thing is known'.[12, 13] Reasoning by first principles removes the muck of your biases, assumptions and dogmatic conventions. It's one of the best and most widely used mental models to improve your thinking. When people encounter difficult problems, a whole range of automatic thought processes kick into gear.

What does first principles thinking look like?   When encountering a problem, new or recurring, our natural tendency is to rely on assumptions we hold to be true, either through experience or anecdote. It's quick and easy to do this, and is a part of our brain's automatic function. We often use these natural assumptions to jump immediately to solutions we have seen in the wild, or applied ourselves. Doing this is efficient in terms of moving from problem to solution quickly, but it also leads to unimaginative and sometimes incorrect solutions that closely resemble whatever has been done before.

Think of a solution to a problem as a cake.

The ingredients are the assumptions upon which the solution is based.

If the ingredients are wrong, the cake will collapse in the oven or taste horrendous when served.

First principles thinking is taking a hard look at the recipe and then ensuring the ingredients are correct, appropriately measured, and of a high quality.

We are imprisoned by the thoughts of others if we're not thinking for ourselves. Too often I've seen teams limit their capacity for impact by settling on projects and solutions which don't maximize impact to the mission, or which totally ignores something which challenges a deeply-held belief.

Consider a limiting belief you have held personally about your work. Something like, 'We will always get a low response-rate on our ENPS survey.

I know because we have always had poor response rates'. If this belief was something you refused to examine, you would remain permanently immovable, with low employee engagement affecting your ability to deliver. Taking a first-principles approach means asking ourselves *why* there is low engagement, and reconstructing a solution from there using quality ingredients. Through reasoning by first principles, your previously limiting belief can become, 'Our team have been less likely to respond to our ENPS survey because it is only sent by email, a tool they may not use in time for the survey's closing date. Also, the team is not incentivised in any way to complete the ENPS because we do not share the information.' You can then solve those two new problems: a better way to send your survey and a new way to encourage your team to complete.

Being trapped by limiting thoughts doesn't only present itself as a benign blocker of good work, but can sometimes be a malignant tool used to encourage bad work. An example of this would be where a member of your team uses anecdotal and dogmatic thinking to encourage a project that does not maximize impact to the mission because they saw it elsewhere. If you find someone in your team saying things like, 'Google has one' or 'someone in the team said they wanted it on a survey', that is a great time to take things back to first principles thinking.

Several years ago, I had some members of my team tell me they needed to arrange and manage the staff Christmas Party, so we had to make sure we didn't plan too much other work over Q4. The reason was that the Christmas Party has always been a People Team job and 'otherwise no one would want to do it'. Oof. Both of these reasons aren't compelling enough to get this onto my roadmap, unfortunately for them, and I pushed back using first principles thinking. The outcome we reached was that, actually, we could establish a set of incentives which encouraged others in the team who loved culture building and socials to get involved. We had some members of the team who had wanted to demonstrate competencies in budget and resource management, some members of the team who had recently taken courses in project management and were keen to put that into action. What we were able to do was assemble a group of folks (including one very enthusiastic member of the People Team) with various responsibilities and incentives, so that our Christmas party enabled our team to achieve through others.

By using first principles thinking, we are able to better assess which projects and pieces of work are most aligned with our maxims and are therefore able to make better decisions. However, this approach is not easy to adopt for everyone. First principles thinking requires embracing a new, and sometimes exhausting, mindset which forces us to identify when our old way of doing things is obsolete. This shift in thinking discards the things that we feel keep us safe, or give us reason for ego – conventional wisdom, experience, dogma – and forces us to question our own beliefs. It's incredibly difficult to kickstart when you aren't used to thinking this way every day. Once you get into a habit of adopting first principles thinking, it comes much more naturally, but the initial transition is enough to exhaust many teams and cause conflict. The good news is there are many simple methods I encourage teams to utilize when first adopting this approach.

THINK LIKE A CHILD: THE FIVE WHYS

Why do I need to eat healthy? Why is my bedtime 8pm? Why are you allowed the iPad?

Any parent out there is an expert at identifying first principles thinking when presented through this lens. If you observe how children naturally approach challenges in the world, you are watching first principles thinking in action. Consider yourself as a child, imagine you too are trying to build your own reasoning around why certain things must be done in certain ways in an attempt to establish a better view of the world.

When someone comes to you with an unexplained solution or point of view, simply ask 'Why' five times (and why not, you can keep going if you aren't getting there and are having fun!).

We see discrepancies in pay which are potentially unfair.

Why?

Men in our team are consistently being paid more than women.

Why?

Our compensation structure doesn't work.

Why?

Because people are negotiating their salaries up after an offer.

Why?

Because men are more likely to negotiate it seems.

Why?

Gender norms and societal reasons.[14] It seems allowing negotiation may be unfair and causing the problem.

Look at that progress! What you have there is a hypothesis you can now test and a potential product iteration to your compensation philosophy. 'What does a compensation structure look like without negotiation?'

If you decide to take this approach, make sure you're very explicit that you are doing so in an effort to adopt first principles thinking by using the 'five whys' or thinking like a child. This will help you to avoid ugly snips of 'let's take this offline' or 'because I told you so'. And if you are a manager who finds yourself shutting your team's 'why?' down, know that being on the receiving end is also difficult, particularly if you feel you've already walked through your own reasoning. Take this as an opportunity to better communicate your position; there should be no fear in defending a well-established stance on something. If someone is asking you 'why?' again then perhaps you haven't explained well enough or got quite to the heart of the problem. Intent is everything when using this approach, which is why using the playfulness of a child is more attractive than using the stern approach of a school principal.

THINK LIKE A PHILOSOPHER: SOCRATIC QUESTIONING

Socrates believed that the practice of thoughtful, disciplined dialogue was the most effective way to examine ideas logically and get to the first principles of a problem and solution.[15] The best way to do this is by having members of your team take on the personas of various types of Socratic questioning as they examine an idea or problem together. If you don't have a team of others, then spend time embodying these mindsets yourself.

The scientist: Look for hard facts and evidence.

- What evidence backs this up?
- What are the sources?
- How did this person come up with this belief?

The photographer: Examining things through the viewpoints of others.

- How would other groups of people respond to this question?
- What would X in the team say?
- How are my ideas similar or different to this one?

The storyteller: Looking for the origin of your ideas and telling it through the medium of narrative.

- How did I come up with this idea?
- What steps in thought me to believe this?
- Has either of our opinions been influenced by something or someone?
- What kinds of experiences made me inclined to think this way?

The lawyer: No stones left unturned, looking into the facts for implications and consequences.

- What if I am wrong about this?
- Is there a right and wrong, or is there a grey area?
- What are the consequences if I am wrong?
- If that happened, what else would happen as a result?

Not every decision you make requires this degree of interrogation. Sometimes it is okay just to honestly ask yourself, 'Am I *sure* about this?' If you are adept at first principles thinking, you start to become more in tune when your decisions are no longer based on solid ground, and will naturally pull yourself up from time to time. When approaching People Operations like a Product Manager, the most crucial points to employ first principles thinking are the times where you are deciding which projects you will and won't invest your time into. Chapter 6 of this book will go into more detail about how you can build first principles thinking in your retrospective and planning process so that you tackle projects with confidence.

CASE STUDY

It was settled, the HR Team at Sprintbox were on a mission *to deliver excellent tech-enabled execution with a caring attitude.* This mission is in service to Sprintbox's mission to make buying, trying and returning effortless for everyone, everywhere.

Yihana and Jan are deciding on their first project to work on together. Yihana has the benefit and burden of being brand new to the team, she comes with little institutional knowledge, but also is open to new ideas which Jan may have otherwise rejected. She has experience using first principles, so Yihana knows she can use this to her advantage. This is all new to Jan, however, and he is still learning how to navigate this new way of thinking.

Together, they begin by listing a range of different projects which they would like to see come to fruition at Sprintbox. Their plan is to then use Eisenhower's urgent/ important principle to help them decide which project is most capable of maximizing impact to the mission. They list things like 'HRIS Data Audit', 'HR FAQ Help Centre', and 'New Corporate Values'.

In this process, Yihana writes down 'Lunch and Learns' and puts that into the 'not important and not urgent' box, indicating that there are other projects which would have a bigger impact on their mission. Jan pushes back and says that he thinks this should be more urgent and that it is much more important than the other items on the list. Yihana finds that interesting and asks him to elaborate.

Jan explains that the team have 'all been asking for Lunch and Learns'. Yihana lets Jan know that she is going to take a step back and ask some more questions to try to get to the foundations of this issue. She doesn't want to prove Jan wrong; she wants to understand why they're coming at this from totally different places.

'Why have the team 'all' been asking for Lunch and Learns?' asks Yihana.

'Because Felicity in Marketing had them at her old company and she told everyone how good they are. Everyone in the team wants them,' replies Jan.

'When you say 'everyone' who do you mean?'

'Well, maybe not everyone, but when I look into the surveys I often see Lunch and Learns mentioned.'

'Would you say those folks mentioning Lunch and Learns are the majority of those responding?'

'No, most of the people don't submit any comments. We only ask ENPS with an open comment box.'

'Have you ever asked about any other kinds of learning opportunities?'

'No, actually. We've only really asked people for open feedback.'

'Do we have other ways to learn at Sprintbox?'

'Not really. Actually, we have never really spoken about learning in the company, so there is a chance Felicity has just filled a void there.'

At this point Yihana begins to agree that framing the problem as 'not offering enough learning' will help them to ship something and maximize impact to the mission. If their mission is to build a caring culture, the People Team must also express a care for feedback and the need to develop the team through L&D. Further, it is clear that the voices calling out for learning, coupled with the company's plans to hire more people and continue to grow, are making the need for development opportunities quite urgent or else there may be a churn risk.

Together, Jan and Yihana decide they will do a project on learning this quarter, with a goal of '100 per cent of the company offered at least three ways to expand their knowledge'. After running through the foundational thinking, Jan has begun to understand the core of the problem. He offers a project idea: he will run a series of interviews with the team, and then sit with everyone interested and create bespoke learning plans for each member of the company. This is something he said he did in his previous role. Yihana likes the heart of the idea, but recognizes this has the potential to become a full-time job for Jan.

Yihana encourages Jan to take the heart of this idea and find a way to motivate others to act, and achieve their aims through others. Together, after a few hours of thinking, they decide to gather some data through a Typeform survey about what the team would like learning to look like, and grouping that into pillars which could easily cover the entire company with only a handful of initiatives. They then begin to source a tech-enabled marketplace tool to offer various learning opportunities to the company, suggested to the team via the power of management feedback.

The key points from this chapter

- Using maxims helps you effectively communicate complicated concepts as you scale and change.
- There are two product management maxims you should use to keep your work prioritized and effective:
  o Maximize impact to the mission.
  o Achieve everything through others.
- Maximizing impact to the mission requires you to have clarity on what your team (and company) mission is.
- You can use tools and frameworks to help you assess a project's impact on the mission. Some of these include:
  o RICE
  o MoSCoW Method
  o Eisenhower's Urgent/Important Principle.
- Achieving everything through others is the process of approaching your programmes so that your POPs team is ultimately accountable, but in a way which distributes responsibility to others to make the outcomes more effective.
- Using mechanistic management, you can build processes and projects which effectively achieve large volumes of operational work through others, such as managers.
- It is not enough to assess projects and pieces of work the way you used to. In order to do a more effective job of rationalizing which work should be prioritized against the mission, you and your team can use first principles thinking.
- First principles thinking is a problem-solving technique which requires the thinker to break down a complex problem into its most basic, foundational elements.
- Tools like the 'five whys' and thinking like a child is a great way to embed first principles thinking when you are first adjusting.
- Use first principles thinking when establishing the right pieces of work for your team and always align them with your two maxims. These three elements alone will do a great service in improving the quality of output from your POPs team.

Endnotes

1 Zelazny, Roger (1975) *Sign of the Unicorn*, ch. 3 [Corwin], Avon Books, New York

2 Goetzmann, Jens-Fabian (2019) Product Management from First Principles https://www.jefago.com/product-management/first-principles-thinking/ (archived at https://perma.cc/Z7YY-69JK)

3 Chu, Brandon (2018) The First Principles of Product Management https://blackboxofpm.com/the-first-principles-of-product-management-ea0e2f2a018c (archived at https://perma.cc/WWK4-3BHE)

4 Also, because there is no such thing as an un-magestic cat.

5 This quote is actually a paraphrasing of a small section in *Alice's Adventures in Wonderland,* between Alice and the Cheshire Cat. Carroll, Lewis C (1865, 2003) *Alice's Adventures in Wonderland,* (Penguin Classics) 9780007578580

6 McBride, Sean RICE: Simple prioritization for product managers, Intercom Blog https://www.intercom.com/blog/rice-simple-prioritization-for-product-managers/ (archived at https://perma.cc/5ZF7-2L8G)

7 Clegg, Dai; Barker, Richard (1994) *Case Method Fast-Track: A RAD Approach.* Addison-Wesley. 9780201624328

8 Clear, James (2022) How to be More Productive and Eliminate Time Wasting Activities by Using the "Eisenhower Box" https://jamesclear.com/eisenhower-box (archived at https://perma.cc/MF9R-VDTW)

9 Eisenhower, Dwight (1954) The American Presidency Project, Speech delivered by: Dwight D. Eisenhower, Speech number: 204, Title: Address at the Second Assembly of the World Council of Churches, Location: Evanston, Illinois

10 *A Guide to the Project Management Body of Knowledge* (PMBOK Guide) (5th ed.). Project Management Institute. (2013) p. 262. 9781935589679

11 The Product Index (2022) Thinking Frameworks for Product Managers https://theproductindex.com/docs/thinking-frameworks-for-product-managers.html (archived at https://perma.cc/CTS5-Y8JA)

12 Aristotle, Waterfield, Robin (2008) *The Physics,* Oxford University Press, Oxford, 9780199540280

13 Irwin, Terence (1990). Aristotle's First Principless, Oxford University Press, Oxford. 9780198242901

14 Eriksson, K and Sandberg, A (2012) Gender Differences in Initiation of Negotiation: Does the Gender of the Negotiation Counterpart Matter? Wiley Online Library, *Negotiation Journal* https://onlinelibrary.wiley.com/doi/10.1111/j.1571- 9979.2012.00349.x (archived at https://perma.cc/J4HV-LYNT)

15 Jacques Brunschwig, Geoffrey Ernest Richard Lloyd (eds), (2003) *A Guide to Greek Thought*: *Major Figures and Trends*, Harvard University Press, p. 233

05

User research and evidence-based decision-making

In many companies I've worked with, holiday booking has presented a frustrating logistical knot. Some members of our teams book too little holiday, others request time off only days before their already purchased flights; teams in Europe want longer breaks over the same peaks in summer and some folks arranged holiday with their manager and entirely avoided any HRIS system, only to be discovered in an audit at the end of year. I've seen many try to solve this problem through the long arm of policy: employees must book holidays at least two weeks in advance, all holidays unapproved will be unpaid and some companies even enforce certain holiday days or require all holidays to be pre-booked months in advance to avoid double-ups. This kind of approach is rarely aligned with the kinds of values modern businesses embrace: trust and ownership, for example. I've never been a big fan of overly parental policies such as these. They dehumanize the workplace and are partially responsible for the un-cooperative and corporate reputation of POPs teams. I am sure you have seen similar 'solutions' in your professional life; perhaps you have implemented them. But have you ever had the nagging feeling that you don't understand a problem quite as well as you thought?

A few years ago, I was working with a company when I was given a strong incentive to look further under the skin of 'solving' the holiday problem. When it came to holiday, I had something eating away at me, saying that the way I'd seen this solved in the past wasn't quite right.

In product management and design thinking, a key element of solving user problems is through user research and with good reason. There's evidence that companies that apply user research and design principles are typically more successful than those that don't.[1] The user research you don't do costs your business opportunities – that's a fact. User research provides opportunities to learn more about your customer, innovate and build usable products quicker. Despite this being something deeply embedded in product management, user research is a relatively unused and new discipline within People Operations. One of the reasons I started out talking more publicly about my work in HR was because I had worked in organizations where I was fed up with the inertia of innovation, but also with the lack of customer-centricity. Too often I saw People teams solving problems, such as the holiday knot I explained earlier, through deterrence and stricter policies rather than user-research and well-executed incentives.

Try as we may, we don't know our teams as well as we think we do. A yearly engagement survey isn't enough to get under the skin of the kind of the needs of those in your team in all of the places we need information. Chances are, your employees aren't going to come to you one day and give you an overview of their deepest needs and desires – maybe your company culture isn't transparent in that way, maybe they worry they'll not be taken seriously or maybe their needs are niche. If you think of your employees as your customers, you know that those you employ are also not the only place you need to be focusing; you also have candidates in the market who you would like to attract into your company now and in the future.

When it came to the holiday problem, I decided to embark on my first project of specific user research inspired investigation into a HR problem area. I felt empowered because in my years in people operations I'd seen a gradual shift in the way we think about feedback from our colleagues and candidates. This change continues even now: yearly engagement surveys have become pulse surveys, pulse surveys have been driven through automation and expertly designed software as a service (SaaS) sentiment analysis tools were being explored. However, one thing I want to see evolve is the relationship between these questions and answers and where they are used to solve problems. The survey data I see collected in HR is often used to identify problems and areas for development. I rarely see user research employed during a project to help guide solution development. Using People Operations as a Product methodologies means this needs to change. User research has to become a foundational part of your team's delivery.

User research in people operations

User research is the detailed and methodical study of a product's users, including exploring their needs and pain points, with the intention to feed insights to product management squads. User researchers regularly use various methods to expose problems and present design solutions, from surveys to user interviews.[2]

In HR, we collect an incredible amount of user data from our team, including exit interviews, surveys and qualitative feedback. Finding a way to systemize these efforts in the same way product management teams are is the key to empowering research in your POPs strategy. User research is a way for POPs teams to make evidence-based decisions, similar to how we spoke about first principles thinking but further into the development process. Consider first principles thinking as the first step in discovering your solution and user research as the methods you employ to refine and deliver it. Evidence based decisions are (and it probably won't surprise you) easier to defend, have better ROI and give confidence in a People Operations team with commercial value. In short, through evidence-based decision making and building we can build better programmes, policies and tools for our business.

User personas   The insights we gain from our teams don't just sit with the People Operations team; we should be actively sharing that knowledge to our leaders and managers. Any targeted research allows us to create user personas to use as tools when explaining or building an initiative.

User personas are examples of hypothetical users with a connection to your company and product. They usually present themselves as a short document outlining behavioural patterns, goals, stills and background. For example, you may have a user persona of Abdul, a Junior Manager who sees their career growth as urgent, and Amelia, a highly skilled technical Individual Contributor (IC) who is difficult to hire and highly motivated by autonomy and technical challenges. You can already imagine that the kinds of things you build and how you communicate these may change depending on which user persona you are interacting with.

From here then, you can use research to map your team's experiences with the company and whatever you are building. This changes the conversation from, 'We need to make some changes to the holiday policy,' to 'We're more likely to retain people like Amelia if we offer stronger positive incentives to holiday booking'. When we can imagine real people behind our programmes of work, we are able to build better products for individuals and for our company.

Diversity in your audience   Today, it is table-stakes that we understand a diverse company is a vibrant and thriving one. The more voices we engage, the stronger our solutions. So too in POPs. In bringing more voices to the design table for our company's solutions and ways of working, our team can shape our product to the benefit of everyone.

Not all POPs teams are large, or have a diverse range of voices within them. Opening up the avenues for customer feedback in what we are building enables richer feedback. Further, having contact with the People Operations team as they design and solve problems is great for teams because they have a chance to be heard. Only by collaborating together and combining our knowledge can we build innovative products for our teams using the power of diversity while we listen and lift our colleagues.

Just like in the holiday knot I've spoken on throughout this chapter, sometimes it's hard for us to see the problems clearly. Solutions which seem obvious to us on the outside may be really difficult for those in our team to understand. User testing helps us to look at a solution, tool, process or communication through the eyes of people who are expected to use or interact with it. Working on building solutions through user tests and interviews, we can validate ideas before launching them, which makes our launches more likely to be successful and adopted.

User research for POPs 101

It seems obvious: user research is a crucial part of a product design process. Intuitively, we know that speaking directly to users and customers is the only way to discover exactly what these users need. For a user researcher to generate crucial facts and insights for a product management squad, they gather data from users through a structured and specific approach:

1 Define the hypothesis.
2 Pick the method.
3 Interpret the data.
4 Tell the story.

For the sake of clarity as we go through the rest of this chapter, let's use the case study at Sprintbox.

CASE STUDY

Yihana has set Jan a goal of '100 per cent of the company offered at least three ways to expand their knowledge'.

From here, Jan conducted some user research to decide what the project would look like to deliver this.

DEFINE THE HYPOTHESIS

In user research, hypotheses can be thought of as testable assumptions – something like, 'If I stay up late, then I will want to wake up later'.

An assumption can be something that we believe is true which we want to prove or disprove, or it can be something that we're expecting to happen and we're aiming to see the outcome. Generally, a testable hypothesis will be based on what we already think we know, as well as our personal experiences or individual viewpoints. Coming to a testable hypothesis or assumption is itself somewhat of an art. Like first principles thinking, there are ways to waste time by testing the wrong hypothesis, or designing a solution around a hypothesis that doesn't get to the core of the problem.

For this reason, using first principles thinking and spending time really committing to the hypothesis you'd like to test is an important step of any user research into a People Operations problem area.

The way we build our testable assumptions doesn't necessarily need to be as structured and clear as used in academia or science, but it is a good place to start to understand how these hypotheses are built as it gives a great foundation for future testable assumptions. Hypotheses propose a relationship between two or more variables. An independent variable is something which you are able to change or control, such as eating an apple a day. A dependent variable is something which you are aiming to observe or measure, like doctor's visits.

Often, a good place to start when thinking of a hypothesis is asking the question the way you would if you were asking someone who knew nothing about the topic. The simpler the language, the more distilled your point tends to be. The question should be focused, specific and answerable. Something like 'employees who don't book time off effectively rarely use email' or 'employees have no compelling reason to book a holiday earlier.' If you're working in a team, this is always a great time to engage in some brainstorming, as it serves as an initial step in the process of user research. You may be surprised to see the varied ways your team may present and frame whatever problem you're facing based on their own lived experiences.

CASE STUDY

Jan got to work on setting his hypothesis:

- The independent variable in this situation was the team's ideal learning pathways.
- The dependent variable is the categories in which these fall.

The majority of our team's ideal learning pathways will fall under an overlapping set of categories, so we do not need to offer an unlimited list of bespoke options.

If you're struggling to come up with a hypothesis you want to test, it is really helpful to do some preliminary research and thinking, asking yourself what kinds of variables exist and how they relate to each other. From here, try to come up with your own presumed answer or ideal solution and frame it as a question that must be proven or disproven. It may also help to look out into the market for other HR teams and research, using that as a starting point to build your hypothesis.

There are a few ways you can phrase your hypothesis. I suggest you start by writing a simple prediction using the 'if/then' form. For example, '*if* we were to find an ENPS survey tool that integrated with Slack, then survey responses would improve'.

Another example: if you approach the problem of late holiday requests with first principles thinking, one of the first questions you may ask is, 'How far in advance do people book travel tickets?' This is something which can be easily discovered outside of your team. Many airlines and travel booking companies keep and present this kind of data. If your company was seeing a huge volume of same-week holiday requests, but you knew that almost 50 per cent of the United Kingdom book their holiday two to six months in advance,[3] you may be able to form a simple hypothesis like, 'People don't request their holiday at the same time they book their travel because they are not incentivised to'.

As you adopt this way of working, your ego around solutions will begin to shift. Many assumptions and hypotheses you present will turn out to be wrong, or at least partly wrong. This is a part of the process, and in Product Management considered to be not only okay, but is happily embraced. As long as we're clear about the assumptions we're making and what we're testing then whatever the outcome, we are learning something about what a successful solution will look like. Being wrong on a thoughtful hypothesis often means we're making progress.

PICK THE METHOD

In user research, we have the same two areas of focus as you do in any research, qualitative and quantitative, which you may already be aware of. Quantitative data is collecting and analysing numerical data, looking for patterns and averages. Qualitative research is the study of behaviour and attitudes. In attitudinal research you should spend time listening to users' words (e.g., in interviews). Whereas in behavioural user research you watch their actions through observational studies. There are many methods of user research within qualitative and quantitative research, with more and more methodologies being shared online.

Quantitative research   Your HR team likely already uses several varieties of quantitative data. The data can be used to monitor employee engagement through ENPS, calculate time and cost to hire, rank employees and functional units by output and to see trends in attrition. If you operate a manufacturing company, for example, you may track quantitative data that details the number of units that each worker produces over a particular period of time. Law firms and other service companies often track the number of worker–client interactions on a daily basis for billing and performance. You can gather data over long periods of time such as a month, quarter or year in order to see trends and develop forecasting. Using quantitative data is a robust way to gather insights into what is happening in your team.

With more-structured methods such as surveys, POPs teams often gather measurable data about what their employees do and care about on ratings scales. This type of quantitative data is particularly powerful across large employee bases and POPs teams can use this data to find patterns within the population over time. In fact, the larger the sample of representative test users is, the more likely you'll have a statistically reliable way of assessing the target user population.

As powerful as it is, quantitative data alone cannot expose deeper human insights, so for this reason I suggest that quantitative data is used in situations where there are large data sets, closed questions and when seeing patterns and trends is particularly important to your outcomes.

Methods of gathering quantitative data

Surveys: the most obvious and well-known way to gather quantitative data. Sending a list of closed or multiple-choice questions that is distributed to a sample (online, in person, or over the phone). One of the mistakes I see from POPs teams is using the survey for many longer-form questions about attitudes, feedback and expectations; save this for user interviews with more time for follow up questions and rich discussion.

Experiments: setting up situations in which variables are controlled and manipulated to establish cause-and-effect relationships. One place that this works particularly well in HR is in recruitment. Setting up two different job ads, for example, one with a salary shown and one without, may be a great way for you to see the outcomes of a more transparent salary framework on the quantity and quality of talent applying for your roles (using volume of positive interview feedback as another quantitative driver). We will talk more about A/B testing in Chapter 7, so if this is a new concept to you it may be worth coming back to this chapter once you've finished the book.

HR Systems: Looking into the back end of reporting for almost any HR system these days, you will be greeted with a rich data visualization and reporting interface. You can use this data to enrich your quantitative user research and problem solving in the People Team.

Qualitative research   Human Operations as I described it in Chapter 2 always comes back around, and if we're making plenty of time for product management thinking, Human Operations is a huge part of the role. Many of us spend our time observing and engaging with our team as they display their behaviours, work habits and needs to us in various forms. In every POPs team meeting I run I have a part on my agenda specifically for 'trends.' This is where our team talks about behavioural, attitudinal and other trends our teams are exhibiting to see if we can connect on a problem area we may be able to dive into.

Many HR teams already have both onboarding and exit interviews which operate very much like qualitative user research interviews as places to gather insights around how to improve the specific onboarding and experience of working in the team. These structured user research interviews can be a method used in building a deep understanding of why users behave the way they do across multiple areas of POPs. For example, why do candidates leave a careers website so quickly without applying?

Qualitative research requires great care as it involves collecting non-numerical data and opinions where your own opinions and bias might influence findings. Being cautious with how you summarize and categorize the data is very sensitive and I often suggest teams work together on exploring the outcomes.

Market data   Today, more and more HR teams are public and transparent with the work they are doing to make their workplaces more engaging and successful. Communities like Lattice's Resources for Humans, People Over Perks by Leapsome and Troop HR are popping up so that People Operations teams are able to learn from each other and share their ways of working. Blogs such as Spotify's HR blog are also wonderful resources bringing the inside out and offering a look at best-practice People Operations work. The team at Learnably have been adopting a People Operations as a product approach and they are excellent examples of building in the open, with an open handbook and a HR team which talks openly about the way they build.

Looking into the market is a fantastic source of data for us as business leaders and creates a rich environment of inspiration for solutions to our problems. I always encourage functional leaders to spend some time looking out into what their peers are doing, not just for recruitment and candidate opportunities, but also to see how other companies are solving problems and how their teams feel about the ways of working.

More than one method   Selecting the method for gathering research around your hypothesis and problem area is key to success. Sometimes one method is more suitable than others, but I always suggest you use more than one methodology and approach to dive deeper into your hypothesis. For example, you can start with a survey, collect some historical data through your HRIS, speak to the market, run some one-to-one interviews targeting your hypothesis, before A/B testing (if you can) some variations of the solution.

CASE STUDY

Jan sent out a Typeform to the company to ask them which kinds of skills they would like to develop through a L&D programme at Sprintbox.

He formulated the survey as so:

- Employee name

- Employee email (if they would like to participate in future research for this project)

- On a scale of 1 to 10 how important are learning opportunities at work to you?

- **Asked three times**

  o   Describe the most (second most and third most) important learning you would like next in your career.

  o   Does it fit into one of the following 10 categories (or other?)

- Is there any other information you think we should consider about L&D at Sprintbox?

INTERPRET THE DATA

User research is an incredibly inspiring and eye-opening area and I often see engaged and curious teams almost bursting at the seams to put their findings into action. However, we need to remember that just collecting the insights is not enough! It is just as important to collect the research as it is to review and interpret the data you've collected. Without doing this, you risk leaving really valuable insights undiscovered, or acting on something which may not be the priority. The process of synthesizing and interpreting the data involves organizing it into ideas, themes, patterns so that it can answer the hypothesis effectively.

When capturing your research data, it is very important to record or take detailed notes so that you are able to document your observations as close to the truth as possible. Be sure to always ask your research participants for their permission to record or take notes and let them know who may see this data and how it will be stored (including plans for deletion once the research is complete).

Whiteboard Workshop   Using tools like Miro is a great way to electronically workshop the themes of your research, but you can also do the work in person using post-it notes and sharpies.

Have everyone in your group read through the research, and if you are in person have a few printed copies for folks to refer back to.

On your post-it notes, ask the question to the group, 'When going through this research did you see any consistent themes?' Write the answers down and place them around the space. Once that is complete, do some work to group your notes according to one (or all) of the below:

1 **Themes:** this idea is in the same category or 'theme' warranting further discussion or analysis.

2 **Equivalence:** this finding is the same as the other.

3 **Hierarchy:** this finding supports another, larger idea or theme.

4 **Association:** this idea is best considered at the same time as this other idea.

5 **Out of scope:** these ideas are interesting, but not relevant at this time. Perhaps should be discussed in another session.

It is particularly useful to take your written notes or quotes and use these directly on the board so you can see how they are directly connected and then easily connect the data later when presenting your findings.

Spend some time discussing; the most important part of this exercise is the conversations you have while organizing your ideas and thoughts into a place where your entire team finds some agreement. This is another great place to use your 'roles' taken onboard using Socratic thinking in Chapter 4. Take some time to group and write each of your findings as 'insight statements' (detailed more below) in order to complete your analysis.

Analysis Sheet An analysis sheet is a particularly useful way to group qualitative data if you are running user interviews or looking at open text in surveys or feedback. This is done by using a Google sheet or Excel doc to group your participants into insights or findings to see where there are groups of shared experiences or ideas. Start with a blank sheet and in each row write a theme or idea you have encountered in your initial research or coming up with your hypothesis. Then, in a new column for each participant, highlight or mark where that theme was brought up. From here you can use this data to inform visualizations or to write insight statements.

CASE STUDY

Jan's Typeform results were in!

When looking at the data, he began by reading through all of the qualitative responses individually.

From there he created an analysis sheet where he looked at the category that each responder had attached to their own response. If they had attached something he disagreed with, he added a new column with his own category. If the responder had selected 'other' he did the same.

He grouped and counted all of the overlapping categories by individual and by category, to see if there was a predominant category, or if he created a set of 'pillars' of L&D if he could cover the entire population.

Finally, he filtered the feedback according to how important L&D was to the individuals and picked out a few folks who would be willing to have further interviews about the project.

Analysis Report   This method can be particularly useful when analysing quantitative data. Create a document with the below questions as a template, and then have each member of the team involved in the research answer them. You can then use this document as the point of reference for further analysis, or use it directly to inform your outcomes.

1 What did you go into this research expecting?

   a) Did you feel this biased you in any way?

2 Did any major patterns and common themes emerge?

   a) Did anyone else see anything different?

3 Did anything surprise you?

   a) What about your colleagues?

4 Where did your participants seem confused by your questions or requests?

   a) Do you have a theory on why?

5 What did they like most about the topic?

6 What did they like least?

   a) Why?

7 What was similar in the group of users?

8 Is it possible there are some users in your cohort who may not have been represented?

  a) How will you address that?

9 How do you think this reflects your hypothesis?

10 What remains unanswered?

  a) How do you intend to address that?

INSIGHT STATEMENTS

Insight Statements succinctly articulate the most valuable learning moments which emerge from your research: they can also be known as 'aha' moments. To get an insight statement, you should take one of your themes or ideas and rephrase it as a short statement that captures the essence clearly. You do not need to write the solution. You should focus on transforming a theme into what feels like a core insight of your research. Insight statements should be:

- Thought-provoking
- Easy to remember
- Actionable.

Example of an insight statement:

Our team has a more positive association with booking training if they are able to do it personally rather than having someone do it for them.

This can even be extended to into subsequent insight statements that support a solution:

This insight is true even when it is company organized or mandatory training, but when they have a selection of dates and options. The more personally involved the team is the better outcomes for attendance, engagement, and learning satisfaction.

If you're struggling to write an insight statement, try using these Three Ws:

1 What is the user doing?

2 Why are they doing it?

3 Wow! What has nobody ever noticed or talked about before?

Remember, as you write your insight statements: just because it's insight, doesn't mean it's insightful. Hold your bar high as to what is useful in your findings. Insights like 'the team don't like poorly written policies' isn't going to get you any points in a high-functioning POPs team.

In the example of the holiday knot we covered earlier, after running through the details of the holiday policy and looking at the quantitative data such as holiday booking, sentiments around flexibility, external market data and then holding one-on-one discussions, I was able to distil two insight statements which lead to the improvement of our holiday policy:

- First, our team struggles with holiday booking because all booking approval is made through an external system and notified via email. Many folks are asking their manager permission on Slack before booking travel, but not having holiday approved until a later date. This means managers forget, or that employee absences aren't included in resource planning, which comes from the HR information system (HRIS).
  - Insight statement: A Slack integration would speed up the loop within the usual work pattern of our team.
- Second, there is no positive reinforcement to book holiday early, so teams were leaving their holiday until the last moment rather than being incentivised to submit it earlier. Even worse, the team didn't see evidence of being reprimanded when they booked holiday late, they considered it to be standard.
  - Insight statement: if we were able to offer incentives to book holidays earlier, people would be more forward thinking.

Both of these insights enable the People Operations team to build something proactive and impactful to solve the holiday knot, rather than issue more policy guidance and reminders – striking to the heart of the problem by empathizing with the users of what we're building.

CASE STUDY

Jan has his data and is able to validate it against his hypothesis. It turns out he was right.

The majority of our team's ideal learning pathways will fall under an overlapping set of categories, so we do not need to offer an unlimited list of bespoke options.

Of the responses returned from his survey, Jan realized that if Sprintbox were to offer learning programmes around management, presentation training, Google

Sheets, and project management, everyone in the company would have at least two opportunities which were covered.

From there, he could offer one more personalized option by working with managers, in order to hit his goal of '100 per cent of the company offered at least three ways to expand their knowledge'.

THINKING ABOUT ANECDOTES

The enemy of solid research is anecdotes. It is tempting to accept the appeal of an authoritative voice in a *Medium* article or a single articulate response to a company survey. However, one warning I give to all HR professionals is to begin to push away from the anecdotal and into findings which are truly backed by numbers and rigor. It is difficult, because anecdotes often pass as evidence in POPs. I've seen my fair share of personal experiences and guess-explanations being used as insights. You only need to spend a few hours on the internet to see intuitive but incorrect explanations spread like wildfire, made appealing by their simplicity rather than their veracity.

The following are examples of anecdotal evidence which may lead you astray, and is the kind of thing that demands first principles thinking:

1 I interviewed this one candidate from Nottingham and they were promoted immediately: we should recruit more people from Nottingham.

2 Google had a programme for recognizing performance that was successful for them: it will be successful for us as well.

3 Kevin never needed management training to succeed: anyone who does must be an underperformer.

This does not mean anecdotes are entirely useless – they can often be used to inform a hypothesis, or as a point of data in your user research (invite Kevin along to a user research interview on great management!)

TELL THE STORY

Human beings are more likely to tell, listen to and remember extraordinary personal stories. In psychological terms, statistical analysis of data, carefully collected from well-designed experiments, lacks that emotional kick. This is why how we present our findings is crucial to their successful adoption.

Communicating user research learnings is a storytelling exercise, and for this reason it is important that you don't stress about the format – focus on your narrative. When you're communicating user research learnings, you're dealing with limited attention spans, competing priorities, their capacity to remember *and* their preference for their own opinion or anecdotes.

When mapping out your findings and insight statements, build them around a narrative in order to build understanding in your audience and to make the research more accessible for others reading. This is also a great place to use the user personas you created, developing a narrative around a specific character that relates to a proportion of your employee population.

Remember that not everyone reading the document or watching your presentation will have the same level of knowledge or interest, so it may be best to present your findings in a number of ways:

- **Executives and leadership:** a brief fact-filled summary of your key findings and their impact on the organization. Detail your methods and some key insights using cause and effect.

- **Managers out of People Operations:** the most important thing here is the team's needs and their preferences, not only those they manage, but the managers themselves. Sharing interview material and your user personas in the form of narratives and case studies may greatly help them understand why the research and outcomes are important.

- **People Partners:** depending on how much influence they have over the final project and outcomes, it's good to help them visualize the outcomes in reality. Share the insights, possible solutions and what success may look like. It will help them make better decisions and be more bought into the insights. This should be the most detailed view, and making it as transparent as possible further gives your insights credibility.

Remember that sharing your insights should be compelling and inspiring for those reading or listening. Finding out useful information which inspires your People Operations team to push further forward is a fantastic win and a true demonstration of the incredible commerciality of a well-functioning team.

Now, let's go forth and build!

The key points from this chapter

- We don't know our teams as well as we think we do. A yearly engagement survey isn't enough to get under the skin of the needs of those in your team in all of the places we require information.

- User research is the detailed and methodical study of a product's users, including exploring their needs and pain points, with the intention to feed insights to product management squads.

- Using user testing can help us confirm if a new feature, process or tool will be easy to use and understandable. This will help us more effectively reach our outcomes through what we're building.

- The insights we gain from our teams don't just sit with the People Operations team; we should be actively sharing that knowledge with our leaders and managers.

- Start all research by creating a testable hypothesis. Generally, a testable hypothesis will be based on what we already think we know, as well as our personal experiences or individual viewpoints. These are used to centre the research so that it remains on track and focused.

- User research can be qualitative or quantitative:

  o Quantitative data is useful for large volumes or detailed analysis.

  o Qualitative research is great for rich insights and user stories.

- You may find that using market data, such as looking at other companies' blogs and speaking to their teams, will give you rich insights into how your HR projects can take shape. Use this as an element of research.

- Using more than one method of data collection allows your insights to be rich and meaningful. Try using a variety of data and collection methods, such as surveys, interviews, market data and historical trends.

- When interpreting the data, you can use methods like a Whiteboard Workshop, Analysis Sheet or by working through a series of questions to structure a report.

- Group your insights into thoughtful insight statements using the 'Three Ws'.

- Avoid anecdotes and personal stories when crafting your research, unless you are using them as a single datapoint or starting point for your hypothesis. Do all you can to push back on the narratives you hold dear, and challenge your own beliefs.

- Use user personas, narratives and storytelling to get your insights into the hearts and minds of those you need to convince towards adopting a new way of working or thinking. Doing this can help them understand not just the solution, but also see what success should look like.

Endnotes

1 Leidtka, Jeanne (2018) Why Design Thinking Works, *Harvard Business Review* https://hbr.org/2018/09/why-design-thinking-works (archived at https://perma.cc/B3KW-EXWL)

2 Usability.gov (2013) User Research Basics https://www.usability.gov/what-and-why/user-research.html (archived at https://perma.cc/RVR6-Q952)

3 Statista (2022) How far in advance did you book your last (main) holiday? https://www.statista.com/statistics/1071600/holiday-booking-in-advance-uk/ (archived at https://perma.cc/Q98N-NKF6)

06

Execute like a product squad

The gap between inspiration and execution is formidable. It's the difference between 'I could have painted that' and a Jackson Pollock and between 'Wouldn't it be great if we could download DVDs' and Netflix. It is one thing to have great ideas, but it takes another set of skills entirely to build up the initiative and discipline to make something happen.

Throughout this book so far, I have given an overview of the kind of thinking a Product Management function employs in order to give themselves a competitive advantage and craft the best products for their customers. Hopefully you've found this inspiring, analogous even to your own way of thinking People Operations teams should run. Often when I run mentoring or coaching sessions on this way of working, the concepts described so far are not those which cause the most concern; it is how to get a team to execute and do it well. Indeed, the craft of product management is more than just theories of discovery and decision making. Diligence, consistency and repetition are what we describe as discipline. One of the things I've always admired about PM and tech teams is their ability to be focused, disciplined and capable of high-velocity, repeatable execution.

Learning about how a PM team *thinks* can only help us so much. We also need to learn how they *work*; how they operate through a series of carefully planned and disciplined check-ins, meetings and working sessions, in order to deliver. This is where repetition and discipline comes in. In any field, focusing on creativity and inspiration will lead to incredible peak moments of delivery, but the practiced and disciplined PM team is going to win out in the long run as they strive to make incremental improvements day-by-day. This is achieved through a carefully designed team set-up and ways of working.

For this reason, when moving to thinking like a PM function, you must also look like one, and work like one. For the purposes of this chapter, this means in your organizational design and your process design (how you design the team's ways of working and calendar).

Organizational design

Effectively building a team requires more than just hiring specific roles. You also need to consider the big picture and ask how all the individuals on your team will work together today and into the future. Much has been written on the 'why' of organizational design: when done well, organizational structure helps improve communication, increase productivity and inspire collaboration. When done effectively, it creates an environment where people can work not just effectively, but also with the behaviours and principles you are trying to operate by.

Organizational design to encourage behavioural patterns

Consider building a team in which you have made a commitment to **quick decision making** and a **lack of hierarchy**. In this team, in order to enforce less hierarchy, it would be important to build an organizational design with a high IC (individual contributor) to manager ratio. If a manager in the team tried to break this norm, it would be reasonable for you to question how this benefits the organizational aims.

Organizational design requires discipline. Without purposely building a structure where management layers are suppressed, it is likely that the principles of a flat hierarchy would begin to disintegrate.

This same careful thinking must be applied to building your People Operations team like a Product Management function.

A key consideration in this new thinking is identifying how your structure can help the team operate as efficiently as possible for their responsibilities of building and iterating on the employee experience product. Even if you cannot structure your team perfectly according to this model, I have given you some basics so that you can begin to offer your team at least some structure as you expand. This will help ensure your people team divides roles and skills by the most effective means possible and can grow to fit an organizational structure which works best for this way of thinking.

Structure in a Product Management team

A reality of Product Management teams is that they are usually split into relatively small groups which operate cross-functionally within the larger teams they work with, such as engineering and design. In Product Management, the idea of doing more with less is not a challenge, but an advantage. Lean, dexterous squads with clear roles can operate in repeatable cycles in order to spend maximum quality time focused towards building and iterating. I'll talk through three different ways these teams can be structured, but the commonality between all of them is that they are cross-functional and independently focused on building a specific outcome.

This approach to cross-functional work is somewhat analogous to how some People Operations teams function today in modern business, particularly those using a business partner model. In HR practice we are learning that integrated People Partners do a better job of truly understanding how and where it can add value, and to identify any challenges and opportunities. You may already have this cross-functional approach in the Human Operations work you are doing, and if you do you will be better placed to understand how your team may shift towards this new structure for the product development style work.

In Product Management I will explore three ways that product squads can be structured, as I think all three of them are interesting to understand while building your People Operations Team. In reality, there is one structure I advocate for, but this is not always possible. This can be due to historical structures which must be slowly changed, specific roles and specialisms which exist in the team, or a lower headcount than what is required.

'All models are wrong but some are useful.' George E. P. Box[1]

PYRAMID: SKILL SPECIFIC

Under this team structure, teams leverage their product managers' different skill sets across multiple products at once. In this model, one product manager might take the lead on market research and developing expertise about user personas across your entire product line and another product manager would be involved in budgeting and resource planning across all areas of focus for the team.

This means that you will have Product Managers who have a discipline of focus within product management itself. This also lends itself to having a more junior team which can move up through the disciplines. An analogous concept here in People Operations would be a team where there is a HR Coordinator, who is responsible for all coordination and administration, a HR Advisor, who is responsible for all employee relations and advice across no specific team, and a HR Project Manager who moves across all projects within the HR function.

This team structure can work well for some companies because they can develop high levels of domain expertise on various aspects of product management and allows a clear 'entry' for developing juniors. However, a clear risk of using this model is that if one member of the team leaves, the entire function will be left without that specific domain knowledge. This means there are 'bus factors' across the success of all parts of the function.

> **Bus factor**: A bus factor is a description of risk whereby if someone in the team was very tragically hit by a bus, no one else in the business could quickly or easily fill their shoes. It is also known as the lottery factor. *If someone won the lottery and left the team today, could we survive without them in the short term?*

STREAMS: PRODUCT SPECIFIC

Here, there is a Product Manager allocated per product or per feature. This is a practical and straightforward way to understand how a product management team can be structured. The model is perhaps most similar to a matrix organization design, where each product or feature would have a product manager overlooking that specific area. You may have three PMs and their teams responsible for onboarding, two PMs responsible for acquisition, etc.

In HR you can consider this similar to a Lead for Reward and Recognition, a Lead for Learning and Development, and so on. This structure scales well, and is often seen in larger companies, as it gives PMs higher autonomy over their product area. This structure, however, is also one which leads to siloed work and specialisms – something which many scaling start-ups cannot afford to lean into due to cost and efficiency of hiring.

SQUADS: GOAL SPECIFIC

One of the most ubiquitous elements of product management is the idea of a dynamic cross-functional *squad*. This idea was born through Agile methodology, and was popularized by Spotify.[2] The product squad is now embedded in tech companies around the world, from Gitlab to Whereby[3].

This generally looks like a team of one product manager, at least three engineers, a designer and a user researcher. This 'squad' will group together to focus on a specific goal of the product, such as improving metrics within the onboarding flow.

What is a squad?

Goal-driven group of cross-functional product and development people who collaborate to find solutions to a specific mission-oriented problem.

Squads generally consist of a team of 6 to a maximum of 10 people with a single leader. The idea of a leader in this framework is leading on the work *output*, rather than managing the individuals within the squad.

Another example of something similar to this model is that of Amazon's 'two-pizza' team structure.[4] The catchy name is dubbed through Amazon's goal to keep the teams lean and able to move quickly, describing the principle that no team should be so big that two pizzas couldn't feed everyone if they gathered together to work through a problem.

The challenge for these squads is that they are relatively autonomous, leading to risks if you don't have the right people operating carefully. Additionally, cross-functional collaboration can be difficult and requires a unique set of skills which the 'best engineer' may not naturally possess. In order to function in this way, you have to ensure your business is set up to support and teach collaboration skills.

Ideal People Operations as a Product Structure

How to make your team work best together is a fun idea to think about. For some of us it can also be overwhelming. *What if I get it wrong? What if we never get there?*

Product Management teams know that the goal isn't to get the product right on the first try. Learning through developing is a part of the journey towards success and it sometimes involves failure. The same is only somewhat true for organizational design. Because human beings require consistency and security as a basic need, we should be careful about frequent changes to the organizational design as it relates to managerial relationships. However, the good news is the squad model I propose does not affect managerial relationships and should only impact the working groups your team are in for project work. This means the teams may have a higher threshold for experimentation. Focus on the goal of getting something out there, learning what may work about it and then making a plan for what is next to make it better. In other words: don't worry if you cannot make this structure work the first time. The journey is often the destination.

As I've mentioned, there is a specific structure I encourage you to think about, if nothing more than a thought experiment for you to decide what works for you. It is worth noting that the structure I outline below makes some pretty bold assumptions:

1 Your hiring managers are accountable for recruiting in the RACI framework.

2 Your people team are multi-skilled across the Human Resources discipline (I call this being T-shaped).

3 Your People Team should be willing to learn about other functional areas such as design, communications and perhaps even development.

4 You need some budget to hire consultants and freelancers for specific projects.

As I said, some of these may be pretty bold. Before you get disheartened, remember that you may not reach this organizational design nirvana in the short-term. Take what you can from the framework and adapt it for your size and stage. The point is that you understand what the ideal structure looks like so that you can move your team in that direction over time – *no one is rushing you.*

T-shaped team members

Being t-shaped describes someone who is both a specialist in one area (such as recruitment, business partnering, or L&D) and a generalist with people skills who can work across multiple projects.

Having t-shaped skills in your HR team means your team is able to move quickly to adapt to new challenges and realities. If you have a team of highly specialized and non-t-shaped recruiters, what will happen if there is a hiring freeze? Now, imagine you focus on t-shaped employees in HR: if there is a change in business strategy your team should be able to move to focus on the new area with fairly limited upskilling.

The ideal organizational design for thinking of People Operations as a product draws on the strengths of the role we described in Chapter 3: Human Operations and People Operations. Remember, People Partners will all have two sides to their role, and this book largely deals with the second half so that your team has more time for human operations work.

The structure is built into squads of People Partners who are also partnered within a function of your organization in which they have either a strong interest, or a professional background. So, this means you will have a People Partner aligned with the technology team for Human Operations work, just as exists within the traditional business partnering model.[5]

ROLES

People Partner A squad should ideally have three People Partners, but this is not a firm rule. There the squad could include a Technical People Partner (who could be an ex-engineer), a Marketing People Partner (who studied marketing) and an Operations People Partner (who is a CIPD qualified HR Professional). This means that each squad will have a function within which they are embedded for Human Operations work, which is also a professional area where they aim to apply to the products and projects they build.

Consider a project on compensation. The Operations People Partner could ensure all compensation data is uploaded and correct, the Marketing partner could write the documentation and internal announcement and the Technical partner could code a simple calculator interface or create an integration with a compensation tool for easier implementation.

> This is a very basic description of how a project could be split, and as this chapter progresses, we will build upon it.

Consultant Functional Expert In this group, there is also a functional expert, who is brought in for a three-month project to support the team and depending on the scope of work decided upon. In the compensation project example, this person could be a Reward and Benefits consultant working on advising the compensation structure. This person would not be the project lead, but would be on the squad throughout the delivery to ensure that the specialist principles are applied correctly and that the team are educated on how to best implement work of this type.

Research This is nice to have for smaller teams. Generally, the People Partners being embedded in the team offer a fantastic opportunity for research in their Human Operations role. However, in rapidly scaling organizations there is a role and need for research as a specialism, where there is a dedicated user researcher working as described in Chapter 5. This means that you will have a member of the squad who is specifically tasked with gathering internal and external data about any specific project area, and to deliver the findings to the team in a way which they can best implement. These profiles are also fantastic at sourcing new tools and frameworks and analysing a project's success or ROI.

THE PEOPLE OPERATIONS SQUAD SO FAR

So far, your squad has three people partners, a consultant expert and a user researcher. Now, you may have more than one of these squads. Each squad will focus on a product area or goal for each quarter, with each of them taking on different roles in the delivery of the project and one member of the squad acting as the 'lead' for the project piece of work. Maybe this lead will be a manager role within the team who steps into a more hands-on project delivery lead position in the squad. If your team is smaller, it may be a rotation of one of the People Partners who steps up to lead each quarter.

I've described the example squad working on a compensation project. Now imagine a second squad working on delivering Jan's L&D project outlined in the case studies in the previous chapter. I will talk more about scaling your squad model in Chapter 9.

FIGURE 6.1 Squad organizational design

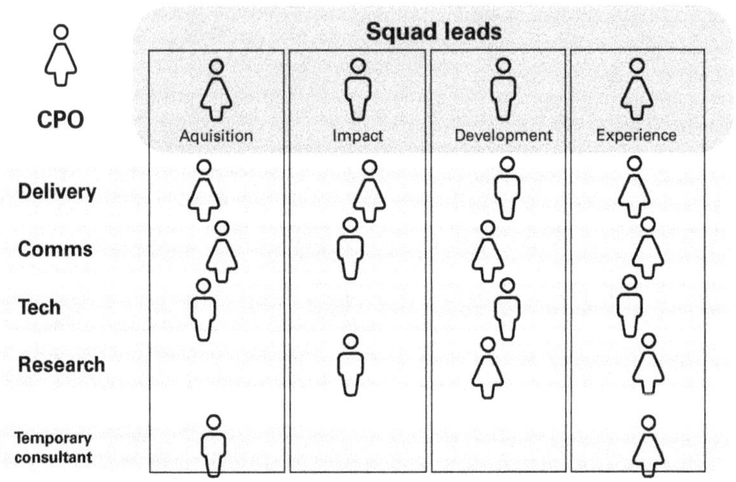

Cross-squad project manager   One role which I have found incredibly useful in my teams is that of a cross functional project manager. This is particularly true if you have multiple squads working on different products in any one quarter, or if you are new to this way of working and your team needs to be upskilled in PM practice. The role here is to assist each team in organizing their goals, following and tracking progress, escalating blockers and assisting with resource allocation and planning. The practicalities of keeping the product management processes tidy and effective can be laborious, but must be respected.

How to transition

I understand if you are looking at Figure 6.1 and beginning to wonder if you can ever make this work. Many People Operations teams are not built in a way which they can easily imagine a transition to this way of working. As I said before, the good news is you do not need to be doing this perfectly straight away to be doing it well. In fact, I encourage you to try to do it in your own way, in a way in which you support your team with education and learning opportunities to grow into more t-shaped roles.

> If you are lucky that you are starting from scratch and instead your concerns come around finding these profiles, then you will be given some more food for thought in Chapter 9, 'Hiring and Building at Scale'.

If you currently find yourself stuck between one way of working and the ideal one I have described above, now is the time to decide what will work for you, and remember that this is an iterative process. Begin by thinking of the team you currently have onboard. Generally there will be one of two problems: too many folks who do not fit the profiles above, or too few and no plans to hire more. Both present challenges we will explore.

A very different team of roughly the right size   I am going to entirely avoid the suggestion of making your team redundant and hiring new team members. I do not propose this because I do believe there is a way to gradually transition your current team while shifting the realities and responsibilities of their roles. With that in mind, this can either be significantly easier or more difficult to solve depending on the profiles of the folks you have in your team. It is not a recent development that POPs teams are being expected to take on more cross functional and modern roles. In the past, many HR teams were built to ensure compliance and decrease liability issues, where today's people teams have a higher expectation to use analytics, be consultative across multiple disciplines, and make complex risk-reward trade-offs. Almost all of the People teams I've worked with in the past are filled with capable and excited people who want to work in these modern and cross functional roles. I believe you can support your team to rise to this new challenge.

Ok, let's start at the top. You have a team that is roughly the right size, but is shaped entirely differently to a squad model. Maybe you are working in functional silos, or perhaps you are geographically split. How do you turn whatever structure you have into something closer to the ideal squad structure mentioned above?

As I outlined in detail in Chapter 3, there are two sides to each People Partner's role: Human Operations and People Operations. The Human Operations side of the role is unlikely to significantly change. If you are currently already using HR Business Partner (HRBP) type roles but rather than assigning them with a function, you are assigning them a region, level or some other means of alignment, perhaps you will elect to keep the current HRBP alignments and to give them functional roles only in the squad. For example, rather than having a 'technology' People Partner, you will have an 'APAC' People Partner, who happens to take a more 'techy' focus in the squad when working on projects. This is a perfectly reasonable way to begin the transition. Perhaps your organization even makes the decision to retain this current alignment until headcount increases, when you can begin splitting regions into functional alignment (Technology People Partner for APAC, Commercial People Partner for APAC, etc). There is no right or wrong answer to how you begin moving your People Partners into squad formations.

Perhaps you have a highly siloed team with few or no HRBPs. You have a Learning and Development specialist, a payroll specialist, etc. This structure will be much more difficult to transition as your team is operating even further away from Human Operations as a part of their role description, and rather are operating as administrators. For the least disruption, I would advise the first step here is to begin to shift towards a HRBP model and retain your team's specialists working in a product management mindset, but not yet in squads. Once the People Partnering element is embedded, you can begin the second phase of transition.

The People Operations, or product focus, is either going to be entirely new or dramatically reconsidered if using the job descriptions outlined in Chapter 3. As I've already mentioned, many competent HR professionals will be motivated and excited by the changes presented in this book. Whatever your current shape, take this as an opportunity to move your team into roles which are more cross functional, technologically enabled and forward thinking than a traditional HR role. The skills and profiles offered to your team in this set up offer a huge opportunity for growth and development. Perhaps you already have members of the team who would like to move to a user research focus, or would like to shift out of a more siloed role generally and start learning more as a People Partner.

First, I would suggest you do what any good leader will suggest and get some feedback from your team directly. Of course, there is some subjectivity in what the team members would say about themselves, and particularly when presented with an upcoming period of considerable change. However, this method is objective and empowering. Ask your entire team (and those they work with) to share their feedback on each other's performance. Ask specific questions around the competencies in Chapter 9, and almost use this as being internally hired into a secondment or trial period. If you place three people together who all seem to have very similar skills, you will end up with a squad that is lopsided. Look to create a squad with an even mix of the skills outlined in Chapter 3.

From there, the most efficient way to train and assess skills is through practice and real-world work. This is a crucial step in demonstrating how important the idea of testing and iteration will become in your team – use it as an opportunity to utilize the new ways of thinking you must fully adopt and embrace. After you have done an initial assessment, use the data to put your team into squads for one quarter of work and use it as an opportunity to test what worked and what didn't. Then come up with possible solutions to continue to refine and iterate the team structure.

Throughout the process, continue asking for feedback from your team members themselves and from those they work with. Remember that if you are moving from a traditionally siloed way of working, your team is now beginning to establish a much more complex web of relationships in their working environment. Before, if someone was the L&D Lead and the team is now working collectively on L&D, they will do so with one squad *lead* and multiple other contributors. This means there will be connections with more complexity (Figure 6.2.1 and Figure 6.2.2). This can lead to greater conflict and a flatter decision-making structure, so will hopefully lead to richer and more collaborative team relationships. Keep this in mind during the initial stages of this transition, as many managers may be caught unaware when traditional hierarchical relationships in their teams are suddenly disrupted by being more collaborative and democratic.

FIGURE 6.2.1 Relationship complexity increases in a squad

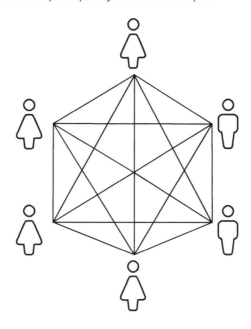

FIGURE 6.2.2 Relationship complexity increases in a squad

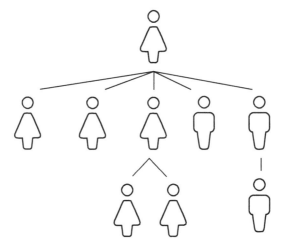

CASE STUDY

BloomLabs

You may remember from an earlier case study that the HRD of BloomLabs, Lottie, decided to adopt Product Management thinking to solve the problem she and the BloomLabs team are currently facing. She wrote new job descriptions for a 12-month trial period, with two key deliverables to aim towards. First, to use this new way of working to turn the tide on the retention trend (aiming for stable retention improvements month-on-month for six months). Secondly, to have an evidenced, replicable understanding of who the 'key talent' (ideal customer profile) in the business is.

This presented a significant change in the People Team's roles at BloomLabs, and one which Lottie knew she would need to work hard to implement effectively.

From here, Lottie and the team began to think about how to structure themselves into a squad. Lottie is lucky enough to have four members of her team already, two of which were in more generalist roles and two of which are in specialist positions (L&D and recruitment).

Lottie's People Partners were not aligned to any specific areas of the business, so the first change she made was transitioning all four of them into People Partner positions (rather than specialisms) and then aligning their roles with areas of the business they had experience working with, or a passion in.

Lottie went through previous role feedback for each individual, as well as assigning them a reflection exercise in order to identify where they may best be suited in the business.

Jean: The recruiter's background was in technology recruitment and their relationships were very strong with the technology managers. Furthermore, the recruiter had expressed an interest in learning more about software development and had requested to take part in a two-week software development night course. Lottie decided to align Jean as the People Partner for Technology, which included all recruitment for the function.

The two People Partners in the team were currently feeling reasonably stretched and were grateful for the opportunity to partner with a smaller group. One had expressed a keen interest in learning more about recruitment, but the other had an aversion to recruiting. This was something Lottie was going to have to work on – everyone in the team now had a role to play in 'full stack' People Operations. This didn't mean that they would be 100 per cent responsible for recruiting (Jean and hiring managers would still have roles to play in this no matter the area of the business), but it was important that all People Partners now took a more horizontally varied and T-shaped role.

Bradley: Lottie assigned the more senior People Partner to Creative, as he had a background in design and had studied some copywriting at university. Bradley didn't like recruiting and pushed back often, but did enjoy and lean into employer branding, so Lottie felt there would be a way to align together over the forthcoming six months.

Niamh: The more Junior People Partner was assigned to Business Operations, a smaller team, but one with a varied range of team members from Finance to IT. Niamh's strength was in operations, coming with a degree in human resources and no other working experience beyond BloomLabs. Lottie decided she would take this opportunity to train them up more on project management, something they'd shown an interest in.

Raif: The Learning and Development partner was an incredibly talented person and had been developing their own training programmes, documentation and internal communications. Lottie assigned this person as the People Partner for the management team – a smaller cohort – so that they also had the time to be more deeply embedded in the user research aspects of the People Partner role.

Now, Lottie had a team who were not only aligned to areas of the business as People Partners, but also to more specific roles within the squad.

Lottie:
Team leadership and direction, product leadership and strategy

Jean:
Human Operations: Technology.
Squad: Recruitment and sourcing, development, systems and integrations

Bradley:
Human Operations: Creative
Squad: Employer branding, copywriting and design

Niamh:
Human Operations: Operations
Squad: Project management, administration

Raif:
Human Operations: Managers
Squad: User research, L&D specialism

Lottie shared these new People Partner roles with the individuals and with the business. She decided it was best to test these roles for two quarters; one for initial feedback and a second quarter for further iterations and refinements following some training she would organize for each member of the squad.

Your team may not have the kind of perfectly aligned backgrounds, as seen above, but there are ways to assess what someone is good at, has experience in and seek feedback and development opportunities. The most important thing is to acknowledge that the role will not only be more t-shaped, but that each member of the squad will be working together to deliver work, rather than focusing deeply on a vertical they align with. This is a great opportunity for your team and should provide them with room to develop further.

But what if I have more people than work in a squad?

There is no hard-and-fast rule on how many folks are in a squad, but I would say two groups of three or four (plus a lead) would be better than one group of eight. This is something which is distinctly not true in engineering and product squads, where a good size is 6–10. The reason I believe People Squads should be smaller is due to the fact there are rarely several engineers, and everyone in the People Squad is working on delivering work which requires less double-up of skills.

That said, there is no better way to see what works for you than to test it over a quarter.

Additionally, you may have a specialist or senior member of the team who bounces from squad to squad. For example, employer branding experts may be utilized across two squads in one quarter, or move between two throughout a year. This is because they would be working on blogs and internal/external content rather than specific delivery.

There is no wrong answer. The value is collaboration, not a rigid structure.

A very small team where you have no way to hire   Not every team has four headcount (or more!) which can be easily shifted into new t-shaped roles. Role changes are a real challenge, but working in a resource-strapped team presents a different set of difficulties which have to be overcome.

CASE STUDY

Sprintbox

Yihana and Jan are two people in a micro-HR team at Sprintbox. Yihana wants to approach their way of working with a People Ops as a Product mindset, but is concerned the size of her team and resources will be a limiting factor.

The way the team is currently working is that Jan covers all People Partnering, and Yihana is a point of escalation. Jan and Yihana share recruitment equally as advisors to hiring managers, who are doing all of their sourcing either themselves or with external agencies. At the moment there is an RPO (recruitment process outsourcing) with the team, who have two consultants working on a hiring spree. This means Yihana and Jan have their role mostly focused on People Partnering and projects.

Yihana's budget for this year is small and she has been told that until the RPO is out of the team or headcount is above 150 people, there will be no further permanent headcount approved in the People Operations team.

Yihana looks at the 'squad roles' and decides the best way to go about this is that first, their human operations 'people partnering' won't change. Second, both of them will wear a few hats when working together to produce work each quarter, as they form a micro-squad with fluid responsibilities. They will be responsible for all user research in their aligned functions, for example.

What they decide to do is at the beginning of each quarter, when planning out the sprints and what they will deliver, they will also assign a 'scope of ownership' to each of them. Furthermore, Yihana has enough in her budget to invite consultants to support on at least two or three of the projects they do, so she will be able to engage an analyst, developer, reward specialist or any other required skills.

Identifying role profiles in your team and candidates

If you've read the above sections and case studies you may be thinking about your own team (big or small) and how they fit. I've outlined a few 'role types' which you may easily be able to identify immediately. These role types tend to correspond with a specific set of responsibilities in a people squad, so they may be a good place to start your investigation.

The coordinator: A natural organizer who excels at delegation and facilitating decision making. Someone with experience in project management. Deadline driven and conscientious, takes pains to ensure quality.

Operations, commercial, project management, planning. This role type is wonderfully aligned to the type of working we're about to embark upon. You will need someone who loves to plan, assess and develop project outlines, monitor goals and keep a team on track. This person is also wonderfully aligned to Operations People Partnering.

The implementer: The practical and innovative thinker who brings ideas off the page and into the real world. Someone who is able to see from idea to production and has experience launching complex projects across multiple stakeholders. This person has an interest in product management, technology and software development.

User research, product management, organizational psychology and design: The role of the user researcher is well aligned to this role, as well as one leading the squad if you have multiple squads. Furthermore, organizational or industrial psychologists use the principles of psychology to develop a more holistic approach to People Operations, and this person may wish to pursue those leanings.

The analyst: Known for logical and thorough judgment and for healthy scepticism. This person seeks data, loves evidence and will constantly challenge presumptions. They may have a background in data or analytics.

HR Analysis, technology, data and product. Data and analytics will increasingly drive the role of People Operations. This is the person who can head the effort.

The leader: Thrives under pressure, a clear role model for the team when things go wrong. Enjoys high volumes of work, pivoting, and communication with the business. They may present as an extrovert who excels at developing contacts outside the team.

Management, squad leadership, dynamic performance coach: This HR specialist will help maximize the individual contributions of everyone in the squad. This person may also want to seek opportunities to coach managers and leaders across the business. They may take on a squad leadership role.

The visionary: Out-of-the-box thinker whom people rely on for creative solutions to tough problems. This person can brainstorm for hours. They have a background or interest in creative thinking, employer branding, copywriting, communications and/or design.

Employer brand, creative, candidate experience: These folks are well suited to partnering with the creative and marketing areas of your business, as well as working on those endeavours within your People Squad. This person will oversee the candidate experience efforts, ensuring that applications do not simply go into a 'black box'. They may be best placed to write and manage most internal and external comms, and to brief in design and creative work on behalf of the People Team.

The specialist: Highly knowledgeable in a particular field or possesses a specific skill set. They are a vertically aligned member of the team in reward, recognition, sourcing and L&D.

HR partnering, dynamic squad consultation: Just because someone has a specialism doesn't mean they aren't a valuable member of your team. You may have a business large enough that requires a full-time reward specialist who moves from squad to squad (one quarter working on performance, the next working on internal recruitment, the following on share option plans). This person may behave like a consultant to the squads working on areas of their specialism, and may be the business partner for the HR team themselves if the function is large enough.

FIGURE 6.3 Flow state

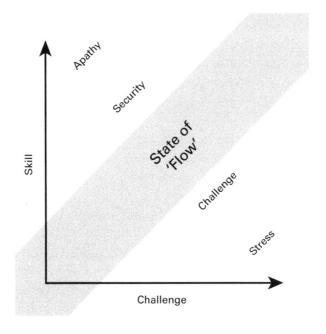

No human being fits perfectly within a box. No one person will be 100 per cent aligned with any of the above and may show traits across all or many of the archetypes. This is totally fine. We are all people who are unique and exciting to work with. If you are trying to identify where your team may fit together, try to think of where someone is most comfortable or most in their 'flow' (Figure 6.3). You can directly ask them, too; don't forget reflection and feedback are not only 360 but come from within.

Process design

Executing like a product squad goes beyond simply being shaped like one. There are many frameworks which must be employed towards the way you work together which will help your People Ops squad bring meaningful work to life.

There is much to learn, and this may be the first time you've learnt about product roadmap cycles, planning, retrospective, sprints and shipping work in iterative stages. The most important thing to know is that, on the most basic level, the primary focus of a product squad is to make sure that everyone's goals are aligned to the mission and that the entire team is pushing towards the same objectives. We've already spoken about the path to build out your mission and vision and doing that work is a big step forward. Now we will begin talking about the mechanisms you can use on a regular cadence to ensure your new squads and vertically aligned People Partners are working on projects which move in the same direction towards your mission.

In addition to your team's new People Partnering and vertical alignment (Technology, Operations, etc.), working as product teams means you have to work on many projects and partners across the business. This means your team will need to understand more about the strategy and where they are aiming towards than perhaps in a more traditional HR structure.

This requires some responsible management from you as a business leader. You should clearly articulate the company mission and provide opportunities for your team to ask questions and better understand how the business works.

REGULAR CADENCE OF EXECUTION

There is a regular cadence of execution which I prescribe, and it may not look dramatically different to what you are already doing. Some of the most important steps may be new, such as retrospectives and setting up work in sprints. Doing all of this planning and discussion may feel counterintuitive to some, particularly when reading everything I've said about moving fast, but the important thing to remember is that moving fast doesn't mean shipping huge pieces of work in unreasonably short timeframes. Moving fast means testing, shipping small, learning and moving quickly when challenges or new priorities arise.

Meetings are considered an enemy of progress by many and I often agree. That said, I do put forward that carefully designed meetings can be *very* effective. It is crucial that you have:

- An agenda shared ahead of time
- A clear attendee list
- A predefined decision or outcome (very important)
- That you give back time if the meeting runs short.

With that pre-warning out of the way, here are the meetings I advocate for the People Operations team running like a product squad.

Daily Stand-ups   A daily stand-up is something you can run synchronously or asynchronously (using a Slack bot, teams channel, or some other mechanism). Some teams I've worked in have effectively run a stand-up twice a week rather than five times a week. These meetings should never be the whole team and should be squad-specific.

Agenda: A very quick check-in on each individual and their tasks. I find a quick Red, Amber, Green works well.

Attendees: Squad members only. Avoid the temptation to merge these with a whole team meeting. These should not have additional people in the conversation unless there is a crisis or concern which is being flagged.

Decision or outcome: Identify any blockers as early as possible.

Time: No longer than 20 minutes.

Sprints and progress updates   Your team should now be working in 'sprints'. This means you should break down your quarter (or term) into composite two-week intervals. These two-week intervals should each have something completed, or some demonstrable progress being made. For example, if your overall quarterly goal is to launch a new 360 feedback mechanism, one two-week sprint may be 'Complete all user research' and the following is 'complete draft 360 feedback forms.'

Sprint progress meetings happen weekly and are always linked to the achievement of goals. Managers should be expected to report on progress and whether the goal metrics will be on track or not. Usually in large teams there is a lot of activity and we often don't take the time to step back and reflect whether we're making progress against our aims, which can cause 'watermelon metrics' (where something looks green on the outside, but it is actually red). Spending time sharing a formal update to your squad lead will help to ensure that you are making progress towards squad-specific and institutional objectives, driving transparency across the team and quickly escalating issues.

Agenda: Restate the overarching goal for this sprint and this quarter. Review the sprint outcomes for the week and forthcoming week.

Attendees: Squad members and the product lead.

Decision or outcome: Is the goal for this quarter on track based on this Sprint's deliverables?

Time: No longer than 45 minutes.

Quarterly goal setting   I am often asked if I prefer OKRs or SMART goals or any other structure out there. The honest answer is I don't really mind as long as your goals are clear, consistently structured and shared broadly across the business so that they reach up into some higher purposes or outcomes. If your business is still not running a whole-company or whole-function goal planning process, don't feel like you cannot make progress alone. Last year was the best time to set clear goals; the second-best time is now.

Set goals by asking your leadership what the overarching business metrics are and write goals that are aligned with achieving those outcomes. For example, if your company goal is to improve customer retention, then it may be important for your team to pay specific attention to Customer Success teams and their needs, or to work on building some onboarding training around the product for those who interact with customers.

If your company already sets goals, your People Ops goal setting can be held in a meeting separate from your quarterly planning outlined below, as I think it should be cross-functional (i.e., not just the People Team). I suggest the agenda, attendees, etc. are aligned with your current cadence. If you don't currently set goals across your business, read up some more on SMART goals and OKRs, and set them within your quarterly planning. I talk a bit more about metrics and output goals in Chapter 10.

Quarterly retrospectives   Those working in technology companies have likely heard the word 'retro' (or retrospective) thrown about by engineering and product teams. A retrospective is something which can be used ad hoc after incidents (such as website outages or restructuring), but should also be added into the regular cadence of your team's development cycles.

A quarterly retro is generally a few hours where your team is allowed to go deep into the work completed over the quarter just passed. This gives a chance to raise any concerns, grievances and feedback. It is also a crucial opportunity to seek adjustments to the way you're working. *Are you having daily stand-ups at a bad time? Are they useful? Should the agenda change?*

Agenda: A prearranged set of retrospective activities as listed below.

Attendees: All squad, sometimes grouping squads together if numbers permit (around 15 people is the maximum I would suggest).

Decision or outcome: Reflect on this quarter and suggest clear improvements for next quarter's work.

Time: Anywhere from 2 to 3 hours.

The list of retrospective activities you can run is long and comprehensive. Miro and other whiteboarding tools provide some great templates for retrospectives if you're running one remotely.

Some of my favourite retro activities:

Sad, Mad, Glad: Have your team write what made them feel sad, mad, and glad this quarter and put them in corresponding sections of a whiteboard.

Shipped, scrapped and snagged: Write every task (no matter how small) and assign it to either shipped (completed), snagged (still working on it, or moving to the next quarter) or scrapped. Talk through those in the snagged and scrapped category, but also spend some time celebrating all of the wonderful tasks and work which was shipped.

Scope of change: Suggest everyone in the team work through the spheres of influence in the company and describe changes they'd like to see this quarter. Start with listing all the changes you would like to see within yourself, move to the immediate team, those within their daily working lives, then leadership, before talking about whole company changes. Spend some time grouping these suggestions together and committing to any new ways of working or suggestions which work.

You can also use or adapt the prioritization frameworks outlined in Chapter 4.

Quarterly project planning   This meeting should come within a day or so after your quarterly retro and should be either at the end or beginning of the quarter, depending how you structure your goal planning. Your quarterly goal metrics should already be set as per above. For example, if one of your yearly People Operations goals is to decrease regrettable churn by 25 per cent year-on-year, you may set a quarterly goal of improving line-management sentiment as you know that 20 per cent of your leavers report a poor relationship with their manager.

In this session you set your squad up with their new goal you set. From there, your team begins deciding how they will tackle that goal by shipping a certain project or outcome this quarter.

Agenda: Define this quarter's project activities.

Attendees: All squad, sometimes grouping all squads together too if numbers permit (around 15 people is the max I would suggest).

Decision or outcome: Choose goal-aligned projects for this quarter.

Time: Anywhere from 2 to 3 hours.

I suggest your team meet together with some base ideas and discussions already about what projects they would like to see worked on this quarter. These base assumptions can come through the Human Operations work they do. I always encourage the team to re-read any survey data, team feedback and the yearly plans and strategy documents so that they are fully prepared for a lively discussion. Remember to use first principles thinking to explore possible solutions and adopt the prioritization frameworks outlined in Chapter 4.

If this is still feeling a little cerebral, I've outlined a quick overview below.

Step 1: Identify your problem

As a People Operations Leader, you have problems you are looking to solve and seeing positive goal movement is the demonstration that the problem is improving. Using the example above, the problem is 'too many regrettable exits are happening in our company', in other words, 'too many good people are leaving us.'

As a first step, have everyone in your team make a post-it with the problem statements as they see it. What do they think it means? How do we define regrettable? Is there a history of management challenges? What is said in exit interviews?

Step 2: Make a list of the reasons why you can't solve the problem

We're going to go off in a tangential direction and write down all the things that are preventing you from solving that problem. This may seem like a negative step, but it is very useful to ensure the team feels heard about what they need to overcome and that you can see if there is anything that requires careful sequencing. It is important to get these out early so that the team is able to move to first-principles thinking, as discussed in Chapter 4. Give room for the team to really open up about the obstructions as they see them. Problems sometimes need to be solved in a certain order and this helps identify that order.

In our regrettable churn example, perhaps your HRIS doesn't allow automated exit surveys, so people aren't always getting them before it's too late. Another issue could be that your team doesn't agree with how you've defined regrettable. There are many things that could prevent solving this issue.

Step 3: Brainstorm

Now set yourself to an optimistic, solutions-oriented mindset. There are always obvious solutions to a problem, but we learnt earlier where first principles thinking can really help. Use the activities in Chapter 4 to work through all of the different solutions to the problem as your team sees it. Tell the team to continue writing more and more solutions, even if they feel the first few are great. Try to use this as a highly imaginative brainstorm.

For regrettable churn this could be anything from new benefits to better exit interviews, to management training. There are so many ways to affect a goal in a positive way and your team's job here is to put all the different options down so that you can select the most impactful path.

Step 4: Structure a plan

Perhaps there is a clear project which stands out. If 50 per cent of your exits have stated poor management relationships, you may not need to explore other solutions. However, if multiple possibilities exist, select a few and begin to align those solutions around hypothesis statements (again, looking at Chapter 4 for inspiration here).

Remember that you need to select something that abides by our two maxims: maximize impact to the mission, achieve everything through others.

For example, if your team identifies that regrettable exits may be due to poor management, a lack of benefits and no career planning (and it is hard to pick which of these is correct due to bad exit interview data), it is a great time to run some user research discovery right off the back to validate the right project. This is exactly what we described Jan doing in Chapter 5.

Step 5: Map out some sprints

Once you have selected a project, or a pathway towards achieving your quarterly goal, you should set up a plan for the quarter to follow along with in your meetings we outlined already in this chapter.

I use a Google doc for this, but there are many tools like Asana, Monday or Notion which are great to use for resource and sprint planning.

Along the top row I place fortnightly sprint dates. Sprint 1 (Week 1–2), Sprint 2 (Week 2–4), etc. I also include the resource plan: Who is away? Do we have any public or team holidays?

In Column A, I have the team add all of the elements of the project we need to complete, in no specific order. Conduct user research interviews, complete Typeform, draft communications, etc.

Then, in column B, I ask that the team begin indicating how many sprints the work will take and roughly when. I ask the team to take careful note of dependencies here.

From here, you can begin to move the tasks into a sequential order, seeing which tasks must be completed before others (Figure 6.4). For example, you cannot send out the communications to the team before they have been written.

This rough sprint plan should only take around 20–40 minutes to complete, and then should be a 'take away exercise' for the squad to complete before presenting their final quarterly plan.

FIGURE 6.4 Sprint-planning roadmap

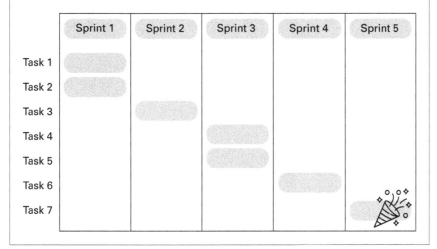

Yearly Roadmap   This may feel at odds with the idea of quarterly planning. 'How do we plan for the year if we're expected to plan what we do during each quarter?'

There are two ways to approach this, which I've described as loose planning and tighter planning. The most important thing is to have and publish a roadmap, any roadmap. This will help to keep your team inspired and really help momentum with quarterly planning.

The first option (loose planning) is the one I'd suggest if you're just setting out with yearly and quarterly planning. The second (tighter planning) is a good place to get to once you're well practiced and have clarity on company goals which nest (as explained earlier in this chapter).

Loose yearly planning   Yearly planning in this way is not a sequential set of projects and deliverables, but rather a laundry list of all of the things the team would like to work on, are working on and have shipped in the year.

What I've seen work quite well is a list of all of the initiatives on a Trello board (or something similar) which are grouped into:

1 Shipped

2 In progress this Quarter (or Term)

3 High priority

   a) This is where all of the projects, goals or ideas which are high priority are listed. This doesn't mean you need to ship them all, but shows any team reviewing your roadmap what is on your horizon.

4 Backburner

   a) Projects which are lower priority, or require sequencing of another project before they can be begun.

5 Cancelled or not a priority

Then, when it comes to your brainstorming in your quarterly planning session, your team is able to review this roadmap as a way to prompt what projects may be appropriate to help shift the quarterly goals. It will also be a useful tool in challenging and creating your quarterly and yearly goals as a functional leader.

Tighter planning   If you already know what your yearly and quarterly goals will be for the forthcoming year, then you can outline these goals in a roadmap with a set of annual ceremonies mapped out (such as performance reviews, compensation reviews, quarterly project planning, etc.).

Then, within your roadmap you can map some rough 'epics' into the goals. This does not mean you are pre-defining the projects exactly, but that you can group them under a rough banner. If you're a team or business which has a lot of practice with planning and goals, you might find that you are able to have some clear insight into what your priorities sequencing already is. This means your project planning sessions are more focused on which solutions you will test, rather than the problem statements or features you plan to look at. For example, your roadmap may simply say 'Quarter 2: Performance Management and Compensation Philosophy', and your planning should be focused on breaking those problems down into hypotheses and sprints.

Roadmaps help with the horizontal alignment of letting the broader business know what to expect from People Operations, but also help to build empathy specifically with smaller People Operations teams. Many businesses simply cannot see how much is on our plate. Moreover, roadmaps delineate clear trade-offs that inevitably crop up as the company grows and new priorities come into view. One final benefit of yearly planning and having a public roadmap is the capacity to share 'shipped' products. Having this on your roadmap is a great way to show the volume of work your team is covering and be used as a point of reference to avoid lots of cross-team communications throughout the quarter. A centralized source of what's happened and what's to come helps keep your team and whole company aligned to the overall mission and strategy.

The key points from this chapter

- Working like a product squad requires a reconsideration of the roles of those in People Operations, as explained in Chapter 3.

- This also requires you to consider your team structure and specifically to move your team into squads working on specific goals and problems, rather than working in more vertically siloed work styles.

- If you're lucky enough to have a brand-new team to build, you are in a very beneficial position as you have little historical structure to rebuild. Chapter 9 will go further to give you the insights you need to do this work.

- If you're working with an already established team, you will need to move their roles into squads, which will require understanding what their pre-existing strengths and weaknesses are:

  o I suggest you conduct some self and team reflection before allocating roles.

  o Do a 'test' for three to six months, iterating on the arrangement before you come to any final conclusions.

- If you have a small team, this may require you to wear a few hats as you work in a micro-squad, but it is important to make sure that someone is always covering the key areas of product development from user research to shipping communications and analysis.

- If you're structured like a product team then you're ready to work like one. Begin by setting up your cadence along these crucial meetings and checkpoints:
  - Yearly roadmapping
  - Company and team goal setting
  - Quarterly project planning
  - Quarterly retrospectives
  - Sprints and check-ins
  - Stand-ups.

Endnotes

1 Box, George E P (1976) 'Science and statistics', *Journal of the American Statistical Association*, 71 (356): 791–799

2 Cruth, Mark (2022) Discover the Spotify Model, Atlassian Blog https://www.atlassian.com/agile/agile-at-scale/spotify (archived at https://perma.cc/2YZH-QUEB)

3 Kramer, A (2022) Starting New Teams, Gitlab Handbook https://about.gitlab.com/handbook/engineering/starting-new-teams/ (archived at https://perma.cc/95MA-U4A6)

4 Hern, Alex (2018) The two-pizza rule and the secret of Amazon's success, The Guardian Online https://www.theguardian.com/technology/2018/apr/24/the-two-pizza-rule-and-the-secret-of-amazons-success (archived at https://perma.cc/N4FR-9YUH)

5 HR University (2022) What is the HR Business Partner Model?, HR University Online https://hr.university/career/hr-business-partner/hr-business-partner-model/ (archived at https://perma.cc/F3QB-RLAU)

07

Iteration of people practices and processes

For a very long time, developing new products was a slow and laborious process, even within the technology industry. Project or product managers moved slowly along what is called a 'waterfall' process, taking each stage one step at a time: planning, user research, collating results, proposing product requirement documentation and launching into engineering work. From there the engineering team would work on delivering the product requirements over weeks, months or even years. From there, markets could change, user sentiment could shift or the project could go an entirely different direction to intention. These ways of working caused the product cycle to be long and any changes could take months or years to get into production and then into the user's hands.

In 2001, 17 software engineers got together in a ski resort and wrote the Agile Manifesto.[1] From there, modern Product Management began to take shape. From this place, the Agile methodology moved into the mainstream, and with it, the idea of iterative process and feedback loops. Iteration is the repetition of a process in order to generate a new stage of an outcome or solution. In its most basic form, it's the idea of launching something small, seeing how it works, taking feedback on board and launching it in a new stage. This may mean starting with a smaller audience or user base. It may mean a less elaborate version of the final product (sometimes also called a minimum viable product, or MVP).

The idea of iterative process development is one of those phrases that automatically makes us think of engineering teams. But most teams iterate in one way or another and you probably already do in some capacity. The difference with how I want to talk about this way of working in this book is that I see it as crucial to iterate intentionally. Intentionally and effectively using an iterative method can help you reduce risk, manage efficiency and approach problems in a more flexible and dynamic way.

What is a non-iterative process?

In a non-iterative process, you and your team would work together to come up with, develop, and launch an *entire* project or product in one timeline. The way this can be described is waterfall. Think of each stage of a project having to fall over a waterfall's edge before the next can be begun. Each phase begins once a previous phase is completed in its entirety and the team avoids changing the project plan as much as possible.

Imagine you're creating a new benefits suite for your team.

You first need to do all of the research into the current benefits and any new benefits the team may be interested in. The next step is to take that feedback and begin investigating the options on the market. The team can begin negotiation and discussion with the new providers before combining all of the details into some kind of page or communication. From there the team can update the careers page and share a company launch.

Each of these things must happen one after another. It is not possible to launch the new careers page without the details of the benefits, just as it makes no sense to begin research after the providers have been selected.

This means you will launch one complete project after the entire process. It may take a month to complete each step, which means that by the time your final benefits package is launched, it has been four to five months since your project plan was made.

You can begin to understand here that this way of working doesn't include time for your team to iterate and find ways to improve what they've developed. This also means that if a project isn't successful, or is a risk in some form, then you have more to lose.

Why we should iterate

I have always seen People Operations teams as some of those with the most promise and untapped potential. I know I am biased, but I truly see the People Ops function as a deeply commercial one, capable of making significant and widely-felt change in any organization and impacting valuations, revenue and business outcomes. However, for many reasons, this potential is not often not realized and HR teams slip into a support function role. One of the reasons I believe this potential remains unrealized is due to the HR team's fears of moving towards more agile and iterative ways of working.

In part, this is a chicken and egg situation and I don't want to be too hard on all of our hard-working People Operations folks out there. Businesses have high expectations of People teams, and they are quite demanding and critical of both the *what* and *how*. From there, People teams feel an immense pressure to launch fully formed and operational pieces of work in order to 'prove themselves' and their contributions and so that the team has positive feedback about the polish of whatever is launched.

What this means is that People teams have to invest a huge amount of time and energy into the initiatives they own. There is simply little room for failure or risk when the stakes are high and fully formed pieces of work are generally deemed necessary, while also being expected to be high quality with low failure rates.

It is not surprising that this way of working will stifle creativity. If a team cannot take risks, they will struggle to try something new or innovative. In HR I often find leaders talking about the need to 'add value' to an organization but often struggle to clearly quantify and define what this value is. It is my opinion that within the space to develop more creativity and innovation is where we truly become a change maker within the business. Innovation is how we drive value for our customers, or candidates, and our colleagues. It goes to say, then, that the best way to create that change is by employing a system of consistent innovation, new ideas and feedback loops.

Most POPs strategies and plans contain complex, broad topics, such as building a diverse and inclusive workforce or designing a dynamic, learning and development programme that scales with your team's experience. While these complex pieces of work are valuable, interesting and worthy aims, the value and scope is so large it may feel insurmountable to many in your team or company. Even worse, it may feel like you are never able to truly make progress in a meaningful time horizon. This is made even more acute when the specifics of the outcomes and goals are left undefined or only linked directly to massive releases once per year.

Working iteratively enables you to break down those problem statements into smaller product launches and ship them quickly, learn from them and then build on what you've mastered so far. This allows almost constant progress towards your goals. However, as I alluded to earlier in this chapter, it requires a mindset change from the People Team and from the business. Gone are the days where People Operations teams launch massive, year-long projects after a waterfall style process. This means your team must overcome their fear of risk and unpolished work and begin encountering frequent constructive feedback from the team.

Different ways to iterate

Iterative processes mean different things to different teams, but it also can mean different things depending on what it is exactly you're iterating on. There are many ways to think about what 'iterating' is, so we'll cover off a few of them to give a flavour for how to use a more iterative approach as you work.

SMALLER USER BASES

One way to think about launching a project or product to a smaller group of users. An example would be a piece of software or a tool, such as a mental health support app. In this version of iteration, the team would launch the app to a small selection of the team (for example just to Marketing, or just to the London office), asking them for feedback on different elements of the service. For example, the team may launch some initial communications and user guides, updating them after the smaller selection of the team has given some feedback.

From there, the team can run a second iteration where the successful tool is shared with the broader employee population.

A/B TESTING

This ties into the ideas we spoke about in Chapter 4 around user testing. A/B testing is the methodology of trying two ideas on smaller segments and seeing which works best. One good example of where A/B testing works well is in recruitment advertising. A People Operations team may A/B test two different versions of copy or employer branding in order to see how they perform under the same conditions. From there you can iterate and continue to see which is more effective.

LESS COMPLETE PRODUCTS

You may have heard of the idea of a minimum viable product, or MVP. This is a term popularized by Eric Ries, founder of the Lean Start-up methodology.

It refers to a version of a new product that allows the team to gather the maximum amount of proven customer knowledge with the least amount of effort.[2] An example of this is launching a careers page with only a link to open roles and the employee handbook, before beginning to build new sections including benefits, testimonials and blog content.

This gives the team the ability to make small, constant changes to the project and avoid launching something after several months of development time which may not be fit for purpose, or could have benefitted from being live and teaching the team something.

Minimum viable product versus minimum loveable product   Over my career I have started moving away from the term 'viable product' and into something which comes from the Spotify and Amazon world.[3] Minimum loveable product (MLP) refers to building something in an iterative way which is really enjoyable, user friendly and loveable.

One of the pitfalls of thinking in minimum *viable* product is connected to what I spoke about earlier in terms of high bars from the business to launch well-crafted work in the People Operations space. If your business expects polished, easy to understand and enjoyable products from the People team, it is likely more productive for you to think of what is minimum *loveable*.

What does it mean to be *loveable*?

Our team and our customers don't just want their needs to be met, they want to be *delighted*. They don't just want to use your tools or product; they want to love it.

Figuring out what is lovable can be discovered through user testing or feedback. Instead of asking, 'does this work? or would you use it?' ask, 'do you love it?', 'do you enjoy it?', 'would you want to use it again?'

Imagine that you go to a restaurant. You order the pancakes. They bring you pancakes from a shake and bake box.

Is it what you asked for? Technically, yes. *But will you love it?* Probably not. Giving you pancakes you love doesn't mean they need to open a maple syrup business, grow blueberries and get a Michelin star for their batter.

It does, however, mean they need to think a little bigger than box pancakes (Figure 7.1).

FIGURE 7.1 Minimum viable versus minimum lovable product

Minimum
viable
product

Minimum
lovable
product

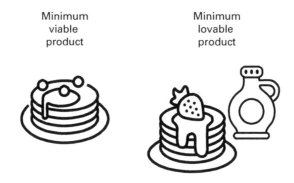

Focusing on an MVP rather than an MLP means your team can spend time thinking about what version of a project represents the minimum that is required for your team to adore a product, rather than merely tolerating it. This shift in mindset means you will still be launching iteratively, but that you will also have to raise the bar of what you're shipping beyond what will be tolerated, but focus on what will bring your team joy.

Creating feedback loops

Feedback loops regulate most aspects of every system in your working life, even if you aren't aware of them. They are built into most of the modern conveniences we have come to rely on, and they're the reason great products succeed.

When you created your first Spotify account you may have noticed your recommendations were a little weak. Over time, you're proven to be a massive Bruce Springsteen fan, so Spotify shows you his best of, and adds some Tom Petty into your regular rotation. You'll notice that the service begins to show you more and more new music which aligns closer to your personal preferences. This is also why your weekly round-up looks a little off-the-wall after you share your account to your younger cousin, or when new couples have a baby and find lullabies take over their yearly Spotify Wrapped.

This is the outcome of a feedback loop. Spotify has designed their whole product around seeking your feedback and applying changes based on what they learn. This is true even if you aren't 100 per cent sure when you are giving insights. Your feedback, in this instance, is the form of what you listen to, when, how often and when you skip or like songs or artists by adding them to your playlists.

Feedback loops are crucial to product development practices and beneficial for quick and effective iteration. An iterative process requires launching something, gathering feedback and then applying that feedback to the next iteration. In order to iterate in any of the manners mentioned earlier in this chapter (testing, smaller user groups or MLPs) you need to set up some mechanism for gathering feedback quickly.

This goes on over and over until, honestly... *forever*. A company is never 'finished' and a project is never perfect. You may, however, reach a point where you're happy putting a pin in any further updates or changes, so that you can focus on other more pressing projects.

What is a feedback loop in People Operations?

In People Operations, we are constantly interacting with our team and we have plenty of opportunities to develop feedback loops. Some of the most obvious ones we see in almost every company is the exit interview. This feedback loop is designed as the closure to the hiring process, engagement, as well as to give insight into retention metrics.

However, there are many other opportunities for tighter loops which give you more real time feedback and enable quicker iterations of projects you're working on. In traditional product management, feedback loops often come in the shape of user metrics or traffic. Things may not be that simple (or even the right place to look) in People Operations. For this reason, I suggest you have some clarity on what exactly you're looking to solve before you begin launching iterative projects or work.

Input and output metrics   This means, when you are doing your project and goal planning, it is crucial that you get some clarity on which output metrics you would like to see move. This is not always easy in People Operations: often our projects are centred around input metrics and deliverables rather than moving a metric directly. This is because tracking data and running analysis is not always something our teams have people dedicated towards. However, with your new squad formation, it is incredibly helpful to not only have someone thinking about this, but also to make sure you're setting up input and output metrics from the start of every project you work on.

Input metrics: An input metric is where you *do* something. An example is 'launch a new careers page' or 'update our benefits offering'. These are a very common style of goal in People Operations and can be very helpful as goals even when you have some clear output metrics.

Output metrics: These are the metrics based on some kind of outcome from what you've done. Examples here (in the theme from the definition above) are to 'improve traffic on our careers page 10x' or 'improve sentiment around our benefits by 20 per cent'. These are the kinds of goals you can see being moved in iterative testing and enable you to see tangible progress towards your higher-level goals via nested goals.

Building feedback into everything you do

It is easier than ever to gather feedback through mediums such as Pulse surveys, Slack, Twitter and LinkedIn Polls, Trustpilot and Google Reviews. If there is one thing people seem to love to give, it's feedback. Use this to your benefit, and harness the power of asking for feedback. From your team, your peers and those out there in the market who may be ideal candidates for your company. I would, however, warn of oversaturating your team with surveys and remember to utilize the various forms of testing and user research described in Chapter 5.

Some ways to think about gathering feedback:

- Create two prototypes and ask for feedback from the team on Slack by requesting they select specific emojis for their preference.
- Run a longer survey to the company on their experience with the new project you've launched.
- Send out scheduled Pulse surveys (or even free on Slack!) to ask for ongoing sentiment on a specific area or question.
- Ask your managers to spend two minutes getting the team to send written feedback at the end of their team stand-ups.
- Organize a focus group to meet regularly on a specific topic of point of interest in your team.
- Demo your project or work in progress in your townhall, invite feedback openly.

- Add a survey link to your email signature inviting feedback, making sure to tweak the questions as you learn from where you can improve (or even change what you're looking to learn!)

How does this differ from user testing?

Gathering feedback is essentially the same family. The idea of iteration and user testing walk hand-in-hand. One thing I would say here, though, is that you should be cautious to feel your feedback exercises have to *always* be as elaborate as I outlined in Chapter 4.

Yes, user testing is crucial and research is a huge part of the work you should be doing in your planning, scoping and product development. However, asking for casual feedback on ongoing iterations of your work does not always need to take the form of structured user interviews and surveys. It's ok to just run a quick survey, as long as you're giving those outcomes the same weight as they deserve (i.e., a little bit).

What if it goes wrong?

This is, undoubtedly, one of the hardest aspects of working with an iterative mindset. As I'd said earlier, the way many of us are traditionally used to working is due to the pinch of requiring complete, successful work. I believe this is the outcome of a trend of mistrust and scepticism towards the HR function as explored in Chapter 1. I don't want to spend too long feeling down about that – this book is all about changing the narrative and turning the tide!

The most important thing I can say is: *learning is the aim here, not success*. This may be a hard pill to swallow, but one of the most important things about iterative thinking is that *sometimes it fails*. And that should be okay, because the amount of time, energy, and resources put into something should be considerably less than a broad-scale project. The great news is that often a failure is not a complete disaster and a project can still be put back on track in a way that any lost time proves itself wisely used.

There is no proponent of iterative and agile methodologies who would suggest everything you do needs to be perfect first go – that's against the very nature of the work!

I am sure everyone out there reading has heard the phrase 'fail fast', especially if you're already familiar with the start-up world and working with the Agile approach. As counter-intuitive as it might sound for some of us trained in waterfall teams, fast failures achieve a much more successful result than aiming to perfect the solution without ongoing feedback and validation.

How to frame failing when you fail fast

You may be reading this in agreement, but struggling with how to share this approach with those who are asking you to contribute work. Getting your leadership on board with the idea of trying and failing may not be as simple for some of us as it is for others. I am sure there are many businesses out there where this idea will be like pushing water up a hill, and there are others where the power of influence can come to your aid. I'm going to try to speak to both of you.

INFLUENCE A FAIL FAST CULTURE

So, you're in a team where you're looking to influence your team and leadership to begin working more iteratively, being more open to failure and accepting learning as a desired outcome. Great! I suggest you begin by using some of the ideas below to craft your approach to influencing anyone who may be on the fence or requires a supportive voice on the matter.

It will save you time in the long run   In an iterative approach, your team starts a new project or task, works to obtain feedback early on, and then analyses whether the project or approach will be successful. If that task is moving in the wrong direction, your squad should be naturally incentivized to stop work as soon as possible and move their focus to something more effective. This means, sure, you spend some time working on something non-viable, but ultimately the value of learning is worth whatever amount of time you go back to focus on better solutions.

It will bring you closer to what works, quicker   Remember that you are servicing the careers and needs of human beings, as well as that of the candidate market (which we talk more about in the upcoming Chapter 8). There is almost no way to reliably predict what people will like. (Trust me, even giving everyone a free Labrador puppy and seating them on linen bean bags won't make people fulfilled and happy in their career.) You need to engage with a very dynamic group of voices (combined with the fact you may also be looking to attract more diverse folks into your team), which means you will need to try various things to get closer to what really works. Any attempt at copying another company may mean you get further from what works or that you entirely miss the mark. An iterative approach allows you to move dynamically with the voices of your team, the market and potential candidates you'd like to bring onboard to achieve your company's mission.

Build it low-key   It is not (not!) easy to change an organization's culture. If you're working somewhere where the idea of failing fast may not float, I understand. I do not think all is lost. I am sure there are many things in this book which you will struggle to implement, but that does not mean you cannot take something onboard. You can absolutely make some changes to move closer to the direction of People Operations as a product.

In this instance, I suggest that you continue working in a more waterfall methodology, but that you begin baking feedback loops into each stage of your project timeline. For example, if you are launching a new benefits programme, begin by asking for feedback from the team and then create a benefits focus group where you can ask them for dynamic feedback as you work through each step of the project. This means you will still launch a large-scale piece of work at completion, but you are more likely to be moving dynamically as you do that. This still isn't ideal, however, because you will spend a lot of time building and not a lot of time launching and learning, but it does give you the upper hand on the best parts of the iterative process.

Shifting the narrative

Communicating failure as a success always feels a little bizarre at first. 'We failed!!!' is rarely exclaimed with triumphant voices. However, it will be your new role to help your team move closer to that direction, specifically when it comes to iteration so that you can learn what is working.

Radical innovation happens when many self-organizing employees experiment consistently and learn what works by seeing what fails. One way I like to frame this with my team is the idea of learning faster. I like 'fail fast' because many people understand it and have interacted with the term before, which makes the curve of understanding quicker. Ultimately, I am not a huge proponent of introducing a new term if the old one is effective.

However, the idea of 'learn fast' is a much more positive way to frame it, so if you're finding yourself struggling to get the team onboard with the idea of failing, try using this instead.

Learning is always a good thing; I am sure I won't have anyone disagree with this idea. Learning something bad or disappointing about the work we're doing may not feel wonderful when it happens, but if you're a person motivated to do better quality work, the discomfort is often overshadowed by the satisfaction of knowing where you stand. Learning quicker enables you to move through challenges faster and also enables you to move to successes quicker, bringing you and your team one more day closer to celebration.

CREATING A PSYCHOLOGICALLY SAFE TEAM

Your team will need to be very comfortable with the idea of trying things out. This is not an easy state to cultivate, and requires a deep respect and psychological safety between your squads. According to a 2017 Gallup poll, 3 out of 10 employees strongly agreed that their opinions don't count at work.[4] Even if you feel you have a very safe and open team, you may still need to put extra work in. This is even more true if you're planning a significant change to this new way of working. There is nothing more compounding on someone's comfort in their role than ambiguity and change.

Psychological safety is the belief that you won't be punished or humiliated for speaking up with ideas, questions, concerns or mistakes. The idea of building a team with strong psychological safety is not new, and it is something I'd encourage every leader to put real time into, regardless of their plans for how they shape their team.

The best place to start thinking about this is the idea of belonging and security. I am sure many of the readers of this book are working in start-ups, and the idea of 'security' is much less certain than at publicly traded or more established businesses. This is not in any way terminal to the kind of security which helps a psychologically safe workplace thrive. Job security in terms of finances is very different to job security related to failure, challenging authority or expressing concerns.

A psychologically safe workplace begins with a feeling of *belonging* and with a feeling that this belonging won't be stripped suddenly without reason. That is what I mean when I say security. Maslow's Hierarchy of Needs shows that each of us require our basic needs to be met before they can reach our full potential and the same is true in the workplace.[5]

Dr Timothy Clark created a very helpful framework.[6] He said that employees have to progress through four stages of psychological safety before they feel free to make valuable contributions and challenge the status quo. I've summarized them below and suggest you read through and think about where your team may currently spend the majority of their time.

- **Inclusion Safety:** Inclusion safety satisfies the basic human need to connect and belong. It is clear that your team feels satisfied with their need to connect and belong. The team are open with their unique characteristics and personalities, and aren't afraid to share what makes their world view unique. This doesn't mean your team is sharing ideas or feedback just yet, but they are comfortable being open with who they are as a person.

- **Learner Safety:** Learner safety satisfies the need to learn and grow. In this stage, your team feels safe to exchange in the learning process, by asking questions, giving (and receiving) feedback, experimenting and making mistakes. Your team will be open to being seen to be vulnerable here, but they may not take risks or challenge others in higher positions on their own.

- **Contributor Safety:** Contributor safety satisfies the need to make a difference. Your team finally feels safe enough to use their unique skills and abilities to make a meaningful contribution to the team by taking material risks and trying new things. This takes guts and you should be proud of those putting themselves out there. Remember that risk taking looks different to different people, and at different levels of an organization.

- **Challenger Safety:** Challenger safety satisfies the need to make things better. Your team feels safe to speak up and challenge the status quo if they think there's an opportunity to change or improve things. This may be something they are comfortable doing in one-to-one forums, or – even more impressive – in public meetings or workshops. This is a gift and having your team at this level you will begin to feel the flow of working well together. However, it is important to know that your team may reach this point at different stages, so be aware of the dynamics between them as they work.

However, you may feel your team isn't quite there even on level one. They may be still interacting and discussing on a professional level, but that any challenges are made through back channels or cannot be resolved constructively. You have seen emails with more than a handful of CCs of senior executives when things get hard and you find complex social situations are often escalated or mediated. At this level it would be difficult to implement a 'fail fast' approach as your team will not likely be comfortable with sharing ideas and seeking open, critical feedback in a healthy way.

If this is you and you're reading through the above list and realizing you have some work to do, I suggest you think about a few ways to improve psychological safety in your team. This list is not exhaustive, and there are many fabulous books, podcasts and blogs on the topic. I'll add some into the resources at the end of this chapter and encourage further reading as this is not an area I claim to be any kind of expert in. With that said, there are a few basic steps you can take to begin to foster more psychological safety at work:

1 Begin from the top

In 2009, Mark Zuckerberg wore a tie to work every day for a year. He did this to demonstrate that it was time to take the business seriously.[7] You have an obligation as a leader to walk your walk, and do things you expect your team to do. Ask for feedback, be open to anonymous feedback at first, and be open about your own challenges, shortcomings, and failures. If you feel you need to get a coach to help you through this, I encourage it!

2 Create spaces for new ideas

Design teams have wonderful spaces for new ideas called Design Crits (or critiques). These spaces are great for sharing new ideas and also giving constructive feedback amongst the team. Integrate an 'idea crit' into your team calendar or hold specific open hours for new ideas. (When I worked at McCann, our two Executive Creative Directors held an hour each day called Elevensies where they listened to any idea from anyone in the business – a fantastic initiative which fostered creativity!)

3 Support and appreciate constructive conflict

If you see a member of your team engage in constructive feedback or conflict, publicly appreciate and support them on this. It is important to do this in a way which does not make the person being critiqued or 'feedbacked' to feel smaller or pushed aside, so make sure you also share appreciation to them for being open to feedback in order to improve.

4 Celebrate risk taking

Feedback and risks are different things. It is easy to give feedback to someone taking a risk, but there is an even bigger challenge in being the risk-taker. Celebrate these members of your team even louder than those willing to offer up feedback and make sure to make space to celebrate when their risks result in valuable learning. Never miss an opportunity to bring the celebration full circle beyond just developing psychological safety, but also towards the idea of learning through feedback.

5 Listen

This one goes hand-in-hand with point 1, and it is the most important point of all, I think. If you are the kind of leader who has received feedback like 'I don't feel heard' or 'I give you feedback and it goes nowhere' then that is a huge red flag. Your team needs to know that you not only hear them when they share ideas, give feedback, and challenge the status quo, but that something will be done with their valuable voices. Start making a channel or forum to demonstrate where you're listening. Even if that is a monthly written 'what I've done with your feedback' update, no matter how clunky. Trust me, the team will value it.

Whatever stage you are at in your journey towards a psychologically safe team and the ability to learn and fail fast, your entire team will benefit from moving towards this new way of approaching problems. You may prioritize this work before moving into a new organizational design. If you do so, I suggest you share this book with them so that they understand that the cultural shift is a necessary one to make them happier and more productive at work, but also comes with the higher purpose of thinking like a product team.

The key points from this chapter

- Iteration is the repetition of a process in order to generate a sequence of outcomes. In its most basic form it's the idea of launching something small, seeing how it works, taking feedback on board and launching it in a bigger way.
- Working iteratively enables you to break down those problem statements into smaller product launches and ship them quickly, learn from them and then build on what you've mastered so far.
- There are different ways to build iteration into the work you do in People Operations:
  - o **A/B testing,** where you launch two smaller versions of something and see which works best.

o **Smaller user bases,** where you launch a project to a smaller group of users to gauge their reaction before moving to a broader user group.

o **Less complete products** – the most common way to think about this is the minimum viable product. This means launching the smallest and least sophisticated version of a solution to learn if you're moving in the right direction.

• We should consider the idea of minimum loveable product rather than minimum viable. This enables our teams to get closer to producing something they're proud of, and raises the bar on user experience of our teams.

• We should learn to iterate because it helps us move quicker, learn quicker and pivot if a project isn't moving towards the metrics we're hoping to impact.

• In People Operations, a feedback loop may look like a survey, poll, interview or simply asking for direct feedback.

• Don't be afraid to consider this as a part of your user research process, but know that you don't need to make every effort to gather feedback as elaborate as a full user research process.

• Make sure you're setting output metrics at the beginning of your projects so that you are able to effectively assess if your iterative project is moving in the right direction.

o Input metrics are the 'doing' such as 'launch a new careers page.'

o Output metrics are the outcomes, such as 'improving traffic to the careers page by 10X.'

• Moving to an iterative approach means you need to be comfortable with taking risks and failing fast. This is not something every person in your team will be immediately comfortable with so may take some influencing.

• In order to move to a 'failing fast' approach, you need to have fostered a team with psychological safety. This isn't easy! Consider the interactions and culture of your team and focus on that while you're moving in this direction.

• If your team doesn't work with a high degree of psychological safety, you may want to prioritize this work above any other changes in order for them to be more effective. Be sure to share that shift in the context of the broader product management philosophy so that the team see a team-wide objective they can believe in.

Endnotes

1 Agile Manifesto (2001) The Agile Manifesto https://agilemanifesto.org/ (archived at https://perma.cc/DG5W-2JBU)

2 Ries, Eric (2008) The lean startup, Startup Lessons Learned Blog http://www. startuplessonslearned.com/2008/09/lean-startup.html (archived at https://perma. cc/K2YT-Q6Q6)

3 Merryweather, Ellen (2021) What is a Minimum Loveable Product, Product School Blog and Podcast https://productschool.com/blog/product-management-2/minimum-lovable-product/ (archived at https://perma.cc/ Q8EX-KEWG)

4 Herway, Jake (2017) How to Create a Culture of Psychological Safety, Gallup Blog https://www.gallup.com/workplace/236198/create-culture-psychological-safety.aspx (archived at https://perma.cc/R668-RX7X)

5 Maslow, Abraham H (1943). 'A theory of human motivation'. *Psychological Review*, 50 (4): 370–396

6 Clark, Dr Timothy (2020) *The 4 Stages of Psychological Safety: Defining the Path to Inclusion and Innovation,* Beret-Koehler Publishers, 9781523087686

7 Zuckerberg, Mark (2009) Facebook Profile Update "Wore a Tie for a Whole Year" https://www.facebook.com/4/posts/10100171126363191/ (archived at https://perma.cc/N4PZ-NFUT)

08

Standing out in the marketplace of culture

I wanted to reach out ahead of our interviews next week and say that, after reading through your public handbook, I don't think this role will be the right fit for me because I struggle in an environment so heavy on written and asynchronous communication.

A candidate withdrawing from a role can feel like a punch in the stomach, but somehow it felt even more acute when I read this email. The team were disappointed too, 'Should we see if we can convince them?'

'No. I didn't think so.'

The reason they'd withdrawn was a clear sign to me that this was the right decision for both parties. Our open handbook had done its job. We had an opinionated and specific culture which (very reasonably) wasn't everyone's cup of tea. If someone had opted out after learning more, we should respect that and continue looking for someone who was a more appropriate fit.

As I've said, every company is building two products. The product you sell to customers, and the product you sell to candidates and your team that is being described in this book as the employee experience. The best consumer-facing products are opinionated and have a point of view, something which can feel hard if you see trade-offs like losing customers who may want something just *slightly* different. Just like selling your product out in the consumer market, you also must *stand out* in the market of culture. If you are not selling something with unique selling points (USPs), then your competitors who do have clarity on their USPs and their market will eat you alive.

In the cold light of day, and with a bit of time in retrospect, we can see what happens when companies don't create UPSs for their culture within the 'Google-fication' of culture in the mid-2010s. Google and many other Silicon Valley giants began building their cultures and employer brand around ideas of bringing their whole selves to work, working hard and playing hard, ping pong tables, free snacks and a more transparent way of working. Many tech companies followed suit and some more traditional companies began to tack those cultural elements onto their (sometimes vastly different) way of working.

It didn't work. You may have seen it yourself or had connections in places where the culture felt inauthentic or even somewhat hollow. I remember going to an event at an online betting company years ago in London. The company had once been a more corporate business and without making any changes to their management or ways of working, they began installing ping pong tables and putting brightly coloured posters around the office encouraging their team to bring their *wacky* selves to work and to fail fast. They were struggling with hiring and were surprised to find that even after their efforts to 'modernize' they struggled with retention. This is what happens when a company tries to homogenize another company's culture without being thoughtful about how they operate differently, and then they fail to either stand out or to retain the team they attracted.

There is no 'good' or 'bad' culture

One of the things I feel truly lucky to have in my life is a group of friends with colourful and diverse backgrounds, who enjoy different things and work in a range of different careers. One of my best friends works in the legal world, another in charity and a few in tertiary education. Sometimes when we discuss projects or conflicts at work, I find myself feeling deeply thankful to work where I work and often I see my friends feeling the same way, with a flash of relief across their face as I describe how we make decisions or pivot often in the start-up world.

I have friends who really enjoy, even love, working at a type of company that I would not just struggle in, but that I would actively dislike. Some folks love hierarchy, some hate it. Some folks cannot tolerate siloed decision-making, others find democratized decisions frustrating. Lots of flexibility and autonomy can be ambiguous, even stressful, for some. If you decide to build a company that is highly structured it is no less 'good' than another company which values loose and scrappy decision-making. People can absolutely be successful (and love) either, but perhaps not the *same* people.

There is no such thing as a *good* culture, just what's good for you. There is almost no such thing as a *bad* culture (unless you are building a discriminatory, toxic or criminal business). If someone has told you differently, it's time to remove that belief from your memory. *ZAP,* Men in Black style. Now, with that gone, it is time to build what is *right* for where you are, not what is *right* for another company. The only way to do this is to form a clear opinion of what kind of company you want to be in the marketplace of culture.

What is a marketplace of culture?

The job market is like any market, filled with a variety of options for those looking. In many ways, the pandemic and events of 2020 and 2021 brought some new spice into the mainstream cultural market by making remote working a more widely adopted approach.[1] Being a remote-first company used to be quite niche, something novel and which only very few businesses adopted with vigour. Now, more and more companies are discussing how they work in a remote-first and geographically distributed way. Even more interestingly, some businesses are using the fact they are fully remote to stand out and others are using the fact they have offices. It has become clear that there is an opinionated set of 'buyers' in the market for any position on the remote spectrum. I have spoken with many Chief People Officers and Directors of HR who have asked me how they respond to their teams' varied requirements and requests when it comes to remote working. This is very much still a fertile ground for differentiation within the market.

My answer when someone asks me if they should go remote has always been that they shouldn't. Well, at least not immediately. The goal should be to decide on where they want to be in the marketplace and to discover what would attract the kinds of candidates they believe are their target market. If a company is a logistics company, with physical premises and local customers, it may not ever make sense to go fully remote and maybe office-based (with some flexibility on home working, of course) is the ideal solution. If, however, you are a video conferencing tool who focuses on remote interaction, it's clear a remote-first approach is aligned.

Remote versus in-office (and all along the spectrum) is just one of the many decisions that you should be making as a leader, founder or head of a

People Team. I would encourage you to think deeply about what kind of company, what kind of 'product' you are trying to build and allow yourself to be opinionated about it. Ensure you have a vision of what you are aiming to develop which has teeth, or you may find you aren't attracting the kinds of people who will push you further as a business.

> I use remote working as a single example of the kind of decision you may make in the marketplace of cultures, but there are hundreds of others. Remote working is a very easy decision to use as an example, where many others aren't so clear – things like your manager-to-employee ratio, how democratized you want decisions to be, how much you value transparency, etc. Your values may give you some great insight into the kinds of ways of working your company favours, so use these as context clues to define your USPs.

What works and what doesn't

What works for you may not work for others. It's important to respect that something that is a brilliant idea for the company you admire posting on Twitter may not work for you.

CONSIDER ALL OPTIONS

What is also true is that you can, in theory, *consider* anything. It may not mean you implement it, but it is often a good idea to spend some time thinking about all of the different types of cultures which may work for you. Just because your current approach is not highly hierarchical, it doesn't mean that may not be the best outcome for your team to start working towards. Spend some real time considering all options for what kind of culture and USP you want to focus on developing.

LEADERSHIP ALIGNMENT

What is also important is that you have agreement from your other leaders that they are aligned with this direction and what it means for their teams, hiring decisions and ways of working. Nothing is less productive than having a Chief Marketing Officer who wants to build a dynamic, flat team of mostly juniors and then having their team try to partner with a Chief Product Officer who has a highly structured team of senior Product folks who detest unstructured decision-making and messy pivots. These two approaches are, independently, entirely valid. It is when they come together that they fail. This makes it your role (along with your CEO) to work with your leadership to identify a cultural approach that works across the entire business and ensure everyone is bought in on what that means.

WORKS WITH YOUR COMPANY

One area I see companies struggle is developing an opinionated culture which feels aligned with the *kind of company they are* as well as what kind of company they are trying to become. As I said before about remote working, if you are a company that is working on building tools for the future of work, it may make perfect sense to be a fully distributed team. If you're working in a book publishing house, it may make less sense. This is directly related to the product you're making and what your whole company is aligned around.

When thinking of the kinds of USPs your company has, you should also be thinking about the mission of your company, the products you create and sell, as well as your People Operations mission you created in Chapter 3. Consider what kind of culture will attract the kinds of people you need to reach the company mission. If you're aiming to be the most awarded creative agency in Europe, perhaps your culture will be defined as highly flexible, creative and built on democratized decision-making. If you're aiming to build a first-of-its-kind artificial intelligence laboratory, then a lean and highly-skilled team with a long tenure will be aligned with where you're going culturally.

How to identify your unique selling points

Reading through this chapter you may already have some clear opinions on where you are as a company and where you want to go to reach your mission. You may even already believe your leadership team would be aligned if you shared this thinking today. If that's the case, fabulous. If not, then it's time to start thinking. Regardless of which camp you are in I would encourage you to do a workshop so that you can be doubly sure of the alignment and so that you can begin publicly and intentionally moving your culture in this direction.

ORGANIZATIONAL DESIGN PRINCIPLES WORKSHOP

When I am consulting, I suggest to all founders and CEOs I work with that they should develop some articulate organizational design and culture principles. This should be a list of five to eight principles which describe the voice and USPs of your cultural voice in the marketplace.

> But aren't these just your values? No. Your values are absolutely a part of this, and I would even argue that they should be informed by this work. If you already have values, they should hint towards your cultural principles but won't expressly describe them.
>
> Where your values describe the heart and mindset behind how you interact together as a team with each other, the world and your customers, your cultural or organizational principles decide the kind of company you want to be on a much more operational level.

CASE STUDY

Whereby's principles:

- **Biased towards top talent:** There are no silver medallist functions in Whereby. Because we run a lean organization, we require top talent everywhere work is done. This means we are biased to top talent and are competitive with the kinds of companies we aspire to be, not the company we are today.

- This doesn't mean we do not hire junior people, but when we look for inaugurate, graduate or associate members of our team we look for those who have a high degree of intellectual bandwidth, ambition and potential to succeed at Whereby, alongside a prior track record.

- This also means we may pass over many candidates at a 'three' before settling on the right talent for our team.

- We are comfortable bringing in consultants to cover skills when a permanent need arises so that we have the time to make a considered choice about who we invite into our team. (See: Flexible)

- **Lean**: We hire a few, highly sought after people rather than many easy-to-hire candidates. We build teams where that talent is stretched and challenged, but not overworked.

- We should often ask ourselves if we need a permanent person or a highly skilled, deeply knowledgeable consultant to teach and guide our team.

- We never hire a permanent team member to only solve a short-term problem. Permanent hires should only be made to consider problems three to six months in the future.

- **T-shaped:** Because we often work in squad-type style, our teams are broadly capable across their function, with a deep area of knowledge or capability. This means our team can work on a varied array of projects, while being able to be called upon when their expertise is required.

- **Flexible**: Because our team is T-shaped, we are able to bend and flex our org design rapidly to meet new challenges. Our team is capable of reforming into project-suitable groups, and are comfortable with autonomy and ambiguity.

- We are also quick to leverage consulting and temporary talent in times where deeper knowledge or expertise is needed, or just over a time where recruitment processes require additional time.

- **Diverse and inclusive:** We hire from everywhere, meaning we can leverage a diverse perspective in almost every role.

- We use this as a competitive advantage, looking for skills, talent and a new perspective wherever possible because we know the best organizations are diverse and dynamic.

- Importantly, it is crucial that we do not add cultural detractors from our team who jeopardize the community, belonging or psychological safety of our team. Even if someone is the 'best in their field' if they disrupt the other elements of our organizational design, it is a non-starter.

- **Tech enabled**: Administration is not a fulfilling role. Because we hire top talent into T-shaped roles, we use technology and interim support to remove or reduce administration as much as possible. We are able to reinvest these administrative role salaries back into technology and rewarding our team.

- Our team, therefore, are aware they need to be operational at time, and know our roles have a responsibility to remove admin and automate inefficiencies where we see them.

CULTURAL AND ORGANIZATIONAL PRINCIPLES

To do a workshop involves half a day with your leadership team where you spend time discussing and debating, before finally deciding on a list of principles. There are many things you can ultimately select from, and it is important to ensure you are realistic about what may work for you from the perspective of your market, mission and current team. If you are a fintech company operating in Seoul, you may not find values around creativity and transparency will resonate with your target market to hire and retain. If you are a fully remote global company, it will be very difficult to have a culture centred around highly democratized real-time decision-making due to time-zones.

One question I ask founders is where their skill and leverage are as indexed against other companies in competition with them. Skill means the technical skills, or experience required for the roles in their team (generally, different teams can move within this spectrum), from entry level high school graduate, to renowned PhD scientist. Often, we find the majority of businesses are much closer to the beginning of the spectrum than the end.

The other axis of this is leverage (Figure 8.1). How much individual reach do each of the folks in your team have? If you have high leverage, you can reasonably expect to attract a more sought-after candidate. If your roles are fairly fungible then you should acknowledge that it is less likely those with the most illustrious career prospects would consider your opportunity particularly enticing (employer brand aside). On one end you have a recruitment agency, where each person creates one node in the financial plan, but has very little impact on the overall product. On the other end you would have Google Deepmind, where each person is involved in a complex and multi-year research and development cycle for their high ROI products.

Getting your leadership team to work together to place your company on this matrix as it is today, as well as where you'd like to be in five years' time, is a great exercise to help you gain requisite clarity on your target audience.

FIGURE 8.1 Skill versus leverage

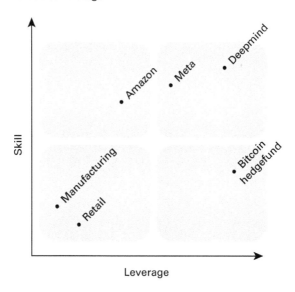

This matrix is, however, just one in the long list of different trade-offs decisions you'd have to explore when deciding on your target market.

Some of the trade-offs you may want to consider:

- Hierarchical or flat management
- Transparent or traditional
- Highly structured or dynamic
- Creative or analytical
- Flexible or rigid
- Remote or co-located
- Democratized or fast-paced
- Synchronous or asynchronous
- Highly social or professional
- Autonomous or interactive
- High skill or low skill.

As you're going through this list you will see that some of the decisions above simply make less sense together. If you're aiming to build a highly-skilled team of PhD scientists, but you are also aiming to build a large, broad team, you may struggle to hire the volume required. Let's explore what some of the sliders do produce.

- **Rigid, traditional, analytical, professional, fast-paced:** This type of culture describes a typical investment bank or larger consulting institution. You may want to build a consulting business which is directly different to this kind of culture so that you stand out in the marketplace, but consider what this means for your key talent you're attracting.

- **Interactive, low skill, broad, highly social, hierarchical:** This sounds a lot like a co-located team with folks in their early careers and several layers of management. It sounds like it describes something close to some recruitment agencies I've worked with, and which culturally worked really well for some folks. From the People Operations perspective, you would need to invest in management training (due to the high hierarchy and presumably low manager to employee ratios), but you'd also be able to develop things like a simple and competitive compensation structure due to one geographical market and lower-skilled teams. It's likely you'd see higher attrition, but less costly recruitment.

- **Lean, high-skilled, creative, dynamic:** This reminds me of some of the boutique creative agencies I've worked with in the past. Again, a brilliant culture for some folks, and if you were building this type of culture in the marketplace, you'd want to focus on giving meaty projects which are intellectually stimulating to retain your team. You'd attract people who are comfortable with ambiguity due to the dynamism, and would build learning programmes around out-of-work skills like strategic development more than skills like people management (where you may not be hiring much due to your lean org where retention is key).

Identify your target audience

Identifying who your target market is for your culture and the kind of company you are trying to build is a less laborious undertaking and should be directly informed by your principles already decided in your workshop above. From here, you need to work out what the ideal customer profile, or candidate profile, looks like out there in the market. The work you have done in user research to define some user personas may be very helpful here.

You will be doing this for two reasons:

1 To ensure you can spot them in a recruitment process.

2 To identify if this feels incongruous to your current team.

> It is very important to say here that this does not in any way mean you should be deciding if this 'ideal customer' is male or female, white, married or any other protected characteristic. What you are trying to decide is the personality which would thrive in your place of work, and personality is not directly informed by the colour of a person's skin, their gender, religion or any other characteristic outside of their working lives.

Many times, I've spoken to ambitious founders and C-suite leaders who struggle with the line between aspiration and reality. I am an advocate for aspirational goals, employer brands and value propositions, but there is a thin line between aspiration and realism, and even between honesty. It is one thing to aspire to be a more transparent company, using that as a pillar in your value proposition while knowing you'd need to attract more folks to help you build that reality. It is entirely another to run on a platform of diversity without any credentials or intentions to bring that into reality. The most common disconnect I do see, however, is that of 'talent and skill'. Many founders and leaders I have worked with have expressed a need to attract and retain talent from Oxbridge, FAANG (or MAGMA), or investment banking.

Small digression: I want to say that I don't believe that there is a correlation between intellect, capacity or potential and individuals who have a history within those three institutions listed above. However, the reputation remains that if you manage to attract 100 per cent Oxbridge graduates with FAANG logos on their CV, then somehow your start-up will succeed where others have failed. *I disagree.*

Once you have spent some time exploring the trade-offs listed earlier in this chapter, and then discovering what kind of person may best suit your strategy, you may find that your ideal candidate differs slightly from what is being touted in the market as the 'ideal' for all companies. There is nothing wrong with going after a different group of people than other companies in your VC portfolio or network. In fact, that is what will make you stand out in the marketplace of culture. Where others may see headwinds with many competing offers, you should see well-suited and happy colleagues.

Stick to it

If you are building a company that loves dogs by default, even if the world's most renowned cat lover wanders into your interview process, you would be well placed to pass on the opportunity and focus on more suitable candidates. 'But what if we want to branch off into Cats!?' I've heard some founders ask. Perhaps you do, but to be sure I'd encourage you all to re-read what I've written about ruthless prioritization in Chapter 3 just in case.

The decision to hire someone who doesn't fit your target audience, or who is not a 'cultural fit' (I, like many others, kind of hate this phrase), is an easy one to make. Someone is a fabulous candidate, has ample skills, an impressive CV, wows the interview panel… it's just a shame they aren't the right shape for your organization; they've got too much (or too little) experience, they don't fully align with your mission, their compensation is way out of scope or they're looking for a role you don't have. 'Well, we can make them a new role!' is something I've frequently seen suggested and rarely seen effectively implemented except in very small start-ups. If you are a first-time founder, or are the leader of a HR team with leadership who are less experienced, this may be something you frequently encounter and should try hard to really interrogate and push back on.

The good news is coming up with your ideal customer/candidate profile alongside with the rest of your executive or leadership team enables you to gather buy-in so that, when you are required to really stick to your guns on your cultural archetype, you are able to do so with teeth.

The question sometimes arises of what you should do if your organization seems way off base. *What do you do if you have already assembled a team which looks entirely wrong?* As I mentioned in Chapter 6, I won't advocate for wholesale terminations or redundancies. I think a much better (and more legal) approach is one of well communicated change management. Some members of your business may elect to voluntarily exit, cancelling their subscription to your business once they realize it's not as transparent, flat or small as they had previously enjoyed. That is okay, although it can be somewhat difficult. You should not consider these exits as regrettable unless you genuinely want to retain them, would rehire them or your team failed somehow to manage the exec appropriately. Communicating your cultural direction widely and frequently is crucial to moving the team towards your new vision.

If you see exits from your business which you are concerned are regrettable, I suggest you do an exercise with your managers answering the following three 'If they left today' questions for each member of their team.

If they left today...

1 Would you fight to retain them?

2 Would you rehire them in the future?

3 Would you have regrets about what lead to that exit (compensation, communication)?

If members of your team are a 'yes' to all three, that requires immediate action (likely from the People Team and the manager) to address the concerns. If the answer is 'yes' to one and two, then this person should be the kind of person you wish to retain in your team now. If someone is a 'yes' only to question 2, or question 2 and 3, then it is clear that perhaps this is not the right time for this employee in your organization. If the answer is 'no' to all three, then you should question if this person is a long-term member of your team.

I personally hate and am sick of hearing about HR vying for a 'seat at the table', but I do believe that Product Management have effectively done so by putting their function firmly in the commercial strategy of the business. The approach of thinking like a Product Manager should allow the HR team to make difficult calls, such as turning down candidates or exiting employees who are not aligned with the strategy of the team and business. All of that requires defining a clear position within the marketplace of culture. This position is what will enable you to make strategic calls about the kinds of products you ship and what kind of organization your people team is helping to build.

The key points from this chapter

- There is no such thing as 'good' or 'bad' culture (with the exception of racism, sexism, or any other toxic, illegal and discriminatory behaviour).

- All businesses exist within a marketplace and should operate as such.

- Businesses should aim to avoid homogeneity as much as possible and focus on building their 'culture' as a product which will attract and retain a certain type of person who is strategically aligned to delivering the business mission.

- You should not be afraid of creating a cultural 'product' which is distinct from others in the marketplace.

- In order to fully understand your cultural product, you should discover and codify your unique selling points (USPs) and target audience.

- Once you have discovered your USPs and target audience it is imperative that you stick to these decisions and avoid diluting or straying from them unless there is a clear strategic alignment.

- You may need to make changes to your current organization to get to your ideal cultural product. Recognize that this is not a simple step and may take months (or years) of organizational change management to get you there.

- Thinking in this more commercially-minded way is the kind of thinking which brought Product Management into the C-suite and spotlight of many organizations and something People Operations teams can learn from.

Endnote

1   Felstead, A and Reuschke, D (2020) 'Homeworking in the UK: before and during the 2020 lockdown', Wales Institute of Social and Economic Research, WISERD Report https://wiserd.ac.uk/publication/homeworking-in-the-uk-before-and-during-the-2020-lockdown/ (archived at https://perma.cc/46WQ-2PHL)

09

Hiring and building at scale

I've been to a lot of tech events, talks and conferences. Sometimes I speak, often I listen. If I were to make Tech-event Question Bingo, the first square would read, 'But will it scale?'.

The downturn in the 2022 markets saw a stark change in tone in venture capital when compared against the previous half-decade or so. For many years, hyper-growth and scale mattered. It mattered so much that headcount figures were often touted as a metric of success, achievement and pride. As this book was written, the 2022 venture economy was showing signs of slowing, with a greater emphasis on a path to profitability, retention and sustainable growth.

I have always lent towards scepticism when I heard a HR leader excitedly announcing they are '200 now but due to grow to 1,000 in the next four years'. I do not see a huge difference in the kinds of people challenges faced at scale, but rather when dealing with complexity. Running a single-entity, single-product SaaS company with 500 heads is much less complex than running a five-entity, multiple product logistics and manufacturing company with 250.

But with that said, scaling matters because in all businesses, growth is crucial for survival.

If you're asking how to scale your entire business in or towards hyper growth, I think there is less advice I can give you that will help your People Practice in this book. I suggest, instead, that you must gather from authors who focus on hypergrowth as a topic, such as Frank Slootman.[1]

I can, however, give you some insight into how to scale your People Operations organization sustainability, hire effectively, and build a team that functions like a product team, well past 500 headcount. When I worked at McCann Worldgroup, I led a team which operated using an earlier iteration of the model I described in Chapter 6. In this team we were looking after significant headcount, and with the product management focus we were able to deliver very high-quality work in an effective way. So much so that, amongst some other honours including gold in our Apprenticeship Programme, we won bronze in Inhouse Recruitment Team of the Year at the 2019 Inhouse Recruiter Awards – no mean feat for a team operating in a unique and experimental way.[2]

Building now is easy, but what about when we scale?

Building a successful team using any organization design requires a great deal of skill and tactical expertise, in that way building using the People Ops as a Product mindset is not distinctive in that way. Even if the method is not unique, hiring folks who will work well in a world where your culture is a product will require somewhat of a reconsideration of the traditional HR structure.

This is particularly true as you scale and grow the team, where you are hiring more than one of the same type of role or individual and require a clear plan for how they work together in a harmonious organizational design as outlined in Chapter 7. You must commit to the maxims even in hiring, so as to avoid hiring administrative roles, ensuring you have the skills to automate and use tools and decentralizing decision making. I speak a bit more towards the end of this book, in Chapter 11, about how to remain focussed on this way of working even when it is difficult.

How to build multiple product squads

In Chapter 7, I outlined an ideal product squad for a smaller team. But if you're lucky enough to be in a growing team, the organizational design I outlined will begin to stretch at around 150 heads. One of two things will happen when you begin to realize it is time to set up another squad, either 1) your People Partners will get too stretched (I generally encourage maximum 50 heads to each People Partner) or 2) you will begin to develop a backlog of high impact, mission-critical projects which require more hands on the ground.

If you are beginning to see those markers it is time to set up a new product squad in your team with the same broad structure as your first. That means another product squad with three to four People Partners and a Lead.

> If, at this point, you have a team of pre-assembled individuals who come from more traditional 'people' backgrounds in your currently existing squad, this would also be a great time to reconsider who is in each of your squads and partner new folks together. Moving folks around from squad to squad helps to extend their skills and create more t-shaped players.

If you're struggling to get the approval to hire another three-plus heads, I suggest you begin by creating evenly sized, smaller squads and building up. As mentioned in Chapter 7, in order for a functioning squad, you require at *least* one People Partner working with at least one squad lead. From there you can hire or include a floating consultant or researcher to support the work.

This advice is also applicable if you have no approval to hire. If you are at the stage where you have one healthy sized squad, with four people partners, a lead and a researcher who are all focused on one roadmap each quarter, then you have two paths you can walk to begin to split into two roadmaps:

1 Hire one people partner to align to wherever the headcount has grown and have one squad of three and one squad of two.

2 Do no hiring and split your team into two smaller squads, with the plan to hire additional consultants to support ad hoc.

Either of these two ideas can, in theory, work. The preference is largely dependent on the hiring plans you have, your financial constraints, as well as the volume of work. Remember however, the ideal structure is three to four People Partners and a product lead.

A word of warning: when thinking for the long term, I discourage you from opting for many small squads over one larger one. Keeping prioritized and focused on a two-stream roadmap is a much more effective way to launch high quality products for your team than moving People Partners back into silos and calling them 'squads'. For this reason, if you identify that your reason for expansion is a hope to make a permanent increase in headcount, thus increasing your operating 'surface area', then I would encourage you to move to option 1 above and plan to hire into the two-person squad as quickly as you can.

KEEPING FOCUS

Two roadmaps, two focuses, two exciting paths for your People team! Keeping focus with one roadmap is hard enough, how do you do the work with two? If you are lucky enough to now have two product squads, you have much more surface area of product improvements across your employee experience.

Splitting your squads to work in similar ways to most SaaS or Ecomm product squads is generally a good start:

1 **Acquisition**: Recruitment, employer branding

2 **Onboarding and Activation:** The first one year

3 **Retention**: Performance, L&D

4 **'Platform'**: Internal People Operations tooling and back office

You can also bunch these into smaller squads, so you have Acquisition and Activation and Employee Experience and HR Ops, for example.

Another alternative is to split your squad by what is closer to traditional HR functions:

1 **Recruitment and Talent:** External branding, recruitment, headcount forecasting

2 **Learning and Development:** Career planning, management pathways, development, L&D

3 **Compensation and Performance:** Performance calibrations, compensation, reward, benefits

4 **Data and HR Services:** Dashboards, payroll, administration systems

When grouping my squads in this way, I also try to think of a product metric associated with them in order to keep the squad focused. For example, Recruitment and Talent may be focused on a metric similar to CAC:LTV (Customer Acquisition Cost to Lifetime Value ratio, find out more in the next chapter, Chapter 10.)

Either of these approaches work and all of them will cross over with each other. The same is true for Product Squads when they are working on products. The important thing is to move folks into product groups which they align well with and which offer them opportunities to work on high-impact improvements to your employee experience.

But what about recruitment!?

Hiring managers should own their own recruitment pipeline and process. This is a big statement, and one which not everyone agrees with. However, I truly believe the most effective way for a hiring manager to truly own their team is to allow them full ownership of their function, which includes hiring, performance assessment, compensation review, etc. This means I see each manager almost as a mini CEO of their function, something which requires them to actively source, plan and assess their team.

Without the right processes in place or technology set up, it is impossible for a hiring manager to do what I am asking here. This is where our People Squads come in.

One of the most disempowering (and ineffective) demands I've heard being asked of my team is to 'just bring me the best people'. Then, the hiring manager wonders why the recruiter is a) asking 100 questions and b) struggling to get it *quite* right. This is because the dynamics of this expectation are incongruous with where the responsibility and accountability truly lie.

The acquisition squad as mentioned above will *not* work as full-stack recruiters. This means they will not be working 100 per cent of their time on sourcing, candidate interviews, interview scheduling and debriefing. There will, however, be some members of the team whose People Partnership role is almost entirely aligned with recruitment activities: briefing hiring managers, advising on process, designing interview processes and speaking to candidates during interviews.

I believe a People Operations professional, or People Partner, working as a full-stack recruiter is at best a waste of time and at worst loses out on an opportunity for your Hiring Manager to truly understand and engage with the candidates in the market. Your Hiring Managers should be fully accountable for the success of recruitment, using their People Partner as a resource to help them get there, rather than the conduit for all success.

This means People Partners in talent roles do two things. In Human Operations they are there to provide assistance, monitor inbound applications through employer branding, design job descriptions, communicate with candidates and to assist at the hiring manager's requests. In People Operations, they will be working in a squad on delivering improvements across the POPs stack; they may be a part of a team working specifically on the infrastructure, documentation and processes of recruitment to better enable hiring teams, or they may be working on onboarding, L&D or performance assessment.

Put simply, the processes, tools and ways of working should be created by the Acquisition Squad and the machinery should be operated by the Hiring Manager with the assistance of the People Partner where extra hands are required. If your current recruitment process has blockers and places where a People Partner *must* be involved in order to move things along, for example a manual role approval or job description drafting, then you should immediately begin working through how to automate and unblock your management. Even further than that, managers should be responsible for sourcing, engaging talent and reaching out to potential candidates.

Reflect

What would your hiring managers say if you asked them to do this?

    Would they be able to seek their own candidates in the market?

    If not, you should begin to work on upskilling and reforming their role expectations and become clearer as an organization what the role of management truly is.

I've heard some People Leaders say, 'I really wish my hiring teams would do this, but they never would, and I don't think I could change their mind'. I understand that it is tough. As difficult as this change is, I do see this adjustment in responsibility as the single most crucial thing separating average talent from joining your team and a world-class recruitment machine. That's right. I believe that this rescoping is more crucial than employer branding, recruitment tools, even your process itself. The reason is because the blast radius of your managers is huge. A great manager is able to understand the talent market, assess their own team, and speak to the employer brand. The hardest part is that you have to raise the bar for both your hiring managers and your people team, and that takes time. I suggest you begin by slowly transitioning to this way of thinking. Start by making your hiring managers responsible for running debriefs according to a standardized template built by talent and work backwards.

Using a framework like the RACI model is a great way to identify how to split the role around recruitment. Remember that there are several tasks within a recruitment process, so you may want to get into further granularity. Below is a rough overall view from my perspective:

- **Responsible:** As it says on the tin, the responsible party is the team member who does the operational work and completes the task at hand, but should be well informed and briefed by the team member accountable.
  - The People Partner is primarily responsible for key tasks along the way, such as scheduling interviews and posting a job ad.
  - The hiring manager may, however, be responsible for some aspects, such as reviewing CVs and creating an interview structure and practical project.
- **Accountable:** The accountable person here is the team member who is accountable for the overall success of the task. There should only be one accountable team member for any task. This person is the hiring manager in this model.
- **Consulted:** The consulted party is the team members who should be consulted on the task and asked to provide their feedback.
- **Informed:** The informed parties are the team members that need to be kept in the loop, not necessarily formally consulted.

At Whereby, we built an automation-assisted hiring request process. If a role is budgeted at the beginning of the year and remains approved throughout our rolling reforecasting, all a hiring manager has to do to kick-off a role is submit a simple Typeform. This Typeform sends an automated email to the Hiring Manager and all of the People Partnering team to let us know that hiring will begin on a role. The Typeform directs the manager to the documentation they require to create a job description with the People Partner, set up a posting, and have a quick one-to-one briefing to come up with an acquisition game plan. Building these kinds of tools takes time and requires your Talent Team to have scope outside of full-stack recruitment and include Product work.

Profiles and roles

Broadly speaking, you have the role types mentioned in Chapter 7: People Partner, Consultant, Research, Project Manager. From here, you may also have someone who focuses more on management or team leadership, or you may have someone who is more of a deep knowledge expert, such as in People Analytics but working in a lead role in the Platform squad. Generally speaking, however, these folks should have a very similar base role as the other People Partners in your team.

In Chapter 7, I identified some key archetypes which you may look for in your current team in order to pivot into a People as a Product organizational design. These archetypes are still broadly applicable, however there are some key benefits of hiring externally which you should explore when posting a new job role. Take a moment to go back and look again at the job description I outlined all the way back in Chapter 2 (Wow, we've learned so much since then!).

Great. You should now have a clearer idea of the kind of profile and skills you will be looking for when hiring. Now is the time to assess your current team or squads, in order to identify where your strengths, skills and opportunities are. If you are lucky enough to have moved your entire team from a more traditional way of working and currently have an engaged squad of People Partners who are covering the fort well, take a moment to look at the functional gaps which they present. It is highly likely you are missing someone more technical or someone with a history working in data, engineering, product or technology more broadly. This is an opportunity for you to look for someone who fills that gap and would like to work in a People Partner role.

Make sure your job description is appropriately angled to attract this type of Person. It is okay to use Technical People Partner or Engineering People Partner and to include requirements such as 'experience writing code and deploying software or web products'.

The question I often get is where to find these people and what they look like out in the market. Not every profile is the same but I can give you a quick run-down of what you may be looking for.

Technical People Partner: If you're hiring for someone to partner with the Engineering Team and to assist with Zapier integrations, automation and some minor development work, then the shape of person you are seeking would suit a Technical People Partner. These individuals have a background in engineering, technical programme or product management, or product development itself. I would generally be looking for someone who would like to move from a technical role into a more managerial capacity, for example a Junior Engineer who is more interested in an Engineering Manager career path. Another great sourcing technique is to look for folks who have been to a coding bootcamp but have struggled to break into the industry, or who have pivoted back into a more managerial or entrepreneurial role.

Marketing People Partner: These folks are much easier to find and generally are either Employer Branding experts or marketing managers who are working in people-centric businesses and start-ups. Look for folks who love to produce content around culture and ways of working.

Commercial People Partner: The scope for commercial people partners is huge and has some really wonderful candidates. This role provides a great growth opportunity for those in Customer Support, or those who have worked in sales but would like to move into a less 'front line' role and into somewhere supporting sales operations and management. You may be able to find these candidates internally! This would offer a wonderful opportunity for career growth while also providing someone to your company who has established connections and understanding of things 'on the other side' of the People Operations systems and status quo.

Research: User researchers come in many shapes and sizes as they exist in the market and you are likely able to hire someone who already is working in user research. As this role is not a People Partner role, there is no need to 'pitch' a career shift like you may have to with a Technical People Partner. However, you will need to explain the way that this role would differ from the kinds of research done on an external facing product, most of which are already outlined for you in Chapter 5. Look for someone who has worked in HR Technology before, or within an 'internal' research team such as in an Engineering Enablement squad.

These profiles are absolutely not exhaustive and should only give you some food for thought on what to go out and look for in the marketplace. Ultimately, as I outlined already in this chapter, you are the one who is absolutely accountable for your hiring success, so enjoy speaking to candidates, building a pipeline and finding the kind of talent that will take your team to the next level.

The hiring process

So much has been written about how to run a world-class hiring process. If you haven't already read *Who: The A Method for Hiring* by Geoff Smart, I suggest you grab yourself a copy.[3] This book is a great read for all hiring managers and I encourage it as essential reading on becoming a manager in any function.

Over the next half of this chapter, I will give a high-level overview of a high-quality interview process for any hiring, but the value I will try to impart will be around how to look for the qualities we're seeking in the People Operations as a product mindset.

OPENING YOUR ROLE

The most important things to get a firm understanding of at this stage are the requirements for the role and the interview plan. You may be hiring directly with no recruitment support, using an inhouse recruiter or sourcer, or partnering with agencies. No matter which path you walk, it is vitally important you spend around 30 minutes to an hour working through your expectations and how your interview plan will unearth that within the successful candidate.

Generally, I've found this works best as a dialogue of questions and answers which are recorded for transparency and for ease of revisiting for yourself or others throughout the process. Generally, creating a Typeform or Google Form is a good way to create the mechanism by which you can roll this out for future roles and keep the documentation of your answers in one place. Keeping these questions for future reference also saves time in future role debriefs. I have, on several occasions, simply pulled a previous role brief and amended it for clarity and confidence. When hiring at scale, these kinds of tips are crucial to make your team more successful and are examples of mechanistic management tools as discussed in Chapter 4.

> Typeform has connectivity with tools like Airtable and Google Sheets, which enables better integration and automation within other processes you're building.

Some of the questions and prompts I suggest you make a conscious note of during your role brief follow:

1 Title for the role

   a) Are you willing to be flexible on this? How so?

2 Level

   a) This can be a range of levels too, as long as you understand the different behaviours and expectations these levels require to be successful.

3 Their mission or focus for the next 12 months

4 Key KPIs or measurements of success

5 Primary strategic responsibilities of this role

   a) Consider the bigger picture this person should be aspiring to change or create within your organization.

   b) This should be inspirational and ambitious.

6 The day-to-day responsibilities of this role

   a) What will this person's general, autonomous work look like?

7 The key projects this role may be working on in the next 6 to 12 months

8 Which software or tools must they have experience in?

9 What kind of projects or work-styles must they have experience in?

   a) Do you require someone with start-up experience?

   b) What about something more industry specific like Manufacturing or Ecommerce?

   c) It's important to not be overly restrictive, and be firm but fair around transferable skills and what are 'nice to haves'

10 Which competencies are crucial that we measure through the process of hiring the right person?

   a) Somewhere between 5 and 10 competencies are important to understand.

   b) If you have a progression framework in your team this should be able to be directly lifted from this document.

   c) *Note*: Don't worry, I will give you some more context coming up in this chapter. You may have competency frameworks built out for your more traditional HR roles, but this new way of working requires a thorough examination of the behaviours and expectations in different roles and levels in the People Team, as outlined in Chapter 3.

11 Would you consider someone stepping up into this role?

12 Would you consider someone stepping sideways, or from another function, into this role?

   a) Remember: this is a large part of what makes People Operations as a product successful. Consider how you can use the transferable skills of someone moving from Engineering Management, Marketing or Customer Support. Instead of blocking the challenge of upskilling, consider the support you can give alongside the upside of additional context and understanding.

13   What kind of person won't do well in this role?

  a) It is important to understand both the strengths and weaknesses of your organization. If your team operates in a highly ambiguous economic market or stage, someone who finds ambiguity uncertain and anxiety inducing is likely not to succeed.

14   Where do you aspire to attract talent from (companies)?

  a) Use this as an opportunity to be self-reflective and critical about why. Is it employer brand? Profile? Great PR?

15   Who have you worked with in the past who does (or used to) match the profile for this role?

  a) Use this to understand the traits, experience and skills you have identified above: Is there a crossover between this person and your brief? Why or why not? Where have you been too strict? Where may you have been too lenient?

16   What's the most exciting thing about this opportunity?

  a) Remember you need to sell this, particularly if you're asking someone to move to your People Operations team from another functional area (such as Engineering or Marketing)

17   Our candidate has an offer from <X Competitor for Talent> on the table… What will they find here which they'll find nowhere else?

  a) Refer to Chapter 8 and use your market positioning in context

18   What's next for this role?

  a) Note: More on this later in this chapter!

You don't need to run through this process every time you hire, and often you may find the answers are 'the same as previous hire', but making sure you at least ask them is a useful exercise in hiring due diligence.

Now that you understand to a greater depth what you're looking for in your open role, the hurdle in front of you is designing a hiring and interviewing process which can best enable you to unearth these requirements while also selling your candidate on your market positioning.

I suggest you use a Miro Board or an old school pack of post-it notes to outline each stage of your process:

1   Who is there?

2   Which competencies, skills, and behaviours are they looking for?

3   Which questions or tools will they use to find these?

4 How long will this interview or stage be?

5 Does the candidate need to produce anything?

6 How will you prepare the candidate?

Some important things to consider when working through your interview structure:

1 Write a list of questions for each competency (following on in this chapter).

2 What would you like to explore during a practical exercise?

3 What form will your practical work take?

4 What kind of scenario(s) should be shared ahead of time and covered in the interview with the candidate?

5 Who will be your 'bar raiser' or value interviewer?

6 Who must attend the debrief?

On practical projects

Giving all of our candidates an opportunity to complete a practical task gives us a unique insight into how they will work within your team. Practical tasks have the added benefit of being focused solely on what really matters for the job and are an excellent tool to reduce and combat unconscious bias and discrimination.

Given you will be building a relatively new way of working, many of your candidates may not be able to perfectly articulate the 'People Operations as a Product' approach. For this reason, practical projects become even more important to draw the analogous skills and experience from a candidate.

It is generally considered best practice to keep your practical work between two and five hours of work at the absolute maximum. Further, it's best practice to make sure you've given all the time and tools your candidate needs to approach the problem with confidence. Please do not try to trick or fool your candidate. An interview should be an effort in mutual success, not an effort to disqualify.

Finally, I strongly encourage you to:

a. Compensate your candidate's time spent on practical projects wherever practically possible. Tax and employment are two considerations which you may need to seek advice on depending on your jurisdiction.

b. Never use your candidate's work for commercial purposes unless expressly agreed by your candidate. Try to build case studies which are more fiction than reality wherever possible. If you are toeing the line, the commitment to paying for the work will always put you into safer territory where you aren't plagiarizing or profiting off a candidate's free labour.

COMPETENCIES

I've placed competencies after your role brief and interview plan because, for many folks, you may already have a solid structure of a progression framework from which to work when you begin hiring.

For some others, however, you will want to 'start over'. I am not a strong believer in hyper 'localized' progression frameworks, where each team, role and function has individually maintained frameworks. The reason for that is they become very administrative and difficult to manage with time. Since you are working on building a People Operations team which operates like a product squad, this would be akin to drafting unique instruction manuals for not only each iteration of each product, but for every operating system, language and version. Building one consistent 'generalized' progression framework is generally the path I prefer to tread, working with managers to build out 'add-ons' for specific teams and functions where there is a real need.

If you're reading this and already have a generic competency and progression framework, you may want to consider what competencies are 'on top' of those you generally look for at each level of your business. If you're starting from scratch instead, I've suggested a base of competencies for People Partners across levels. How these behaviours are displayed and the sophistication in which they are employed tends to be the main differentiator between levels.

I generally break competencies into two areas: what you do and how you do it.

What you do is really about the skills and experience the candidate is able to demonstrate.

How you do it is about the ways of working, behaviours and also the values.

What you do (examples):

- **Business Impact:** At the lowest levels, you can expect your People Partners to reason about how decisions impact business outcomes with some guidance. At the most senior levels you can expect an active contributor in setting function and organization specific goals, as well as evidenced examples of helping team members translate these goals into actionable items that move your team closer to achieving their objectives.

- **Planning:** Someone at the more junior end will be able to run a single process (for example recruitment) or project consistently with guidance. Someone very senior in a People Operations team should be able to run a full strategy and planning process from start to finish. They can challenge the roadmaps of other divisions with insights and commercial validation when needed and are able to consolidate and share ideas which resonate at the company level.

- **Building:** Junior members of the team can make daily contributions to the team's work to a high standard and meet milestones and deadlines. Further, in People Ops as a Product we'd expect even the most junior team members to be capable of making minor adjustments that improve how the team works. This means interpreting and updating documentation, how-tos and frameworks created by others in the team. Senior members of the People Team demonstrate their capacity to make contributions to your team's work, while also building tools your team can learn from and build upon. Further, they can give examples of identifying resources that may be missing to help enable your team's autonomy, growth and success.

- **Culture Contribution:** A crucial point for all People Partners! Your junior People Partners are active contributors to the team and functional culture. They are able to take on some coaching and Human Ops responsibilities. This may be one of the most important from a Human Operations perspective: your senior folks are accountable for aligning their squad with your company's culture and values. They are responsible for providing suggestions and feedback on improvements for your ways of working, planning and leading the company. Furthermore, your senior partners can lead culture initiatives with senior leadership, challenging presumptions and the status quo.

From here, it is easier to visualize and align on what these competencies may look like in action when a candidate answers a question or produces a piece of practical work. These competencies and the levels at which you expect the candidate to behave should provide a relatively consistent and predictable method for your interviewing panel to triangulate someone's suitability.

Note: Some more competencies which are more specific to People Operations as a product were listed in Chapter 3.

THE INTERVIEWS

Interviews should have a clear and articulated purpose as outlined at the beginning of your recruitment briefing. You should do all you can to avoid adding additional steps, particularly meet-and-greet steps where a panellist has the capacity to give feedback or veto a decision, but does not have a clear role in the structure of your interview process.

Interviews should, generally, be no more than one hour and should follow a consistent structure each time.

CASE STUDY

BloomLabs

Lottie and the team at BloomLabs have been successfully working in their squad setup for two quarters now. The team are beginning to find their feet coming into their third quarter of working in their new product squad and roadmap and the business is continuing to grow.

It is clear that the business will hire a new Business Development and Sales function, for which Lottie would like to hire a new People Partner. BloomLabs has hired a new Global Head of Sales, Frederic. Frederic has a strong vision for the Business Development (BD) and Sales team, and is looking for someone who he can partner deeply with as he expands his team and builds out new structures like commission.

Lottie sits down and writes her role brief, interview structure and gets clarity on the competencies she requires for her People Partner. Two of which are below:

- **Commerciality**: Our new People Partner will have a broad, complex and commercial view on how the BD and Sales function contribute to the BloomLabs mission, vision and strategy. They will play an active role in improving the current ways of working in the team, including partnering with our Sales Leader to build new People Products such as commission. Further, this role will require commercial acumen around ROI on recruitment, headcount planning and how to prioritize certain people ops projects within the squad.

- **Communication:** Our new People Partner can create cross-functional communications about impactful changes and updates in the BD and Sales function. This People Partner's teams' progress and outcomes have support and visibility at the executive team level. They can include stakeholders in key decisions and make stakeholders an extended part of the team. For this reason, this People Partner must be able to influence company-wide strategy, prioritization, resourcing and headcount planning.

From here, Lottie sets up her second-round interview where Frederic will interview the People Partner candidates alongside Bradley, the Creative and Branding People Partner.

From here, Lottie selected a few questions from a long list she and the team had developed in a previous sprint. Each interview would contain an introduction, three questions, space for the candidate's questions and then an administrative wrap up (next steps, etc).

1 How would you go about explaining a complex idea or problem to a stakeholder who was already frustrated?

   a. A good answer will demonstrate the candidate can communicate to people across different functions, not just their own or stakeholders which they regularly deal with.

      i. The candidate may mention specific roles such as, 'I would do X with Sales, and X with executives' or may be more nuanced such as, 'I would build out different methods of communication to capture all groups'. A great answer will also mention the lead up to involving others in the process, showing that communication is not a single-pronged approach and involves preparation and ongoing touchpoints, including feedback on how it lands and continues to develop.

2 Talk about a time when you made a point or shared an update that you knew your colleagues would be resistant to.

   a. A good answer will show the candidate understands that sometimes the strategic 'greater good' requires an element of change management which, naturally, can create resistance.

      i. The answer should outline a path which takes a team through the journey of providing data behind a decision, sharing with and involving others for buy-in, collecting feedback and delivering a message in a sensitive way. A great answer will go on to explain that, for the most resistant in a team, some changes may be not possible to overcome and there is a certain 'point of no further returns' where the business must continue with a change through the resistance and, perhaps, manage an exit or change in role.

3 Use an example to explain how you prioritize strategic wins against operational needs.

    a. A good answer will demonstrate that operational needs contribute to a successful strategy.

        i. There is no one without the other and balance is crucial. The candidate should give a detailed overview of how they interlace strategy with planning and delivery. This includes listing tools, frameworks, or ways of working they employ to be successful. A great answer will give examples of a time of failure, learning, or how they were able to measure the ROI of a trade-off they made.

From here, Frederic and Bradley were able to run an interview process and easily identify when a candidate was meeting the required standard for the role. This level of preparation took Lottie around one hour, was able to be stored in an interview library for future use and saved around two hours of deliberation time for each interview loop (group of interviews).

WRITING GREAT FEEDBACK

Taking the time to think through and write balanced, structured and unbiased feedback is important in helping a hiring panel fairly evaluate a candidate.

It's also so important to the candidate themselves and in today's marketplace of cultures I would strongly encourage all businesses to offer every candidate a chance to hear their feedback alongside some suggestions for their personal development wherever possible, including how to improve in further interviews. This may not be something that can be offered at the initial screen stage, but once a candidate has spent time on a practical test or longer interview loop, it is even more important to make the time for a call, video meeting or simply sending over a reading list and some written feedback.

Slightly less charitable, the feedback written for your successful candidates will be a great help for you to shape your new starter's three-month onboarding plans.

I have a few controversial opinions (as I'm sure you've ascertained). One of them is that *there is no maybe*. If you *maybe* want to hire someone you have not interviewed effectively. Push yourself to a clear point of view and decision. This does not mean you have to have made a hiring decision in every interview, but you do need to be clear on whether or not you think the candidate met the expectations of the *interview you were a part of*. One of the biggest flaws I see in inexperienced interview panels is framing their feedback with a 'would I hire this person?' mindset rather than a 'does this person meet the expectations I have been asked to explore?'.

Some other top interview feedback tips   Do not make blanket statements without adding rationale or explanation. Saying 'too junior', 'bad on process', or 'weak on visual design' doesn't help someone reading your feedback and won't be fair to the candidate.

Provide rationale and specific examples. Remember the candidate will receive this feedback and will want to know why you've made the decisions you have, as well as context on how they can improve and grow.

Remember to write tight (clear and concise) feedback, loaded with examples.

DEBRIEF

It's really important that you spend some time and get together while the interview is still fresh in your minds and opinions aren't biased by other people's thoughts. Once everyone in the interview team has shared their feedback and formed their initial opinion on the candidate, you should arrange a debrief meeting to talk through the candidates in any loop. This should be an effort to make a hiring decision on a candidate only and not used when moving a candidate from stage to stage – the interview feedback should be sufficient enough to make that decision. Remember, there is no maybe! If you believe a candidate met the expectations, but you still believe there are questions around certain values or behaviours, you should have made a note of them in your interview feedback and trusted the process would explore them. It is a good place to bring those concerns to light in the debrief to be sure they were dealt with.

OFFER

Great news. You're ready to invite your new team member into our team. This is such an exciting time and we want to make sure that you are able to be involved in delivering the great news. Remember to give your candidate positive feedback, talk through the offer package and be thorough again on the role and opportunities.

Many candidates are exploring multiple opportunities, so using the work from Chapter 8 as a framework for outlining *why you* is really important.

If your candidate decides this opportunity isn't for them, be sure to take this as an opportunity to gather some feedback; why is your 'ideal customer' not purchasing your product? How can you improve? This feedback is likely (and hopefully) very anecdotal and not quite enough to build a consistent and particularly rich data pipeline, but it is very helpful to look at this feedback as objectively and consistently as possible. This is true for every team, not just People Ops.

What's next for your team?

One of the questions you will get asked by candidates, and specifically those moving functionally, is around what this will spell out for their career. I am a strong believer that career planning is a two-way street and requires just as much input from the employee as it does from the manager, but being able to give some previously explored or encouraged paths should strike a great balance and inspire confidence in your candidates and team.

MANAGERIAL

This path is for People Team who find their greatest satisfaction in leading, supporting and coaching others. This is probably the most commonly understood path for progression – moving from an individual contributor (IC) and into a managerial role.

TECHNICAL

This track is for people who are invested in developing specific, function-based knowledge which is crucial for every role. This means choosing tools and processes that are best suited to the goals of your team. This track is for those of us that enjoy being subject matter experts (SMEs) and sharing knowledge. Examples here would be a People Partner wanting to become a Squad Leader for an L&D squad or People Data and Analytics.

ENTREPRENEURIAL

This track is for people who enjoy thinking about the big picture, looking deeply at systems and processes and thinking about how to make the organization more efficient and better connected. This would be moving into a more and more senior product manager, moving into a senior IC role leading multiple squads, building roadmaps and ways of working which become more and more complex and ambitious.

LATERAL AND INTERCOMPANY

Of course, your People Partners don't need to stay in People Ops for ever. This is one of the most appealing paths for some of the folks who have worked in my team, who can see a path into Engineering Management or perhaps even Business Operations, Product Management or Strategy. The skills you are offering your team are no longer strictly connected and siloed to the HR world and are more t-Shaped and adapt across the business stack.

The key points from this chapter

- Scaling matters. Because in all businesses, growth is crucial for survival.

- Hiring is a huge part of scaling, but should not be the only metric for success. Be sure to look for more metrics to define your team and business success. I will discuss more in the following chapter, 'Metrics for success'.

- Building a team in any way requires a great deal of skill and tactical expertise. Hiring folks who will work well in a world where your culture is a product will require somewhat of a reconsideration of the traditional HR structure.

- A single product squad organizational design I outlined will begin to stretch at around 150 heads. This means you should explore hiring and forming a new, lean squad, or growing your People Team and raising the delivery expectations from one squad.
  - If you choose to split into two squads there are a few different ways you can split the work; along the employee lifecycle, or against themes such as impact or development.

- A big change in your organization at this stage may be how you think about recruitment. This model rejects the idea of a full-stack recruiter with no project (People Operations) work.
  - This means Hiring Managers must be responsible for their recruitment, and use the People Partnering team as a resource to help them be successful.

- The most effective way for a hiring manager to truly own their team is to allow them full ownership of their function, which includes hiring, performance assessment, compensation review, etc.

- Hiring managers require the guidelines, tools, and advisory support of a People Partner in order to successfully recruit, and you must build that as the head of the function.
  - o Using a framework like the RACI model is a great way to identify how to split the role around recruitment.
- When hiring for your new People Partner roles you may be looking to hire along the lines of a few archetypes:
  - o People Partner, Technical, Consultant, Research and Project Manager.
- Being highly prepared and methodical is crucial in building an effective and scalable hiring and interviewing process.
- Begin each interview process with a role brief and interview plan:

  - o The interview plan should be built around some core competencies which are explored more in Chapter 3.
  - o Run practical assessments (and if you can, I encourage you to compensate your candidates!).
  - o Give your candidates evidence-based, constructive feedback.

Understand the 'selling points' you have in the marketplace by reviewing the work from Chapter 8.

Endnotes

1 Slootman, F (2022) *Amp It Up: Leading for Hypergrowth*, Wiley, 9781119836117

2 In House Recruitment Awards (2019) Award Winners in 2019 https://www.inhouserecruitment.co.uk/awards/hall-of-fame/2019-winners/ (archived at https://perma.cc/5J73-ESY6)

3 Smart, Geoff (2008) *Who: A Method for Hiring*, Ballantine Books, 9780345504197

10

Metrics for success

As I type this, I have written 55,925 words. At the purported average reading rate of 238 words per minute, this means you should have spent 3.9 hours reading this book.[1] At £29.99, that means you have paid £7.68 per hour of reading (so far), a cost per hour metric that is improving with every new word you read (and every time you come back to this book!)

Of course, if I were to write a longer book, it doesn't necessarily correlate with more value per hour or pound spent. In fact, I am almost certain that many of my readers, and indeed the lovely editing team at Kogan Page, would prefer I said more with less. Just like roasting potatoes at 200 degrees for one hour will cook your potatoes to perfection, but roasting the same potatoes at 400 degrees for 30 minutes would leave you with coal, not all metrics tell a compelling and honest story about how you should behave.

In People Operations, as well as Product Management, what to measure, how to measure it and how to know things are going wrong before they can no longer be amended or stopped are all a mix of science and art. Even outside of what to measure, I am often met with pleading questions around which tools to use and how to collect data on a 'data budget' (when you don't have elaborate software and dashboarding tools).

This chapter aims to explore not only how to collect crucial data, but also what to look for, what to report on and how to think about storytelling using data in People Operations.

Why is this important?

If you are *any* business leader, from People to marketing to product management, one of the biggest challenges you are likely to face is how to demonstrate that your team is making a significant contribution to a company's top-line, bottom-line and strategic targets. The introduction of new suites of SaaS (software as a service) tools for seemingly any business or operational application has embedded an expectation in every team towards tracking, assessment and tighter links between investments and results.

In most businesses I have worked for in the past, there is a direct line of sight between a leader's performance and their ability to tell compelling stories about their team's effectiveness and performance. This is not just expected via qualitative data and anecdote, but also getting under the skin of KPIs and performance data of a more quantitative nature. This may seem simple in functions like Sales where there is a direct and individual connection between outcomes, but in functions like People Operations, management and leadership, many of the tasks and outcomes are described as esoteric and nebulous.

Like the Peter Principle, where someone is promoted to their highest possible point of competency (or failure) within an organization, I often see HR leaders fail through what I am calling *a gut principle*. This is where they are promoted, or succeed, to the highest possible outcomes of their own intuition or gut reads on a situation.

The Peter Principle[2]

The Peter Principle is an observation that states an organizational tendency towards promotion until the final point of failure.

In simple terms, a person performs well in their job and is promoted to the next level of an organization's hierarchy. From there they will be promoted again and again, until they reach a point where they are no longer performing adequately enough to be promoted. This means they are in a role which they are lower performing in, having met a level of respective incompetence.

The Gut Principle

We've all seen it – someone who has incredible intuition. They are capable of seeing a situation and making a capable and educated guess on what to do. However, as you promote that person based on their success, and they continue to not invest in analytical analysis, they will eventually reach a stage of business scale and complexity where they become incompetent.

People functions should be data driven and quantitative, including a varied diet of metrics beyond those standard in the industry such as attrition. That said, coming up with these metrics can be difficult when so often your business has made decisions based on your intuition, anecdote or out of creativity while your business scaled. As a business grows and matures in complexity, leadership will inevitably begin to have higher demands on the reporting capabilities of the People Operations team. It is, of course, logical that boards and investors understand the returns on investment into People Operations, the efficacy and the value of the business's people overheads.

At times, I've seen this pressure mount on People Ops leaders in a way which results in 'tuned-out' behaviours and dark patterns. These dark patterns mean focusing on the wrong thing and encourage or even enforce poor decision making. For example, a recruiter focused entirely on time to hire, but with no offsetting metric such as interview feedback quality, is encouraged to hire quicker and disregard performance or success of hire beyond the offer stage. Ultimately, people do what they are measured on. This is what is called Goodhart's Law.[3] Goodhard's Law states, 'When a measure becomes a target, it ceases to be a good measure'.

> ### Goodhard's Law in practice
>
> Congratulations, you're now a baker in a Parisian Boulangerie. The head baker has set a target for 'most cakes baked'. If your team happens to top the performance metrics, and bake over 500 cakes, your bonus will increase.
>
> You and the team get together and decide to bake cupcakes.
>
> This is a somewhat silly example of Goodhard's law in practice, but it gives a good sense of the kinds of behaviours your metrics can push a team towards. If you don't mind cupcakes as the outcome, perhaps you're onto a great metric, but the lesson is to be aware of which direction your metrics will push your team and what patterns they may create.

Supposedly the management guru Peter Drucker said, 'If you can't measure it, you can't improve it'. This quote is regularly misattributed to Drucker, and is in fact more likely to have been stated by Dr W Edwards Deming. However, the accurate version of this quote as it was written by Deming reads, 'It is wrong to suppose that if you can't measure it, you can't manage it – a costly myth'.[4]

Reading this quote in the context of understanding Dr Deming and his career somewhat, I understand this quote as acknowledging the importance and value in using data to make improvements, while also understanding that measuring and looking at data is not enough *on its own*. There are so many things to consider: massaging data (using data to present a somewhat or fundamentally inaccurate outcome), ignoring or disregarding that which cannot be measured, vanity metrics and so much more!

Further, as we will discuss more in Chapter 11, we are working with human beings. Human beings are not able to be perfectly distilled into averages, data points and clicks. We must keep a holistic mindset around the work we are doing in People Operations, while using data to drive us in a beneficial direction.

CASE STUDY
Data is a compass point

An example of this in practice was with a previous consulting client of mine within a large VC-backed technology company. The client was a senior leader who was struggling to justify the performance and spend on recruitment efforts. She came to me earnestly asking how to unpick the data in her applicant tracking system (ATS). She had identified that one recruiter was achieving a cost per hire of $20,000, and a close rate of over 90 per cent from offer to onboard. Another in her team was closer to $50,000, with a close rate of under 75 per cent.

It was clear, she proposed, that one was significantly under-performing despite glowing feedback from their hiring manager and candidates. As we dived into the raw numbers, we didn't see anything which indicated why the gap should be so significant. If the data was to be taken on face value, we had one disproportionately expensive recruiter.

However, as mentioned, experienced leaders should understand that data alone is the compass point and not the compass. When prompted, it was revealed that one recruiter was hiring exclusively into customer-facing roles and the other was hiring into engineering. The talent market in London was experiencing a shortage of engineering talent and a boom in technology businesses recruiting into the region. It was clear that we were not comparing apples to apples.

If the business leader were to have made a decision on data alone in this instance, they would have made a grave error.

I have already mentioned a criticism I have of some People Operations practitioners is their inability (or unwillingness) to measure and be data driven. So how do I reconcile that with the advice to use data as a mere guide, rather than a map? Please don't disregard the criticism. Instead, I would like readers of this book, and future practitioners of People Ops as a Product, to understand that gut feel alone, just like measuring data alone, will not suffice in building something prosperous and scalable. You must utilize *both* focused judgement, creativity and sometimes guess-work alongside careful measurement, testing and analysis.

DECENTRALIZING DECISION-MAKING

Experience offers the benefit of speed of decision making. (Remember, this can sometimes be detrimental to quality work, so please refer back to our discussions around first principles thinking in Chapter 4.). When used appropriately, experience and speedy decision making can offer the agility of moving from problem to solution with haste.

The issue with team building, and specifically as a product squad, is that experience is not evenly distributed. Members of any successful team have various knowledge and experience sliders which you should be utilizing together. This grouping of t-shaped individuals is the superpower towards achieving a holistic team, greater than the sum of its parts. You may remember we spoke about this previously in Chapter 3 and Chapter 9.

Building a team this way gives you a broad base on which to build your products serving your team, but it also requires a more generous and transparent sharing of knowledge so team members with varying degrees of experience are able to make rational decisions reasonably independently.

Utilizing data effectively is one of the best ways to ensure this system's success. Have you found yourself frustrated by a team asking a question which you saw as straight forward? Something like asking why employees seemed most discontent and likely to resign in early spring? For you, having experience working in People Ops over a long period of time, you may be able to make some educated assumptions: budgets are opening up in the new year, more hiring and poaching activity begins and folks may have begun job searches in the new year as a part of personal growth. You also know that people are more likely to resign around their work anniversary and most hiring in your organization happens in the second quarter of the year after budgets are released in Q1.[5]

These are reasonable, experience-driven assumptions. If your team member is not as experienced as you, they may not make these same educated guesses. It may take them more time to understand the patterns of a business and to connect the dots. This is a part of mentoring and leading a team, but it can be frustrating if you feel you are holding the keys to this information and your team cannot self-direct without distraction.

If you are building a team which tracks, analyses and discusses this data, you should find that your team is able to self-serve these answers. Further, you should be pleasantly surprised when your team unearths something your experience does not tell you! This is the true joy of leading a modern People Operations team – learning from those you lead. Building data into your decision-making helps decentralize those decisions, encourage creativity and enables your team to act with more autonomy and authority.

Since we're on the topic of data – there is significant evidence to show that teams who are able to act with autonomy are less likely to experience burnout.[6,7] By offering your People Operations team access to data, you are improving their working lives and offering them higher degrees of accountability and opportunity. For many People Operations leaders in my past, I have seen a kind of fear exist around transparency: what if people are disgruntled by salary information, spooked by high attrition or unable to reconcile executive decisions? Transparency is a powerful catalyst for change in People Operations, and while data privacy and sensitivities must be protected, HR leaders must face their fear of transparency in order to ascend into the commercial position they seek.

People operations metrics: what to look for

There are broadly two types of data measurement I will dive into today: Success Metrics and Operational Metrics. I will also speak again about input and output metrics, already defined in Chapter 6, so if you are fuzzy on those definitions, I suggest you head back and brush up before reading further.

Operational metrics

Data indicators that measure and track core performance. These metrics provide an ongoing report or bird's eye view of how a company, team or function is performing along their key deliverables. They primarily track efficiency, quality, spend and are used for identifying trends or areas of focus, rather than tracking success against a specific goal. Operational metrics may take the form of a dashboard or reporting to the board or management team, and are often standardized and longer term.

Example: Employee headcount

Success metrics

A quantifiable measurement that your team uses to track if a project or strategy is successful or effective, and by how much. These may also be framed within key performance indicators (KPIs), objectives and key results (OKRs), or SMART Goals. Success metrics may be tracked long or short term and may be bespoke to a project or period of time, often formulated at the beginning of a project or strategic milestone.

Example: Profit per headcount

Operational metrics

All teams in a business, from People to Product, will ultimately be judged by the financial successes and outcomes of the business on the whole. The most widely used example of this are revenue targets (such as annual recurring revenue or ARR).

There are consequences of putting too much focus on financial metrics, such as profitability or bottom-line revenue growth. For one, many of these metrics are 'lagging metrics' which means they are those which take a long time to impact or measure. Further, using retrospective and high-level metrics such as these may have a negative effect on team morale due to a feeling that they cannot control or be held accountable for the outcomes. Simply put, so much feeds into your revenue (market activity, sales, product pricing, user adoption, etc.) that your team will struggle to identify their own successes in the noise.

An understanding of financial measurements of success at the executive level is crucial, but your team and function should be looking at the operational metrics, or 'measurements behind the measurements', which are leading indicators of greater company success. Your role as a leader of the

People Operations team is to identify the relationship between operational measurements and relevant financial measurements. Doing so will not just motivate your team, but can bring more predictability to your company's financial results.

There is a baseline of data which almost all People teams should have available to you through your HR information system (HRIS) and applicant tracking system (ATS). Beyond this, you should also be engaging with your employees through surveys and feedback tools such as Lattice, CultureAmp, Peakon or Leapsome. It is also possible to build simple (and free!) survey tools using Typeform, Google Forms or Survey Monkey. More and more HR and productivity software, such as Asana, Slack, Pleo, FirstBase and Rippling, are able to offer fully integrated data extraction and visualization tools.

This rich pool of data and information you are collecting should put you in an effective position to create compelling dashboards of metrics which are able to inform high-level trends and context around decisions. Remember, you do not need to purchase new tools if you do not have the fiscal capacity. Consider focusing one of your People Ops squads on data for a quarter or two, setting them an output metric around decision making speed.

When thinking like a Product Manager, and breaking the hiring, onboarding and engagement process down into a funnel akin to a product journey, there is an easy and effective way to draw inspiration from the commercial and product teams in your company.

Ask your Marketing and Product teams which metrics they look at during each stage of the funnel.

For this chapter, I have focused on applying my inspiration from Marketing and Product teams. Using that, I have built a comparison below where I propose and present HR metrics in a more product-centric fashion, rather than reporting them for reporting's sake. This means each metric is contextualized against a product outcome.

We will explore more a little later in this chapter about how to build a dashboard using HR data, but for now let's explore what kinds of metrics you can utilize for operational metric dashboards and reporting.

TABLE 10.1 Hiring and acquisition

Metric	Affecting
Recruitment, probation, performance feedback quality (Feedback per stage, tracked on an individual basis)	You should look for a healthy progression of positive feedback and a relationship between recruitment and ongoing performance assessments. Use this metric to look out for employees with strong recruitment scores and low probations, for example.
Strongest feedback to accepted offers relationship	Conversion rate of key 'customers' Use this metric to ask your team, 'where did we see strongest feedback from hiring managers resulting in high volumes of accepted offers?'
Interview failure rates per funnel stage	You should look for a healthy transition from first to final interview in terms of hiring manager feedback. Aiming towards limiting the volume of interviews, but also indicating a higher-quality understanding of the role by the hiring team.
Budget and headcount forecasting within range	Efficiency and execution of our headcount plan. Look at cost compared to plan and final start dates being within a range of plan. This should show markers of a recruitment team operating effectively with planning.
Hiring managers effectiveness (Hire to probation passing ratio)	Hiring channel efficiency, learn where your strongest hiring managers are. Identify the hiring managers with the highest volumes of passed and strong probations, and strongest recruitment > probation > performance relationships. The same is true for the inverse, look for the lowest performing hiring managers.
Hiring source effectiveness (Hire to probation passing ratio)	Quite a standard recruitment metric now, and very similar to marketing metrics around channel efficiency. Look for the hiring channels and platforms where you are most likely to find successful candidates, so that you are able to better invest.
Cost per hire	Similar to cost per acquisition in marketing. This can be reported as fully loaded (i.e. including the cost of recruiters) or as only the investment outside of your cost of business. In some teams this may include employer brand efforts, or may change on a campaign basis (for example, if you were doing an apprenticeship campaign where you included branding activities and events). In marketing, CPA reflects the cost of a single customer moving from the first touch point to ultimate conversion. The same can be considered in recruitment.

(continued)

TABLE 10.1 (Continued)

Metric	Affecting
Cost per hire to tenure	What is the relationship between high cost to hire and tenure within your organization.
Cost per hire to salary ratio	What is the relationship between high-cost hire and salary.
Cost per hire to performance	What is the relationship between high cost to hire and performance outcomes within your organization. This requires you to have a quantitative measure for performance, and asks the question, 'is there a higher relationship between cost to hire and how effectively they perform?'

TABLE 10.2 Onboarding

Metric	Affecting
Activation metric	In product this is called the 'aha moment'. Each company may have a different activation metric.[i] For example, Spotify may use 'liked three songs' or 'created a playlist' as their aha moment. You may use something like 'recorded a professional goal in Lattice' or 'completed a 360 review'. *Ask yourself:* Does this metric demonstrate some kind of commitment to the company long term? Does this indicate that the employee is engaged in the team? Is this metric related to onboarding and the first year of employment? If the answer to all three is yes, then the metric is a great one to measure and investigate.
Onboarding satisfaction	A simple entry interview during onboarding to understand how the process is serving the onboarded team. You can use ENPS (detailed in the Table 10.4 'Engagement') or simple calculation such as 'Did you find this onboarding met or exceeded your expectations?'
Time to efficacy	Very similar to product metrics around activation. Ask for managers to log performance of key role duties on a weekly basis. This can be as simple as 'is this person independent in their role?' on a scale of 1 to 10, and have your manager respond to this weekly in an automated poll. The time where the employee begins meeting expectations of their role independently is the time to efficacy.

(continued)

TABLE 10.2 (Continued)

Metric	Affecting
Regrettable attrition during onboarding	Stickiness and activation. Look for those who exit your team during onboarding. This can be effectively used when your company is going through great scale and should be considered alongside anecdotes and qualitative exit interview data.
Probation failure rate	A percentage of failed probations where performance did not meet expectations. Layer this with recruitment data to get a richer understanding of where things went wrong.

[i] Bush, Wes (2022) How to Identify Your Product's Aha Moment, Product Lead Blog, (Online) https://productled.com/blog/how-to-identify-your-products-aha-moment

TABLE 10.3 Performance

Metric	Affecting
Revenue & profit per employee (Revenue during Q/ number of employees during the quarter)	Rough ROI of the workforce to the revenue generated and retained by the business. Work out the profit contribution for each employee in the team; this is particularly useful when measuring and forecasting the value in brand-based recruitment campaigns and headhunting. When layered with performance data, if you can reasonably accurately assess the increased productivity or output of higher performers, you are able to forecast what further recruiting efforts return.
Internal promotion and growth (funnel)	Like a marketing funnel, consider the promotions as ongoing 'upselling' of your target candidates. Look at promotion rates year-on-year from the date on joining and develop a funnel of those who move and develop internally.
Performance per level, gender, tenure and team	An average assessment of performance across some key splits. This assists you in discovering bias and ensuring you are addressing areas of enquiry into poor performance averages for management.

TABLE 10.4 Engagement

Metric	Affecting
Regrettable attrition	A lagging metric around low engagement within the team. The important thing here is understanding how to assess what is a regrettable hire using three criteria: – Did we offer/act to retain? – Would we rehire? – Do we have regrets about how this exit came to be? (Ours or their behaviour) If the answer to all three is yes, this offer is *highly* regrettable. Two yes responses and the exit is regrettable. One yes is *somewhat* regrettable. If the answer is none, the exit is non-regrettable.
Employee Net Promoter Score (ENPS) (Percentage of promoters – percentage of detractors = ENPS)	A very common metric used now and graciously taken from product and marketing, asking 'how likely are you to recommend a friend to work at this company?' can give a high level read on overall engagement and satisfaction with the workplace. Those who mark 9 or 10 are considered promoters, and those who report 1–6 are called detractors. All other survey results are passive and not included in the calculation.

TABLE 10.5 HR administration

Metric	Affecting
HR shipping to plan	Team focus and delivery, the ability to meet KPIs and goals, and specifically success metrics, within the required time and costs.
From identification of issue to date shipped by HR	Speed to market. The ability to identify a HR issue in a survey or user research, and act on and deliver that project. This requires a tool like Asana or some kind of project management tool to effortlessly track, but can also be tracked at the end of a project as a lagging metric.
Turnover costs	How much it costs to hire, train and onboard a new employee for each exit.

As you can see above, I have made some suggestions of metrics which give a more nuanced view of the HR operations than simply the number of unplanned absences and attrition, although I still encourage you to use those when required. The metrics above are specifically formulated through thinking like a product management team, and using the product management analogy, to understand what success may look like.

Some of these metrics may seem difficult to calculate, or superfluous to your size of organization (for example, I would not recommend looking at median-to-mean performance ratio, or onboarding stickiness to any company under 250 people). If you are thinking some of these aren't quite right, *great*! The key here is choosing a few key metrics to keep an eye on and which have a strategic impact on your business outcomes. Then, after you've done that, you should find ways to spend less time tracking and more time acting upon the found data. We'll talk a bit more about that later in the chapter when I explain how to build some basic dashboards.

SUCCESS METRICS
Chapter 6 talks in depth about how to execute like a product squad. Within this approach there exists a specific and disciplined focus on projects and executing in sprints of 'shippable' work. During the process of Quarterly Goal Setting, the primary goals your People team should be looking at developing are Success Metrics.

Even if your team are looking at moving the needle or status of an operational metric, for example shifting Cost Per Hire from $20,000 to $15,000 (down 25 per cent), the way that this is framed is as a metric for success, i.e., 'When we achieve this, we will have succeeded.'

We defined input and output metrics in Chapter 7 already, and your success metrics can take either form. That said, a common mistake I see in People Operations teams is to lean too readily on input metrics, for example, 'Shipping this project'. Focusing on input metrics is an easy way to measure 'success' as it relates to completing a task, but not as it relates to thinking through your work using the first principles practices outlined in Chapter 4. When you are exploring your project for the quarter, really ask yourself and your team, 'What is the problem we are trying to solve?' and then, in order to begin outlining and exploring possible success metrics, ask next, 'What are the indicators we will see that we are solving or making progress on solving it?'. Sometimes the answer may be an input metric. For example, if the problem is 'we don't have worker's compensation insurance' the success metric may be most simply defined as the input 'purchase workers compensation insurance.'

Most often, however, People Operations problems are directly impacting effectiveness, efficiency, engagement or some other measurable outcome. This is where I implore your team to think deeper and identify an output metric to impact. Using an output metric enables your team to better offer solutions through first principles thinking, unlocking creativity and innovation.

From this headspace, allow your team the requisite room to be creative. Creating success metrics, although a generally quantitative piece of work, comes through the process of exploring what solutions and behavioural changes may look like. Some success metrics may be obvious due to the nature of the problem. Using Cost Per Hire again, if the problem is 'hiring is costing us too much,' then a very natural progression to what success may be is 'we will reduce cost per hire from X to X.' However, there may still be more to unpick here. Allow yourself and your team time to ask questions using the methods shared in Chapter 4, such as the Five Whys. It may uncover a more specific metric which engages your team more effectively to solve the problem.

Some examples of possible success metrics and problems are below for your consideration:

> It is important to note that success metrics can have another metric pushing against it, but try to avoid setting a success metric where you are moving two data points at once. Doing that will cause confusion as to where your campaign or project has been effective.
>
> Do use: A reduction in time to hire in our sales team from X to X while maintaining the quality of feedback at the offer debrief stage.
>
> Don't use: A reduction in time to hire in our sales team from X to X, while improving the quality of feedback at the offer stage from X to X.

TABLE 10.6 Hiring

Problem	Success metric
Key candidates are not accepting our offers.	Increase in % of candidates with high feedback from offer to onboard.
Our candidates are primarily coming from recruitment agencies, and not engaging with our employer brand.	Increase % of successful hires who have applied directly through our careers page. Increase % of successful hires made through referral.

(continued)

TABLE 10.6 (Continued)

Problem	Success metric
Candidates applying to our job advertisements are primarily of a homogeneous gender and/or ethnicity split.	An increase in job applications from diverse backgrounds from X to X. An increase in diverse candidates at first-round interview stage to X%.
Our average time to hire in the Sales team is too long.	A reduction in time to hire in our sales team from X to X while maintaining the quality of feedback at the offer debrief stage. An increase in candidates in our qualified candidates pipeline from X to X or by X%.

TABLE 10.7 Onboarding

Problem	Successful metric
Our onboarding process is time-efficient, but our onboarded team members do not feel sufficiently capable.	Improve onboarding structure, to maintain within the timeframe of X weeks, while improving 'time to effectiveness' from X to X.
Our onboarded team members do not have requisite clarity on their performance expectations.	Ensure X% of team members successfully passing probation are able to.
Our onboarding process takes too much time from our HR team.	A reduction in HR administration time by X%. X% of our onboarding process is fully automated or partially automated.
Our onboarding is too generic; certain teams are spending too much time building additional onboarding tracks.	An increase in fully-automated onboarding messaging and onboarding from X track to X tracks, covering at least X% of our teams with more bespoke onboarding content.

TABLE 10.8 Performance

Problem	Successful metric
Our team are not regularly reviewed for their performance.	X% of the business reviewed for their performance on a quarterly basis.
Our performance process is inefficient, and managers are spending their time on administrative tasks.	X% of our performance feedback process is fully automated or partially automated. An increase in management satisfaction with the operational performance process from X to X.

(continued)

TABLE 10.8 (Continued)

Problem	Successful metric
Our team do not have a sufficient understanding of what good performance looks like.	X% of the business report that they understand what it means to be a strong performer in their role. X% of managers report they are capable of identifying strong performance in their team. X% of managers believe their peer managers are measuring performance by the same benchmarks.

TABLE 10.9 Engagement

Problem	Successful metric
Our team's engagement dips after two years of service.	An improvement in ENPS after two years service from X to X. An improvement in performance ratings between one and two year performance cycles from X average to X average. An increase in retention of high performers in their third year.
Our team does not believe management is living the company values.	An increase in leadership sentiment from X to X. An increase in leadership performance on values behaviours from X average to X average. An improvement of leadership engagement in Community Volunteer Days by X%. An increase in management nominations for values based behavioural awards by X%.
Our team are struggling with recent changes in our organization, feeling burned out at key times.	An increase in our Gympass membership from X% to X%. An increase in team Gympass usage to X engagements per week. A decrease in unplanned absences from X per month to X per month.

TABLE 10.10 HR administration

Problem	Successful metric
Key areas of the business are struggling to correctly resource their team during peak periods.	Lowering conflicting three-plus days holiday absence rate per manager in any rolling calendar month. Operating to plan, reporting on managers operating within X% of their resource planning at the start of a quarter. Increasing percentage of holiday days booked more than 30 days before planned absence.

(continued)

TABLE 10.10 (Continued)

Problem	Successful metric
Payroll processes are inaccurate more regularly than they should be.	A rollout of a X% automated payroll process, reducing payroll administration from X to X. A decrease in critical payroll errors to <X%.
Training expenses per employee are not effectively tied to performance.	An increase in the relationship between high performance and training within the prior quarter from X to X.

How to build a dashboard

Great, so you have a small collection of key metrics you would like to look at on an ongoing basis (and some success metrics you will look at during this quarter at least).

In order to easily convey this crucial information to decision makers in a way which is easy to understand and engage with, you need to embrace the power of reporting dashboards. Reporting dashboards provide a snapshot of your key KPIs and metrics in a visible and often interactive format.

Word of warning!

Reporting dashboards for the sake of dashboards is not an effective use of time or resource. This is the area where I am the loudest advocate for the minimum viable solution mindset. There is no need for your team to develop complex dashboarding and reporting if your metrics regularly change, your business is so small your exec team do not regularly interact with them or if you have higher priorities. Do the bare minimum to easily report the information you need and no more.

In order to build an effective dashboard, you need to embrace visualization, storytelling and simplicity. The processes will be effective if you anchor the purpose towards easily connecting with the audience, be that your team, the whole company or the board. Easier said than done!

The metrics you have selected in People Operations are most likely across a range of tools and platforms. Your applicant tracking system (ATS), performance tool, and HRIS may all have their own inbuilt reporting and dashboarding and they should generally allow you to download a CSV file.

In order to build a cross-system dashboard, it is necessary to either extract the data manually, or pull it via an application programming interface (API) or integration. Now, anyone who knows me knows I am far from being an engineer, so I will not be detailing the intricate and extraordinary ways in which engineers have made our operational lives easier by building APIs and integrations, but I hope to tell you a little about how to effectively use them.

APIS AND INTEGRATIONS

API integration

The way two or more applications connect, via their application programming interfaces, that lets the systems exchange data between each other.

Think of it like a hose being taken from one system to another, allowing data and information to flow between them in a format each system understands.[8]

If you have data across multiple systems such as ATS and HRIS, you may discover a need to bring that data into one centralized dashboard. The easiest way to do this is by licensing a data visualization tool such as Looker (a Google tool), Amplitude, Tableau or Mode. These tools are SaaS tools which enable the automatic creation of visual and interactive data using data already imported into a centralized company database.

Building a dashboard using this method is likely to require: a budget, IT and data privacy approval, an update to your employee data retention and usage policy, and the assistance of your data or engineering team (in order to build the pipeline and API between your different systems). For many businesses, and specifically scaling businesses, this resource load may be too high to effectively implement in the short term. Remember what I said about minimum viable solutions, and think carefully about what level of complexity best serves your organization.

Manual dashboard

If you have thought about it and find yourself in the 'this is too much' camp, but still have some budget and technical capacity, utilizing tools such as

Airtable and Zapier enable the automation of data integrations. In this way, you can hack a database of key moments and data to collect in a single Airtable, Excel file or Google Sheet. From here, you can build data visualizations using this data, creating a live dashboard!

If you do not have the budget or IT approvals to onboard a new system for your employee data, or to build integrations using automation, all is not lost!

A very cost-effective way to build a dashboard in the People Team is by pulling data through scheduled or saved reports, and then manually uploading them to a Google Sheet which has data visualizations built in. This means you can report on metrics on a daily, weekly, or monthly basis, whenever you pull your report and upload new data.

HOW TO PRESENT YOUR DATA AND METRICS

Once you have accurate and up to date data in your document, or in whatever tool you are using to visualize your data, you need to make some decisions about how to present that data to tell a compelling story and effectively communicate your progress. There are many ways to present data, but I'll give some of the most commonly used below.

Bar Chart: Bar charts (Figure 10.1) are ubiquitous, sometimes nauseatingly so. Bar charts are an easy to read, simple and generally effective way to look at data. They are particularly effective for representing things like comparisons, cohort analyses and trends.

Line chart: Line charts come in many forms, and the most commonly used is a connected story of a single point of data, such as a trend line of ENPS on a month-on month-basis. These can be easily used to show the progression towards a success metric and when used correctly are generally an easy chart to interpret.

FIGURE 10.1 Bar chart

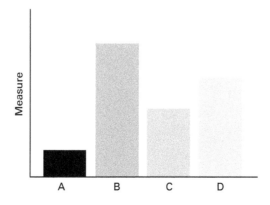

FIGURE 10.2 Area chart

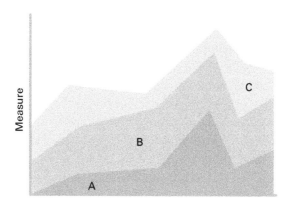

FIGURE 10.3 Pie chart

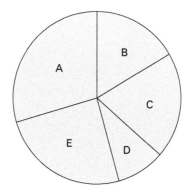

Area chart: An area chart (Figure 10.2) is a similar visual tool to a line chart, but the specific type of area chart I believe is useful in HR is the stacked area chart. A stacked area chart is a great tool to show proportions of a trend. For example, 'headcount growth each quarter' broken down into tenure.

Pie chart: Some of us (myself included!) love to hate pie charts (Figure 10.3). Pie charts are incredibly effective in a very narrow set of use cases. You should only ever use pie charts when representing proportions of a whole and only ever – and I stress this – when your total numbers are exactly 100 per cent. Pie charts are a poor use for comparison data in many circumstances, and particularly when there are many segments of comparison.

Scatter plot: Scatter plots (Figure 10.4) are fantastic tools for taking large amounts of data and representing it as a single story. A fantastic use for a

FIGURE 10.4 Scatter plot

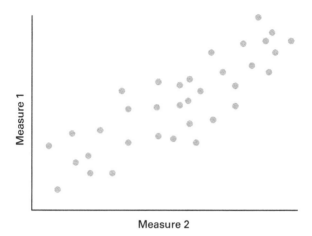

scatter plot would be to map performance of a large cohort of your team in a specific quarter. Scatterplots are particularly effective visualization tools for operational metrics and can be used in pairs to represent data such as performance comparison by gender or level.

Whichever method you use, gathering feedback from your audience and running some light user research on the legibility of your dashboard is a really excellent way to ensure you're able to engage your audience. Using and engaging with metrics and data, as I hope this chapter has explained, can be used as a really effective tool to guide your team towards building truly effective products for your business. More so, it can be a creative and engaging exercise across the team if you are able to build compelling and easy to understand dashboards and reporting.

Due to the highly qualitative nature of many People Operations professionals (a description with no criticism – I count myself in the same camp!) many of us can be apprehensive about building and managing metrics, particularly those around areas of the business which feel more human and less numeric, such as culture and engagement.

I understand these fears, and my most compelling argument against this natural response is to remind you that data is a compass point, not a compass. Remember, these are tools to give you insights, tell human stories and lead your team towards more compelling and human-first solutions.

Our next chapter, 'Prioritizing people', will go into detail on how to consider this human element and how to build with people first.

The key points from this chapter

- Collecting, interpreting and using data and metrics are high priorities for business leadership across all functions, including People Operations.

- Without engaging in data as a method for prioritizing work and measuring success, HR leaders are likely to fall into a version of the Peter Principle called the Gut Principle, where HR leaders are promoted, or succeed, to the highest possible outcomes of their own intuition.

- Data is crucial to making decisions, but is not a decision or revelation in itself. Data must be interpreted and used in conjunction with rational judgment and sound decision-making frameworks.

- Democratizing data enables your team to scale more effectively, self-serve when confronted with problems and opens their capacity for creative problem solving.

- Teams who are able to effectively self-serve using data are more likely to operate with autonomy, a key factor in reducing burnout and increasing effectiveness and engagement at work.

- Deciding on which metrics and KPIs to track and measure is a science and an art and can be split into both Operational and Success Metrics:

  o Operational Metrics should be tracked on an ongoing basis and are generally lagging metrics used to identify trends and tell stories about past work.

  o Success Metrics are used to drive future behaviour and move a team towards a target or outcome.

- Building a dashboard to report these metrics and goals is an effective and necessary way to tell stories to those you are engaging with, from your team to your board.

- Building a dashboard does not need to be expensive or require new tools and engineering help. A People Operations Partner with a solid understanding of Excel should be able to build a manual dashboard using CSV downloads from your HR tools such as Lever, HiBob, Typeform, Lattice, Gympass, Recruitee, Lever, Ben Benefits, etc.

Endnotes

1 Brysbaert, M (2019) How many words do we read per minute? A review and meta-analysis of reading rate, Journal of Memory and Language, Volume 109, December 2019, 104047 https://doi.org/10.1016/j.jml.2019.104047 (archived at https://perma.cc/PQ9Q-3TXY)

2 Peter, L J (1969) *The Peter Principle: Why Things Always Go Wrong,* Pan MacMillan, 9780330025195

3 Goodhart, Charles (1975) Problems of Monetary Management: The U.K. Experience. Papers in Monetary Economics. Vol. 1. Sydney: Reserve Bank of Australia

4 Deming, W E (2018) *The New Economics for Industry, Government, Education,* third edition, The MIT Press, 9780262535939

5 Talent Point (2020) 3 times when employees are most likely to leave https://www.talentpoint.co/resources/3-times-when-employees-are-most-likely-to-leave (archived at https://perma.cc/FV4L-5UGH)

6 Moss, Jennifer (2021) To Prevent Burnout, Stop Micromanaging and Give More Autonomy, Worth.com https://www.worth.com/prevent-burnout-stop-micromanaging-give-more-autonomy-jennifer-moss/ (archived at https://perma.cc/PKN9-NS9M)

7 Moss, Jennifer (2021) The Burnout Epidemic: The Rise of Chronic Stress and How We Can Fix It, *Harvard Business Review Press,* 9781647820367

8 RapidAPI (2022) API Integration – What is API Integration? https://rapidapi.com/blog/api-glossary/api-integration/ (archived at https://perma.cc/866K-4YB7)

11

Prioritizing people

People Operations teams are losing trust.[1] Crucial Learning reported that just 25 per cent of 1,000 individuals surveyed say their HR leader is trusted as 'one who cares about the needs of employees.'[2] The reason for this degradation of trust is, I believe, compounded over years of People Teams administering themselves into reward and punishment roles. Too often I've seen teams' success measured by how vigorously we defend management and corporate gain and not enough on how we build for strategic outcomes and impact.

We are also losing trust on the business side, due to our inability to consistently provide quantitative measures of our success or valuable contributions to the commercials of the business. It seems the effort to win the business over has failed on both accounts, as discussed in Chapter 2.

The sooner People Operations teams can move away from these stereotypes the better. The better for businesses, the better for the profession, *and the better for human beings you work with.*

Working in People Operations is a highly commercial and strategic role – one which takes an analytical and business-forward approach. It also requires a huge deal of personal empathy and a high bar for professional ethics. It is a role which has the capacity to be highly trusted by the business as caring about the needs of employees, as well as delivering value for the business.

I propose that moving towards an approach of thinking like a Product Manager will unlock a better way of working within you and your team, something that will fire-up your capacity to build meaningful and impactful work for your organization and to get better results. I also believe it is one of the best ways to put our customers, our colleagues, at the centre of everything we do for the greater good of the business and the future of HR.

The move into a product-centric mindset does *not* make human beings the product. We must remember that! Our culture, our ways of working and our business is the product. At the end of everything we build in the People Operations teams, are real humans, their lives and very often their families and loved ones' livelihoods. We must take that responsibility seriously as we build.

HR is about empathy

Ultimately, the products we are building require us to understand, to care for and to connect with the human beings around us. While building the product our colleagues engage with, we must not lose sight of the forest through the trees. Building a product which affects human lives (and families' livelihoods) requires more consideration than launching a new ecommerce business selling your macrame pot-plant cosies.

I want to use this penultimate chapter, now that we have explored data and the need to be highly attuned to telling stories with numbers, by reminding you that there is a bigger picture and that at the heart of this, your capacity for and expertise in *Human Operations* will remain one of your most valuable assets.

In Chapter 3, I mentioned that Human Operations work – the human-first, coaching, discussing and connecting – was perhaps a primary motivator for your entry to this field. It definitely is for me. Even in the most difficult times – redundancies, difficult feedback, even facing grief within a team – it is the work I can do making work better for other people that keeps me motivated.

I spoke deeply in Chapter 3 about how if you put thinking like a product manager at the centre of everything you do, knowing your customers are your colleagues, then you are likely to make fantastic human-first decisions. However, this doesn't mean abandoning Human Operations entirely. In fact, it requires you to nurture those skills just as deeply as ever, but with a new approach to helping people.

The ethics of product management

Just like People Operations leaders, Product leaders must make ethically sound decisions when they go about building new products for their customers. These ethics and how problem solving is approached is not dissimilar to People Operations ethics and how we must apply them to the work we do every day.

Building products means you must continuously take the position that the work you are doing will evolve and improve over time. There is no final state of 'completion'. We should begin to think in terms of 'shipped' and 'not shipped' (and, as you continue to grow and progress, 'depreciated'). This mindset means that we may fall victim to missing how incomplete products can cause harm, confusion or anxiety to those who use them. This problem is perhaps less acute when someone is downloading a photography app, but it can be incredibly harmful when the product is a compensation calibration.

The work we are building has real-world outcomes and impacts not just folk's enjoyment of their role, but perhaps their livelihood. This means we have a higher degree of responsibility to maintain when we are scoping, designing, building and shipping. This responsibility comes in the shape of our personal and product management ethics.

At a minimum, I suggest two golden rules when building ethical people products:

1 Will this cause avoidable harms or confusion if we were to ship in its current state?

   a) To whom? Do these folks align on an axis of gender/ethnicity/religion?

2 Would we be ashamed if the outcomes of this failing were made public?

If your team is constantly asking these questions, not just of themselves, but of each other, many avoidable hurts may be prevented. This doesn't mean that you should be afraid to ship, just that you should be responsible, intentional and mindful of the individuals who will interact with what you ship.

Your team will disagree

We are not seeking total agreement when we deliberate, what we are seeking is *avoiding harm wherever possible*. Sometimes that means making an additional communications plan for certain individuals, sometimes it may mean sharing with managers before launching to a team, or it may mean a longer testing cycle.

> People can and will disagree about ethical options because our values, experiences and politics vary.
>
> Your team having passion for the ethical rules you set should be seen as a privilege. Be grateful your team trusts you enough to challenge the work you're doing. Accept their views as crucial data points in helping you ship higher quality work to your team.
>
> Ensure that wherever an ethical argument is complete, the team have all verbally agreed or disagreed, but committed to the outcome and solutions put in place.

This section alone should give you some clear reasons why a diverse team brings better outcomes as a business. Having a team with many, varied viewpoints may be the stop gap between shipping something harmful or not.

If you do, on your journeys, happen to ship something which is criticized for being hurtful or disrespectful in some way, I implore you to listen to new voices, accept responsibility and continue to use those examples of improvements in your capacity to build effective work. A simple and honest sorry is often enough, as long as you and your team demonstrate a consistent commitment to ethical building.

Building for wellbeing

Chapter 10 was all about metrics. Many of them were quite directly related to company and individual performance and very few related to human beings' emotional or personal needs. This does not mean you should dedicate 100 per cent of your People Operations team's focus and attention to performance metrics. Wellbeing, health and personal enjoyment are all still parts of People Operations work.

Ryan Bonnici, CMO of Gympass, spoke with me on a panel in June 2022, titled 'how to measure the ROI of a holistic wellness programme.' A difficult task indeed. Our panel discussed this at length, speaking of triangulating certain metrics to gather an understanding of employee wellness as leading indicators for performance and, therefore, business success.

During the event, Ryan said something I found very profound: 'building your wellness programme with your team is like brand marketing. You may never fully grasp precisely how much revenue is generated by a brand alone, but you will see indicators it is working, and all good CMOs know that it is crucial to invest in brand in some capacity.'

> As a product-minded HR leader, you must use both sides of your expertise to build compelling cases for not just highly quantifiable work, but for work that makes humans happier, healthier and helps them live better work lives. Employee wellbeing, and particularly the idea of holistic wellbeing programmes, are very difficult to pinpoint to a specific metric, but that doesn't mean you shouldn't build these programmes.

You can and should be able to produce evidence that an employee wellness programme has some positive effect to effectively engage your employees.[3] The same can be said for diversity, equity and inclusion efforts, or raising your employee's engagement in their community action programmes.[4] Take this as a starting point and build from that. Instead of your metric being 'increase performance to X through the implementation of Gympass,' make it 'increase the percentage of our employees activating their Gympass membership,' or 'number of high performing team members sharing that diversity is a key driver for them.' And if someone asks, 'What business metric does this relate to?' you can explain that, like brand marketing, some activities in People Operations can be most effectively measured through happiness and wellbeing, rather than direct output.

Ultimately, this balanced approach will serve you and your team as what is best for the business, best for the team and best for the long-term wellbeing of those you build for – *your colleagues*.

People aren't machines

I hope you are reading this book and feeling motivated and inspired to launch change upon your People team (and whole business!). Perhaps you are already mentally scoping project improvements, considering how you will adjust roles and brainstorming the exciting roadmap of work for the coming year.

Remember that your team, both in People Operations and beyond, are human beings. This needs to be thought about in the context of change management, communications and through operating your team to deliver work.

Communication is touted as a soft skill, but I would say it is one of the most complicated and nuanced skills a leader requires. People Operations leaders can be some of the most effective and empathetic communicators I have worked with, but that skill shouldn't be taken for granted. I have equally seen ineffective and even toxic communications come from within experienced People Operations teams.

Before you start anything, I would like to gently remind you of what was shared in Chapter 3 about your responsibility to respectfully and responsibly manage change. Consider the time to shift to this new way of working as work itself and schedule accordingly. Change is part communication and part operations. I suggest you address both of these points as they were addressed in Chapter 3, while remembering some important truths about how human beings work together.

My good friend and executive coach, Laura Tacho, tweeted one of my favourite threads on management and team organization, beginning, 'Scheduling your team at 100 per cent capacity is a great way to ensure that nothing will be delivered on time.'[5]

It may seem logical from the outset to schedule a team to capacity, but there is some simple maths behind why this is a flawed approach and why giving your team more time (not just through periods of change, but specifically then!) is required to complete work as quickly as possible. In order to understand why this doesn't work, consider traffic jams, lines at the post office, or waiting to enter a music venue and this is explained by Queuing Theory, called 'last in first out'.[6]

Queuing theory

Imagine you are working at the ice cream store, and each customer takes an average of five minutes to be served. Conveniently, a new customer arrives at the ice cream shop every five minutes on average.

Great, you may think. You'll have a swiftly moving line if you schedule one employee to serve your customers.

However, that is not what happens because of the word 'average'. What happens in reality is some customers come in in pairs, some customers take 15 minutes trying every flavour and some customers take a minute or two at most.

What happens quickly as these irregularities occur is the system begins to break under the pressure. Soon, some folks may see waits of up to an hour because the delays begin to compound on each new arrival.

The lesson on queuing theory about working with human beings is that what seems to be an 'ideal estimate', taken as gospel, ultimately costs your overall efficiency.

A sick day, urgent request, unexpected complexity or distraction to the team may cause significant delays and disruptions to your project schedule. Keeping your team able to cope with interruptions – particularly the human kind – enables your team to more effectively meet their requirements and ship great products.

Remember that your team are human beings. You must be aware of differences of background, emotional state and perspective when you communicate. You should be cautious about how different individuals approach change. It is wise to consider the human elements of working together to schedule and operate as a team. No team is infallible to the disruptions of human life, so plan accordingly and be forgiving of yourself as a leader when human lives disrupt efficiency.

Enabling managers and leaders

We've all heard the statistic that 82 per cent of workers would consider leaving a role because of a bad manager.[7]

The blast radius of a manager – good or bad – is undeniable. The delta between your best managers and your least effective managers may be causing real damage towards your capacity to hire, onboard and retain the kind of team you need to succeed. Often, I have seen People Operations teams lean in where bad management fails and become pseudo managers. This means either through building processes which require a great deal of HR assistance to run, or through stepping into every management activity on behalf of, or alongside, managers. These practices are unacceptable to the People Ops as a product mindset. They build bloated POPs teams and ineffective tools.

Like Tolstoy once stated, 'all happy families are alike, but every unhappy family is unhappy in its own way.'[8] Something similar can be said for management. Very often, the similarities between great managers are so strong they are almost identical: their capacity for human engagement, their ability to set clear goals, a knack for asking good questions and listening. The differences and variations in bad management are almost impossible to list in this book.

We've almost certainly experienced a few bad managers in our time; think about the different reasons these managers struggled and how you can learn from this in your work. One thing which can positively impact all of your managers is your People Operation team's ability to lead and guide them using the products you build. When done effectively, a People Operations team can build management tools to enable amazing People Managers across an entire business.

In Chapter 4, I shared details on the need to build mechanistic management practices into your products and tools in the People Operations team. The idea that People Operations teams need to enable managers and step away from the day-to-day work is crucial to maintain a lean People Operations team who are able to continuously build and not be operating machinery on a manager's behalf.

This means raising expectations for your managers. People Operations teams should be seen as vital advisors in their Human Operations work, there to help managers understand themselves and the individuals in their teams better. People teams are also there to set these expectations and challenge managers to grow. This should be through the tools they build: performance assessments, feedback mechanisms and progression frameworks. Baked into all of these tools should be some clarity on where managers are accountable, and People Partners are consulted.

Commit to it

This new way of thinking requires commitment and real changes to the way you're working, speaking about your role and shipping your work. I've spoken in depth about the trade-offs you may have to make around an individual's role in your team, how your team works together and how the function is structured. I hope I have given some solutions that work for teams of all sizes and allow you to move to this model over time if you are shifting your ways of working gradually.

However, one thing which is not possible is living this in half measures. You cannot consider the People Operations function both an administrative centre and as a source of value creation. Yes, your role will have some administration, but your mindset must shift around how you implement and manage that administration as you scale.

For example, there will be *many* folks who may tell you that hiring a Payroll Assistant is a more fool proof way to solve your compounding payroll administration, more so than building an automated payroll process, something which requires engineering support you don't have to hand. However, if you begin walking down the path of hiring administrative roles to operate machinery your People Ops team should be building, you will begin to backslide into the ways of working you are attempting to avoid.

These kinds of benign regressions are easy to tolerate; your team is working hard and you've got so many things on your to do list. However, consider again our subscription product and solving problems through first principles. Headcount is an effective way to solve *some* problems, absolutely, but new headcount should primarily be used to solve complex problems, such as building multiple tools and products for a growing roadmap, not just patching a hole in a pre-existing process or way of doing things. That said, temporary solutions, such as hiring a temporary worker or consultant, can often be effective mechanisms to inspire action.

Keeping up momentum towards a new way of working is hard, and it is always more difficult at the beginning. If you're feeling yourself or your team begin to drift from the ways of working discussed in this book, I suggest you pick it up again and give it a quick flick through. If you're really stuck, don't be afraid to reach out to me on Twitter or LinkedIn. I'm here to help on your journey towards thinking of People Operations as a Product!

The key points from this chapter

- People Operations teams require real human empathy and connection with the teams they work with every day.

- This empathy and understanding comes through building products that meaningfully connect with the problems in your organization and through building them ethically and with humans in mind.

- Moving to a People Operations as a product mindset doesn't mean you see your colleagues as a product. It is your culture, your ways of working and the business at large. *Never forget that!*

- For many of us, the most important part of our role in People Ops is the role of Human Operations.
- Human Operations is one of our most valuable assets to ensure our work is valuable.
  - Human Operations should never be abandoned in our quest for efficiency and effectiveness.
- Consider building ethical product management practices and safeguards into your ways of working and always be on the lookout for new commentary on ethics in Product Management and technology.
- Allow your team space and psychological safety to disagree on what and how you build for your workplace; allowing this kind of productive dissent is helpful to build a more ethically ambitious culture.
- Although performance, effectiveness and efficiency are the primary drivers for building world-class products, you will still find yourself prioritizing products for employee and human wellbeing.
  - Some of these products do not have an easily calculated ROI. consider these like brand marketing – an effective and crucial part of a qualitative and quantitative team's roadmap.
- Human beings aren't machines, they require space and time to creatively solve problems.
  - Inevitably, your team will bump into roadblocks, distractions and unexpected obstacles. There are mathematical reasons why you should allow your team time to be creative and not schedule other tasks for 100 per cent of their time.
- Managers are one of your most crucial assets, so ensuring you and your team build products that enable their success is paramount.
  - Do not allow your People Ops team to become the pseudo managers by building tools and processes which require People Operations to function.
- Be cautious of backsliding into old ways of working. Be intentional about how you solve problems with a product mindset. It will be hardest at first and get easier once you and your team have fully adopted the ways of working.
  - Don't be afraid to pick this book up again and read through to remain on track.

Endnotes

1 Granny, J; Cullimore, D (2022) How HR Lost Employees' Trust — and How to Get It Back, *Harvard Business Review* https://hbr.org/2022/10/how-hr-lost-employees-trust-and-how-to-get-it-back (archived at https://perma.cc/26QN-JEDP)

2 Christiansen, J (2022) Lack of Confidence: Employee Concerns are Going Unheard by HR, Crucial Learning https://cruciallearning.com/press/lack-of-confidence-employee-concerns-are-going-unheard-by-hr/ (archived at https://perma.cc/MJY8-VZC6)

3 KFF, 2021 Employer Health Benefits Survey (2021) https://www.kff.org/health-costs/report/2021-employer-health-benefits-survey/ (archived at https://perma.cc/GHG7-AS6V)

4 Cheeseman, Gina-Marie (2017) Engaging Employees Around Community Action, Business Pundit https://www.triplepundit.com/story/2017/engaging-employees-around-community-action/56396 (archived at https://perma.cc/X3FC-GM8T)

5 Tacho, L Twitter. https://lauratacho.com/ (archived at https://perma.cc/5CLT-FH48)

6 Queueing theory, Wikipedia https://en.wikipedia.org/wiki/Queueing_theory (archived at https://perma.cc/W59S-BUCD)

7 Korolevich, Sara (2022) GoodHire, https://www.goodhire.com/resources/articles/horrible-bosses-survey/ (archived at https://perma.cc/3HRY-J9XJ)

8 Tolstoy, L (1995) *Anna Karenina* (A Maude & L Maude, Trans.). Wordsworth Editions

12

Closing thoughts on the future

In Chapter 1, I lead us through the history of People Operations, from the industrial revolution to 2022. Now, I want to spend some time looking into what the future may hold.

I am proud of this profession, and I am incredibly impressed with the progress we have made through a turbulent history supporting labour unions, standing alongside the fight for equal rights and adapting to major global upheavals such as the 2020 coronavirus pandemic. Remote working, the internet, the printing press, even the iPhone – all of these inventions disrupted our ways of working, shifting and changing our perception of what it means to contribute to the body of work the human race has been striving towards for thousands of years. We're nowhere near finished.

People Operations and HR have progressed a great deal in the lifetimes of all of us reading, and I hope to see a more purposeful and widespread shift towards working like product teams as one of the next advancements. I truly believe that the ways of working explored in this book have the capacity to unlock creative new approaches to work, management, performance, leadership and culture.

Product management itself has too, alongside HR, adapted and changed as human beings have used the principles described in this book to invent new tools, collaborate on new frameworks and launch new businesses. Working in a way which is customer-centric, domain-driven and agile enables us all to work on more meaningful solutions to problems, be more creative and adaptable and allows us to move away from the HR roles of the past where we were seen as behavioural police or data entry.

Writing this book has been a great joy for me. I have interviewed and observed many People Operations professionals to gain insights on how they manage teams and build tools using these practices. I am sure, however, that this way of working is just a stepping stone into the future of what is next for People Operations.

What's next?

Emerging HR models are more adaptable and network orientated than before; the decentralized autonomous organization (DAO) has just begun to rise to prominence, and the world is finally adapting to remote work and culture.[1]

GPT3, Dall-E, Stable Diffusion – we're at the forefront of AI. Humans should spend time on value-rich creative, strategic and architectural work and human-to-human connection. More and more tools are using these systems as a base to improve copy, expedite mock-ups, and collaborate on ideas. People Operations teams must respond to this move away from the idea of menial or repeatable labour, and towards the idea of craft and creativity. AI will automate more and more tasks we currently assign to humans and it will disrupt, augment and improve many of the existing work processes. As a result, humans in People Operations and management roles can focus more on the people within the organization.

People are beginning to demand more freedom, flexibility, decision-making power and ownership. This is an affront to the traditional business structures many have grown up inside. How ownership models and capitalism react to these shifts will have tremendous implications in the world of People Operations. Increasing entrepreneurial expectations, salary transparency and output-based performance may shift compensation philosophies towards co-ownership, profit sharing and higher equity pools.

Workplaces such as YouTube, TikTok and Patreon, where creators are 'owners' of their own content, brand and work, are beginning to emerge as a serious potential career path for young people today. Forbes has reported that 67 per cent[2] of users on social media platforms have indicated that they would like to be a professional influencer. With these career paths emerging, where does People Operations sit? There could be a new industry of independent People Operations roles working with independent businesses and creators, helping individuals understand personal growth, career and performance within the context of their own business, rather than on behalf of another owner.

The year 2022 brought mass layoffs unseen for over a decade, with tens of thousands of technology workers losing their jobs within a few months.[3] From this emerged the new archetype of the People Ops team working together as a form of employment cooperative, sharing pre-populated spreadsheets or even websites designed to help their alumni employees find new roles. These kinds of community-driven tasks and responsibilities are somewhat new in the world of HR and prove that with great adversity comes adaptability and human-centric change. The People Operations leaders of today are demonstrating a great deal of creativity, community and care.

People Ops matters!

When I entered the world of People Operations, I did so with almost no idea where it would take me in life. I knew I loved working directly with people, I was motivated by the broad and dynamic scope and I was inspired by using relationships to inspire business change. To say that this career has continued to inspire and surprise me would be an understatement. I am a passionate advocate for our community, our value and our capacity for innovation.

Using People Operations as a Product thinking enables your team to have a greater reach into the commerciality of a business. It allows you to operate with a greater access to the quantitative and performance-driven approach businesses demand. Further than that, it matters because People are often the greatest investment your business will make. Over 60 per cent of most tech businesses' monthly spend goes towards headcount, in consulting and service businesses you are literally selling your people. Building tools and practices with these humans in mind as your final customer, all the while driven through product principles, is just good business sense. More than that, People Operations work matters because our teams are more often being involved in building meaning and direction into the work businesses are doing, crucial work in a world facing a global climate catastrophe, racial injustice and global income inequality. Purpose at work matters.

People demand their workplace contributes to a greater good – something more meaningful than the drive towards pure capitalistic aims which were previously upheld or tolerated. The People Operations team has a commercial duty to incorporate ethical and purpose-driven methodology into compensation and performance decisions, community and social responsibility programmes, into the brand and values which attracts employees and into the policies and ways of working which benefit all of your team with equity at the forefront.

Go forth and innovate!

For years I have been reading articles and books which explain that the future of HR is more data and analytics, more SaaS platforms or more automation. It feels hollow. It's not enough. In my opinion, that does not describe an inspiring future for a meaningful function like People Operations.

I struggled to put my dissatisfaction into words, to really articulate what I wanted to see change in this profession. Once I began to work in start-ups and scale-ups, I was able to make the connection to the kind of innovation I wanted to see in our field.

In my humble opinion, the future of HR is building cultures like Product Managers and Technology teams build products – agile, in squads, T-shaped – and with People Professionals acting like holistic and operational builders, rather than administrative agents in a machine.

I've written this book to inspire the kind of innovation I believe we are capable of in People Operations. This book was written with one aim: to help you innovate.

If you are out there building businesses, influencing cultures and leading teams, I hope that, in adopting a product management approach, you will have a better chance of successfully doing what I aimed to do as a young HR graduate: build a better working world than that which we entered.

I *cannot wait* to see what you create. I cannot wait to be inspired by your work.

Endnotes

1 Glaveski, S (2022) How DAOs Could Change the Way We Work https://hbr.org/2022/04/how-daos-could-change-the-way-we-work (archived at https://perma.cc/AA98-KZ3M)

2 Suciu, P (2020) Is being a Social Influencer a Real Career? https://www.forbes.com/sites/petersuciu/2020/02/14/is-being-a-social-media-influencer-a-real-career/?sh=f45f3cf195d1 (archived at https://perma.cc/NV47-5Y4U)

3 Lee, R. https://layoffs.fyi/ (archived at https://perma.cc/V83G-GCLY)

INDEX

Note: Page numbers in *italics* refer to tables or figures